Springer Proceedings in Business and Economics

Springer Proceedings in Business and Economics brings the most current research presented at conferences and workshops to a global readership. The series features volumes (in electronic and print formats) of selected contributions from conferences in all areas of economics, business, management, and finance. In addition to an overall evaluation by the publisher of the topical interest, scientific quality, and timeliness of each volume, each contribution is refereed to standards comparable to those of leading journals, resulting in authoritative contributions to the respective fields. Springer's production and distribution infrastructure ensures rapid publication and wide circulation of the latest developments in the most compelling and promising areas of research today.

The editorial development of volumes may be managed using Springer's innovative Online Conference Service (OCS), a proven online manuscript management and review system. This system is designed to ensure an efficient timeline for your publication, making Springer Proceedings in Business and Economics the premier series to publish your workshop or conference volume.

More information about this series at http://www.springer.com/series/11960

Tim A. Herberger · Jörg J. Dötsch
Editors

Digitalization, Digital Transformation and Sustainability in the Global Economy

Risks and Opportunities

Springer

Editors
Tim A. Herberger
Andrássy University Budapest
Budapest, Hungary

Jörg J. Dötsch
Andrássy University Budapest
Budapest, Hungary

ISSN 2198-7246 ISSN 2198-7254 (electronic)
Springer Proceedings in Business and Economics
ISBN 978-3-030-77339-7 ISBN 978-3-030-77340-3 (eBook)
https://doi.org/10.1007/978-3-030-77340-3

This Springer imprint is published by the registered company Springer Nature Switzerland AG
The registered company address is: Gewerbestrasse 11, 6330 Cham, Switzerland

Contents

The Means Justifies the End? Digitalization and Sustainability as a Social Challenge. A Plea for an Integrative View

Tim A. Herberger and Jörg J. Dötsch

1 Initial Situation

It is still not so long ago. Even in the second half of the last century, there was no shortage of forecasts predicting a bright future for workers in the developed world as a result of the use of new technologies, especially automation: higher productivity with considerably less working time and, of course, more time for the essential things of life. Whatever that was. Anyone who dares to take a look at only slightly earlier prognostic efforts will not be able to avoid a smile in view of the visionary omnipresent use of the internal combustion engine. And we haven't even mentioned the role models assigned to the meaningful use of efficiency and time gained. Be that as it may, this much is certain: where technical possibilities lead in interaction with economic and social developments has always been surprising in the end.

The fact that the social sciences have become aware of this phenomenon at all is, in any case, relatively new in its breadth. This has not only to do with the acceleration of technical development per se, which is perceptible within less than a generation, but also with its scope and with the increasing technical and social complexity. The first decades after World War II brought reflection on the importance of technology to a wider audience, which eventually found expression in political movements. Before then, it did not seem generally required, nor was it widely known, to reflect on, for example, "the limits to growth" (Meadows et al., 1972) and to perceive global developments as the result of human action, not human design, in the context of man-made technology as phenomena affecting everyone. However, today it seems

T. A. Herberger (✉)
Chair of Business Administration, specifically Entrepreneurship, Finance and Digitalization, Andrássy University, Pollack Mihály tér 3, Budapest 1088, Hungary
e-mail: tim.herberger@andrassyuni.hu

J. J. Dötsch
Chair of Economic Policy, Andrássy University, Pollack Mihály tér 3, Budapest 1088, Hungary

T. Herberger and J. Dötsch (eds.), *Digitalization, Digital Transformation and Sustainability in the Global Economy*, Springer Proceedings in Business and Economics, https://doi.org/10.1007/978-3-030-77340-3_1

that we are less in control of the situation than ever before. The nuclear physicist and philosopher Carl Friedrich von Weizsäcker saw one of the reasons why man is a spectator of development and a technical actor at the same time in the fact that modern technology is—still—"untechnical": because it has not sufficiently understood what technology actually is, namely a *means to an end*. He justified the danger emanating from technology in the atomic age in such a way that until now technology had been an end in itself or a means to an end of particular interests, of economic or political power. And he concludes from this in general: "A culture cannot be robust whose means are by a scale better developed than the consciousness of their ends" (1977, 104, own translation). This statement is perhaps more relevant than ever today, at the beginning of the digital age, when *sustainability* is one of the most important issues worldwide.

However, technical development has not only accelerated even further since then. Digitalization as applied IT—technology!—brings with it a completely new dimension. It has exponentially increased the technical possibilities at all levels. And this can be experienced directly. Digitalization permeates every niche of our perceived reality. It is not for nothing that it is mentioned in the same breath as the term transformation—and it is immediately apparent to everyone that the two terms are indeed inseparable. No digitalization without transformation. The pandemic of 2020 has made it abundantly clear that life without digitalization, at least in the developed economies, would simply no longer be conceivable. However, this fact is by no means self-evident.

2 Digitalization, Digital Transformation and Sustainability—An Attempt at Definition

It has long been recognized that digitalization and digital transformation are among the greatest challenges facing business and society today. But do we even adequately understand the processes triggered by this technology? Are we sufficiently aware of the interrelationships of various social subsystems that are undergoing radical change as a result of digitalization? Do we know how to use the potential of digitalization in such a way that it serves the long-term good of our societies and does not take on a life of its own in the service of particular interests? Or is this technology by a scale better developed than our consciousness of its ends? This question is neither aloof nor is it trivial. People around the world are more aware than ever of the fact that they are facing a whole series of challenges globally, challenges that have been caused by humans as technical actors, but which have not been planned by anyone. Just think of the threats to our natural environment, biodiversity and climate. Efforts for sustainability, the preservation of our natural habitat with all its diversity or climate protection are high on the agenda worldwide. If digitalization denotes such a technical option that potentiates the possibilities within different technical and economic fields and thereby changes societal partial systems, then it is of greatest general interest to gain clarity on how to work towards sustainable development. Thinking about digitalization must include thinking about sustainability.

What does this mean exactly? There is actually no single definition for sustainability. It is a purely relational concept that can in principle be applied to all kinds of object areas when goals of certain actors have to be brought into a long-term, balanced relationship with the goals of other actors. Economic goals, such as the profit intention of companies, can accordingly be evaluated in a context with, for example, social goals, environmental goals or governance goals (ESG-goals). In this context, the term goes beyond conceptualizing the circle of stakeholders as broadly as possible. Nor is it a matter of considering competing goals as complexly as possible, but rather—also quite selfishly—of integrating the temporal horizon of all stakeholders as thoroughly as possible: it must be in the interest of every company to still be able to generate profits the day after tomorrow. The enormously rapid development of technology, as we have already briefly theorized above, has made this view increasingly problematic in times of ever more intense competition and leads to tensions in managerial decisions (Wasieleski et al., 2021, 6). Sustainability is hence always about values, organizations, and institutions (see Dedeurwaerdere, 2014, 1). Sustainability is about awareness (see e.g. Hildebrandt, 2020). And "Sustainable development" is therefore not by chance an inflationaryly used pair of terms in the course of the observably massively accelerated global development since the 1980s at the latest. In the well known "Three Bottom line"-framework sustainability means a harmony of economic, environmental and social objectives. However, achieving precisely this harmony between three three fields is a challenge in practical implementation, because it also involves harmonizing the different motivations and interests of various stakeholder groups (see e.g. Wissenschaftliche Dienste des Bundestages, 2004). In this context, leadership can prove to be an important competence to achieve this harmonization. It does not seem inappropriate to us to take up the concise definition of the International Institute for Sustainable Development here as a working definition: Sustainable development means to meet "the needs of the present without compromising the ability of future generations to meet their own needs" (IISD, 2020). That sounds nice, and it makes the problem blatantly obvious: a high-tech start-up of three people will not be able to include all future generations in its daily struggle for survival; a conglomerate constituted as a stock company will not always want to. Neither the one nor the other is completely avoidable—but the fact that digital technology will provide even more acceleration and change in this context is undisputed. So it's obvious: digitalization actually only makes an understanding of the possibilities and necessities of sustainable action even more urgent. But where to start? If we want to find a meaningful approach, we first need to be clear about what digitalization actually means.

However, this project still faces considerable difficulties. Even though the current inflationary use of the terms "digitalization" and "digital transformation" documents a strong awareness of the problem, they remain vague on the one hand, and on the other hand there is no uniform nomenclature at all or an appropriate definition that would enable understanding across disciplines. The relationships between the terms remain unclear. The only thing that is agreed upon is that they are particularly important matters. Rather, there is merely a framework of different views and partial aspects to be differentiated from one another. While digitalization is understood to mean the introduction of new solutions based on digital technologies, digital transformation addresses the implementation induced by digitalization and the associated challenges as well as the changes resulting from digitalization compared to the initial situation, which ultimately determines the consequences for the stakeholders also beyond the implementation issue (Herberger & Zoll, 2020; Hess, 2019). Consequently, digitalization and digital transformation as terms can be placed in a chronological sequence: digitalization (e.g., of a process module step) is the first step, heralding the change of a state. Digitalization is followed by digital transformation in the form of a transformation process that ultimately leads to fundamental changes in a business model (e.g., by replacing activities previously performed by humans with IT-based processes) and in extreme cases, it can even lead to the obsolescence of the business model. This, of course, inevitably leads to spill-over effects on societal systems (Herberger & Zoll, 2020).

How intensively a business model competes in an industry can be illustrated based on Porter's "Five Forces"-model (Porter, 1980). The question here is how digitalization, digital transformation and sustainability are taken into account in this model. It originally describes the intensity of competition in an industry, which is determined by the influence of the "threat of substitutes," "intensity of competitive rivalry", "threat of entry", "bargaining power of suppliers" and "bargaining power of buyers/customers". Intuitively, it would be quite obvious to integrate e.g. digitalization into the model as a "new" sixth force as a possible extension of the original model, since digitalization and the ability of companies to adapt to it as part of the digital transformation have a lasting impact on the intensity of competition in this industry. However, this would overlook the fact that digitalization is not a player (force) in its own right in the competition within an industry or emerges from the interaction of players (forces) as an independent force. Rather, digitalization is a factor by which all forces or players are equally affected. It is the same with sustainability and corresponding efforts.

Let us first look at the five forces successively. Digitalization as a form of technical change is accelerating change both on the supplier side, with a view to the faster development of new products, and on the customer side. Customer behavior is changing faster, and the Internet is making markets more transparent. In addition, uncertainty is growing in every industry, because superior substitute products can be expected not only from the best in the industry, but also from companies completely outside the industry as digitalization progresses. The "threat of substitutes" is growing exponentially and disrupting all conventional concepts of industries. Moreover, sustainability considerations are increasingly coming under time pressure.

The industry-disrupting power of digitalization is clearly visible to customers, as there are more and more diverse products from new companies. This clearly shows that not only has the "intensity of competitive rivalry" grown considerably, leading to price reductions in many areas and the shrinking of certain industries; the parameter of the "threat of entry" also has a completely different dimension than it did just a few years ago: For tech-giants as google or apple, the automotive industry seems to be 'just one click away'.

The parameters of the bargaining power of suppliers as well as the bargaining power of buyers/customers are also undergoing fundamental change across industries: new dimensions of market transparency, substitutability and the sheer growth of digitally well-positioned players are putting tried and tested concepts from theory and practice under pressure. In the age of the platform economy, supplier-customer relationships are sometimes based on a completely new foundation.

The fact that this is not merely a shift, but a qualitative change, is made abundantly clear by the strategy types of differentiation, cost leadership or focus developed in Porter's approach: none of the strategies is conceivable without meaningful use of digitalization. A digitally well-positioned company will master all strategy types, even if it is foreign to the industry.

Therefore, digitalization, digital transformation and sustainability in economic activities (e.g. industry competition) are not to be interpreted as "new" forces in their own right or as an expression of existing forces (e.g. threat of substitutes), but rather as cornerstones of a canvas in front of which competition takes place. The reason for this is that all three concepts influence the existing forces in equal measure and thus change the industry as a whole and also the competition there at the same time, which is ultimately also due to the fact that both the existing forces and the canvas are interrelated.

In order to successfully counter these fundamental background changes within an industry as well as the social spill-over effects, special management areas such as change management (e.g. Lewin, 1947) and the corresponding leadership effects (e.g. Kotter, 1996) are receiving increased attention.

3 Our Interdisciplinary Approach

This volume is basically the result of a multi-day international conference held in Budapest, Hungary, in the fall of 2020 with the generous support of the Hanns Seidel Foundation at the Andrássy University. In times of pandemic, the conference became a tangible example of its own subject matter: it took place online, contrary to the original plan. On the one hand, the conception of the event was aimed at gaining clarity about the phenomenon of digitalization and digital transformation, and on the other hand, it had the goal of helping the discourse reach a higher level of constructiveness in light of the increasingly urgent need for sustainability.

This is a concern of particularly high social relevance. After all, societies can only achieve sustainability if the awareness of their means is better developed than the means themselves. However, since digitalization is changing the most diverse areas of the economy and technology and thus also has an overarching impact on all social subsystems, this also had a direct impact on the discourse-oriented design of the event. It is not possible to proceed nominalistically and work through individual problem areas on the basis of a synthetic concept of digitization. In order to make progress here, two things are essential: On the one hand, it is necessary to adopt a cross-disciplinary perspective in order to capture the complexity of the phenomenon and to develop meaningful insights from there. On the other hand, it is imperative to include practice as much as possible to open the protective zone of academic work to initiate a problem-oriented, fruitful conversation. Accordingly, these two aspects have been the guiding principles of the present volume, and we hope that it will not only reflect the vital exchange across borders of the conference, but also further promote it.

Accordingly, by presenting a selection of the papers submitted for the conference, this volume aims to address the opportunities and risks of digitalization and digital transformation for our global economy in a structured manner, taking into account as many aspects as possible. In concrete terms, this means including micro and macro level and combining practice and theory in a meaningful way. This also means creating space for disciplinary different approaches as well as for both, scientific or practice-oriented contributions. Experts from the field identify and critically analyze areas of tension and development potential in connection with new business models and sustainability efforts in our society. This claim results in the structure of the volume, which covers four subareas:

First, the possibilities offered by the new technologies and the challenge they pose to public regulation are discussed. Jona Stinner and Marcel Tyrell focus on the emergence of crypto-currencies, their technical basis, their perception and their role in relation to traditional currencies. The contribution of Piotr Kasprzak deals with tokenization of residential real estate assets as an element of the process of a financial paradigm shift.

The second part deals with the possibilities of digitalization for public welfare. Martina Eckardt uses an Evolutionary Economics approach to information and communication technologies for discussing the impact of ICT on policies, politics, and polities. Jens Geißler's contribution brings globalization, digitalization and sustainability in his focus on the role of Digitalization in Providing Health Care and Health Insurance Coveragein developing countries together.

The third part focuses on management challenges arising from the current changes. This concerns the key competence of leadership, new requirements and possibilities for Corporate Social Responsibility and the transformation of public management. As already indicated above, digitalization is always a very concrete challenge for management. We have tried to take this into account as much as possible by providing one section for "Managerial Issues in Theory" and one for "Managerial Issues from a Practical Perspective". The first section opens with Erik Pelters' contribution. Entitled Corporate Digital Responsibility, Understanding & Applying, it examines the ethical dimension implicit in the term "sustainability" from a practical perspective. Katja Posselt discusses the transformation processes taking place in the field of public administration and includes the challenge of the COVID-19 pandemic in her review. Sonja Sperber analyses the connection between managerial influence and innovation, which is central to competitiveness in the global economy. The section "Managerial Issues from a Practical Perspective" provides concrete impressions and considerations from a consistent practical perspective. The object areas discussed here are again oriented to the overall concept and come on the one hand from the area of academia (Jürgen-Matthias Seeler et al.), in which without a doubt a profound change is taking place, and on the other hand from the practice. Angelika Kölle discusses the latter and focusses on the question of "Digital Sustainable Leadership".

Although the fourth section is the last, it should not be understood as the concluding or closing section. It, too, seeks to express the cross-cutting impact of digitalization, digital transformation as well as sustainability. This is also what its title strives for, addressing the multidimensionality of "analytics" in the age of digitalization. The first contribution by Zoltán Bánhidi, Imre Dobos and Madina Tokmergenova is devoted to the problem of measuring and ranking the phenomenon of digitalization—and directs attention to a part of the globe that one associates only to a limited extent directly with digitalization: Russia. Tim A. Herberger and Christoph Litke explore the "Impact of Big Data and Sports Analytics on Professional Football" by means of a "Systematic Literature Review from a Sports Management Perspective" and thus also establish the connection between academic systematics and a section from practice, which inspires masses with an analog game. Daniel Lorberg and Holger Janusch take an overarching, political scientific perspective with their contribution "Digitalization, Transnationalization and the Transformation of the Global Economy: A Historical Explanation" and also contribute an ingredient to the interdisciplinary recipe of this volume.

As the very essence of this volume, all subsections ultimately contribute to the creation of an expedient interdisciplinary basis for further research into the concepts of digitalization, digital transformation and sustainability. It becomes apparent that these terms do not simply run parallel to one another but are mutually dependent and ultimately also need to be orchestrated together. Who is the conductor? Ultimately, this should be all of us, all stakeholders in societal systems, because ultimately, we as humans will always be the analog anchor and thus the interface between the digital and analog worlds. The latter, after all, must be managed in a particularly sustainable manner.

References

Dedeurwaerdere, T. (2014). *Sustainability science for strong sustainability*. Edward Elgar.

Herberger, T., & Zoll, F. (2020). Das Immobilienmanagement der Zukunft: Ein Überblick zu neuen Anwendungen im Kontext der Digitalisierung und Digitalen Transformation. In T. Herberger (Ed.), Die Digitalisierung und die Digitale Transformation der Finanzwirtschaft; (1st ed., pp. 197–237). Tectum Verlag.

Hess, T. (2019). *Digitale Transformation strategisch steuern* (1st ed.). Springer Fachmedien.

Hildebrandt, A. (Ed.) (2020). Klimawandel in der Wirtschaft: warum wir ein Bewusstsein für Dringlichkeit brauchen. Springer Gabler.

IISD = Institute for Sustainable Development. (2020). Online: https://www.iisd.org/about-iisd/sustainable-development. Last access January 21, 2021.

Kotter, J. (1996). *Leading change* (1st ed.). Harvard Business School Press.

Lewin, K. (1947). Frontiers in group dynamics: Concept, method and reality in social science; social equilibria and social change. *Human Relations, 1*(1), 5–41.

Meadows, D. H., Meadows, D. L., Randers, J., & Behrens, W. W. (1972). *The limits to growth. A report for the Club of Rome's project on the predicament of mankind*. Universe Books.

Porter, M. (1980). *Competitive strategy: Techniques for analyzing industries and competitors: With a new introduction* (1st ed.). Free Press.

Wasieleski, D. M., Waddock, S., & Shrivastava, P. (2021). *Management and the sustainability paradox: Reconnecting the human chain.* Routledge, Taylor & Francis.

Weizsäcker, C. F. v. (1977). Der Naturwissenschaftler, Mittler zwischen Kultur und Natur, in: Idem: Der Garten des Menschlichen. Beiträge zur geschichtlichen Anthropologie (pp. 91–106). Carl Hanser Verlag.

Wissenschaftliche Dienste des Bundestages. (2004). Nachhaltigkeit, 06/2004. Online: http://webarchiv.bundestag.de/archive/2008/0506/wissen/analysen/2004/2004_04_06.pdf. Last access March 24, 2021.

The New World of Blockchain Economics: Consensus Mechanism as a Core Element

Jona Stinner and Marcel Tyrell

1 Introduction

Roughly a month following Lehmann Brothers' bankruptcy at the peak of the financial crisis in autumn 2008, a brief article, titled "Bitcoin: A Peer-to-Peer Electronic Cash System", appeared in a cryptographic mailing list. Its pseudonymous creator, Satoshi Nakamoto, envisioned an electronic cash network as an alternative to the traditional financial system, which at that time faced existential distress (Nakamoto, 2008). Inconspicuous at first glance, the whitepaper paved the road to the first cryptocurrency "Bitcoin", presently valued with ≈$40,000/BTC (January 2021) and a market capitalization of nearly $1 trillion.[1]

Bitcoin is an explicitly decentralized, digital peer-to-peer network, which allows participants to exchange financial value in the form of virtual currency tokens (Nakamoto, 2008). Such tokens combine the benefits of a digital settlement infrastructure with some qualities commonly associated with cash, including third-party anonymity, quick payment finality, small transaction costs and mutual exchange between parties, however, and that is important, without the (direct) involvement of any intermediary as trusted third party.[2]

Transferring these properties to a purely digital currency has historically been challenging, as illustrated by the juxtaposition with cash: First, cash transactions

[1] Data from https://cryptoslate.com/coins/, accessed in January 2021.

[2] See Narayanan et al. (2016) for one of the earliest comprehensive descriptions of PoW-consensus.

J. Stinner (✉) · M. Tyrell
Department of Philosophy, Politics, and Economics, ISIC—The PPE Institute for Social and Institutional Change, Witten/Herdecke University, Alfred-Herrhausen-Str. 50, 58448 Witten, Germany
e-mail: jona.stinner@uni-wh.de

M. Tyrell
e-mail: marcel.tyrell@uni-wh.de

T. Herberger and J. Dötsch (eds.), *Digitalization, Digital Transformation and Sustainability in the Global Economy*, Springer Proceedings in Business and Economics, https://doi.org/10.1007/978-3-030-77340-3_2

can be easily processed and verified between any physically present individuals. Instead, digital accounts are at constant risk of fraudulent access (i.e., cyber-attacks), requiring enhanced validation processes. Moreover, digital processing needs a mediating provider, who adjusts the accounts according to the initialized transfer and manages the underlying infrastructure. Second, digital settlement often induces a delay between goods provision and payment finality.[3] This delay exposes the seller to risks if payment reversibility is a feasible option, whereas cash transactions guarantee conclusive compensation. Third, electronic files can be duplicated effortlessly and at negligible costs. If unrestricted, this allows individuals to inflate the currency at will and spend amounts multiple times (referred to as "double-spending-problem") (Berentsen & Schär, 2018). While central banks have developed anti-counterfeit features to prove the authenticity of cash, guaranteeing this quality for electronic money is a non-trivial exercise (Deutsche Bundesbank, 2017).

The advent of modern asymmetric cryptography provided solutions to validate the legitimacy of digital communication (e.g., Hellman, 2002; Naor & Yung, 1989). Providers of virtual payment systems employed those innovations to ensure reliable account access and validate transfers, thus overcoming the first described obstacle of a trusted validation. But to counteract the double-spending problem, earlier implementations of electronic cash[4] and conventional monetary and payment systems had to rely on a central intermediary as trusted third party. However, as became apparent in the cause of the global financial crisis (i.e., the collapse of Lehman Brothers 2008), centralized systemic relevance of a single or profoundly connected set of entities can cause undesirable externalities and substantial problems.

In contrast, Bitcoin bypasses the requirement for a trusted third party by (i) removing the autarchy of a central record keeper in favor of a publicly shared ledger; and (ii) shifting system stewardship to a set of anonymous and widely distributed nodes. Record-keeping and transaction settlement in the Bitcoin network is built on a novel digital infrastructure, termed "blockchain". A blockchain is a cryptographically secured, distributed ledger that is copied a thousand-fold across any network member willing to download and operate it. Each copy of the blockchain stores a complete history of transactions in an interlocked chain of blocks, according to the rules of an underling protocol (Nakamoto, 2008).

Some nodes, called "miners", perform the process of altering the record when new transactions are initialized in the network. Miners verify and bundle pending transactions into block candidates in a cryptographically robust way and broadcast them to the network. Other nodes express their acceptance of a valid candidate, by appending it to their version of the ledger and continuing on the expanded sequence (Böhme et al., 2015). This process allows the network to exchange transactions in a continuously enlarging ledger. However, to provide a solution for the double-spending problem (and obtain a genuinely decentralized ecosystem) the network must consent upon a unique state of ownership among the arbitrarily distributed participants and numerous copies of the ledger. Nakamoto's core innovation is the

[3] In particular, if multiple entities are involved such as in an international money transfer.

[4] E.g., DigiCash or e-gold.

incentive mechanism under which this decentralized process operates (more or less) frictionless.

Bitcoin's consensus protocol replaces trust in a central entity's honesty with cryptographic principles and economic incentives, designed to align participants' selfish economic interests with collectively intended behavior. Such a protocol is fundamental to the architecture of each permissionless cryptocurrency, but some advancements have been made regarding its specific technical and economical design. In fact, the invention of Bitcoin initiated the formation of a universe of currently $\approx$2500 cryptocurrencies with significant proliferation and substantial heterogeneity in the approaches to obtain consensus (Irresberger et al., 2020).

This article aims to illustrate the fundamental structures of two of the prevailing consensus protocols, namely proof-of-work (PoW) and proof-of-stake (PoS), and to highlight some important distinctions. In particular, it describes how the rules stated in each type of protocol enable the members of a self-sufficient cryptocurrency to coordinate to and agree on a unique state of ownership. Section 2 describes proof-of-work, which gained considerable attention as the first functional consensus protocol in a decentralized ledger technology. Since their evolution is closely related, Sect. 2 includes Bitcoin as an example of an applied PoW mechanism. Section 3 continues with a short description of one widely discussed alternative, the so-called proof-of-stake mechanism. In Sect. 4 we point to some nonstandard consensus protocols, particularly the group of committee-based-consensus/Byzantine Fault Tolerance mechanism and provide concluding remarks.

2 Proof-of-Work Consensus

A consensus protocol consists of a set of rules that, when applied collectively, formalize the conditions under which new transactions are attached to the ledger of a decentralized payment system. By design, network participants are strongly encouraged to follow the specified rules, as conformity maximizes individual gains and is thus in their best interest (Huberman et al., 2017). To understand how the PoW mechanism of a blockchain creates such a precondition, we examine its constituents with regard to the most prominent example, the Bitcoin network.

The transfer of virtual currency in the Bitcoin network is organized as follows: A participant willing to conduct a transaction broadcasts to the network that another wallet address should be the new owner of a specified amount of Bitcoins. Public-key encryption guarantees the sender's legitimacy and integrity of the encrypted transfer information when the initialized order is distributed among the network members. Slightly simplified, the underlying principle is based on a cryptographic pair of keys. The public key identifies a specific Bitcoin address (i.e., comparable to an account number) and is apparent to all network members. The owner of the address keeps the private key secretly (i.e., analogous to an account password). When initializing a transfer, the owner uses the private key to assign a digital signature to the transaction message before spreading it across the network. Any network member is able to decipher the signature with the respective public key and inspect or alter the contained information at will. However, restoring the signature requires the private key, which is solely known by the owner, rendering the message invalid in case of (malicious) modifications. Hence, a valid signature proves both the sender's authenticity and the immutability of the contained information (Schär & Berentsen, 2020).

To append transactions to the blockchain, miners collect pending messages, verify the signature's validity, and include them into a block candidate. In order to become accepted by other peers (and subsequently be included in their version of the distributed ledger), block candidates must (i) contain only valid transactions and (ii) correspond to the target of a difficulty criterion, as explained shortly. The standardized integration of public-key authentication makes it straightforward for miners to meet the first condition. The second condition, however, intentionally provokes substantial effort in the form of repeatedly operated hash computations. The devoted work and associated costs are essential for maintaining the network's trustworthiness and security. However, before examining this implication in more detail, the hashing operation has to be described in more detail.

A cryptographic hash is the output of a one-way function that transforms an arbitrary length input into a fixed-length value.[5] Some properties of hash values make them particularly useful for the application in cryptocurrencies: First, a hash value uniquely identifies the input (somewhat analogous to a digital fingerprint). Even infinitesimal modifications of the input lead to a substantially and unpredictably different hash value. Second, hash values are drawn from an astronomically large distribution of possible manifestations. Hence, it is stochastically implausible to receive a colliding value for non-identical inputs. Third, hash functions are non-invertible, i.e., it is infeasible to reconstruct the input if only the hash is visible. Conversely, due to the quasi-random transformation of the function, it is impossible to selectively customize the input to obtain a desired output (Al-kuwari et al., 2011).

A critical application of hash functions in the Bitcoin ecosystem is to guarantee immutability of past transactions. Miners propose a block candidate by hashing its entailed transactions together with the hash value of the preceding block. Since each block is interlocked with its predecessor, this forms a tamper-evident chain of blocks, i.e., a blockchain. Altering any contained information implies changing the hash values across the entire chain and being notified immediately. However, multiple branches of the ledger may emerge, if, for instance, miners integrate different transactions from the pool of pending ones. That means, different block candidates will be formed (Biais et al., 2019). Therefore, the protocol restricts the generally permitted solutions by accepting block candidates only if the corresponding hash value starts with a certain number of zeros. As we will describe in the next paragraph, the number of starting zeros expresses the difficulty of generating the required hash

[5] Hash functions exist in a variety of specifications (e.g., SHA-1, mumur32 or MD5). Bitcoin is based on the hash function SHA256, which assigns a hash value of 64 digits for any practically length of input. For Instance, the SHA256-hash of the term "Bitcoin" results in "346f1bd1c9f195e21e81d662123c3c94c9df4fa728223459216f8e3a19862c2d", while the term "bitcoin" (notice the small deviation) gives "d67509e37480c61b46c6bfc26f66f6a1884614763f08db3ab45616c8c3c12983".

value. Given the quasi-random nature of hash functions and the current technology level, brute-force[6] is the exclusive strategy to find such a suitable hash value for appending a block to the Bitcoin blockchain. In practice, miners repeatedly adjust a random number within the block candidate, called "nonce", and compute the hash function until a value appears that fits the hurdle rate set by the blockchain algorithm. Of course, computational power (and a bit of luck) is the primary determinant of success (Schär & Berentsen, 2020).

Adding a "difficulty" to the puzzle (e.g., in the form of required zeros) ideally should lead to the result that a single miner (presumably the fastest) first broadcasts a valid candidate to the network. Nevertheless, multiple valid versions of the blockchain may occur, if (i) different miners simultaneously find a suitable hash value (which is statistically unlikely but happens occasionally) or some network members decide—for unspecified reasons—not to follow the first proposed solution. Preventing perpetual disagreement in this context requires a fundamental consensus rule: For the Bitcoin network, participants consider the most extended block sequence as valid. Forks (i.e., valid alternative branches of the ledger) may still exist temporarily if simultaneously proposed candidates result in multiple chains of equal length. However, since block creation follows a stochastic process, one branch necessarily exceeds the others sooner or later and is subsequently adopted (Halaburda et al., 2021).

Considering the longest chain as valid is clearly beneficial for each participant, who expects other network members to behave accordingly. Obviously, any potential benefits from working on an incompatible blockchain cannot be utilized and are therefore worthless, while its operation requires costly computational power. By proposing a candidate with a generally accepted hash, miners prove an externally verifiable commitment to the blockchain's current state. This fundamental principle of proof-of-work makes a fraud endeavor prohibitively expensive. For instance, without mining costs, miners may create undisclosed parallel chains in order to double-spend currency. If such a private chain is provided with valid hash values, it is adopted by the network as soon as it exceeds the publicly shared blockchain, following the longest chain rule (Savolainen & Ruiz-Ogarrio, 2020). Suppose an attacker with enough computational power to outpace the honest network uses her currency on the main chain to purchase goods or services. After receiving the benefit, she publishes a secretly mined private chain, which is accepted by the network (Eyal & Sirer, 2014). The attacker makes a profit since she never moved her funds on the private chain, which allows spending the same amount of currency again (Budish, 2018).

Such an attempt becomes exponentially difficult for any miner controlling less than 50% of the total computational resources. Nevertheless, when abstracting from mining costs, expected returns of a double-spending-attack remain marginally positive even for smaller stakes. Establishing mining costs in the form of proof-of-work,

---

[6] I.e., the enumeration of potential candidates until a solution is found.

however, dramatically changes this simple calculation to the attacker's disadvantage.[7] A fraudulent miner then has to weight the uncertain return from an attack against its costs and the profits from honest behavior. Moreover, accumulating the computing resources required to conduct the described attack with a sufficient probability creates itself a substantial and irreversible financial burden for any potential attacker. The essential economic principle to note here is that the blockchain's immutability increases with the expenditures incurred for mining (Budish, 2018; Ma et al., 2018).

To attract a sufficiently large number of contributors willing to incur those costs, the protocol allocates a reward of currently 6.25 BTC and any attached transactions fees to the miner, who first appends a generally accepted block to the ledger. Reward levels bisect approximately every four years (more specifically, every 210,000 blocks) from originally 50 BTC to ultimately zero with a limited total supply of 21 million BTC. Since mining is permissionless (i.e., anyone can deploy computing power to mine blocks without any special permission), its market structure is characterized by pure competition. It follows that the presence of rewards encourages market entry until expected returns equal the incurring cost. Since only the winning miner (pool) is rewarded, the mining process is akin to a repeatedly executed tournament with free entry.

The incentive compatibility of PoW inevitable demands such a computational contest. However, this consensus design contains some obvious drawbacks: Bitcoin exhibits low scalability, as analyzed thoroughly by John et al. (2020), and requires substantial amounts of resources (de Vries, 2018). For instance, Bitcoin's aggregated energy consumption for the year 2021 is estimated at around 111.3 TWh—exceeding countries such as the Netherlands or Austria (Rauchs et al., 2021). For this reason, several recent projects in computer science have emerged to invent other consensus mechanisms that are more cost-effective and scalable.

3 Proof-of-Stake Consensus

One of the early developed alternatives, and nowadays still the main contender of PoW is the Proof-of-Stake (PoS) consensus protocol, which for example is used by Cardano and Binance Coin (Irresberger et al., 2020).[8] The fundamental principle of the PoS protocol is the following: Instead of relying on competitive forces, as implemented in the PoW protocol, the PoS mechanism authorizes a randomly selected stakeholder, called "validator",[9] to update the ledger (Saleh, 2020). This means that

---

[7] In particular, fraudulent miners have to take into consideration that the attack probably has an adverse impact on the market value of the cryptocurrency.

[8] Irresberger et al. (2020) document a growth in number and relevance of the PoS blockchains, both in absolute numbers and also relative to PoW blockchains.

[9] Nodes, which are selected in the PoS system to update the ledger are also called "validators" since their task primarily consists of validating transactions, whereas PoW consensus requires nodes to repeatedly execute complex hash-computations.

no incentives exist for validators to engage in a computational contest, which—at least in principle—for the following reason could threaten or undermine the ability of the PoS design to generate consensus: Even though the PoS mechanism specifies that a validator is offered an explicit monetary reward,[10] no explicit monetary cost must be burdened to gain the authority to update the blockchain. Therefore, from a design perspective, the PoS consensus mechanism does not couple the benefit of earning the block reward with an explicit cost component—in contrast to the PoW mechanism. Critics argue that this creates incentives for the validator to always add a block to the chain, irrespective of whether the update induces perpetual disagreement among users. This is what these detractors call the Nothing-at-Stake problem. Of course, if true, that would destroy the PoS's long-run viability because in that instance an initial disagreement would persist indefinitely (Halaburda et al., 2021; Saleh, 2020).

This issue is theoretically analyzed by Saleh (2020), who, however, concludes that the Nothing-at-Stake problem is not valid in general. He makes the following reasoning: One key component of a PoS blockchain is that such a blockchain possesses a native coin (token) that must be used to facilitate exchange on that blockchain. Therefore, a stakeholder of a given blockchain refers to the native coin holdings of that individual. The PoS algorithm will consider nodes to append to the blockchain based on the number of tokens they put at stake. Thus, each node will be selected based on a probability distribution, which depends on the respective amount of tokens staked. The stakeholder who has most "on stake" therefore also has the highest probability of being selected to append a block candidate to the blockchain. The selected node adds the next block and receives the sum of rewards and transaction fees of the transactions comprising that block (Halaburda et al. 2021).

Saleh (2020) argues that proponents of the Nothing-at-Stake problem implicitly assume price-taking behavior by a validator, i.e., the validator does not take into consideration the effect her decisions will have on the native coin value of that blockchain. However, this seems not to be an appropriate behavioral assumption for a validator: If the validator chooses to update the blockchain in a way that perpetuates disagreement among nodes, she imposes a cost on all stakeholders. Such an action undermines users' ability to exchange the native coin since the coins' ultimate ownership history cannot be clearly determined. The validator creates a fork. As a result, the value of the native coin will decrease, given that its usage as an exchange medium is clearly hampered. Note that by taking such an action, a validator also imposes at cost on herself. Therefore, if she adds a block to the blockchain in a manner that leads to persistent disagreement, she herself has to incur a financial cost, which in term of magnitude depends on her stake in the blockchain. Thus, the stake might signal a validator's intent to behave honestly. This means that not only for the PoW but also for the PoS consensus mechanism, a financial cost is coupled with the benefit of grabbing the block reward and the transaction fees.[11]

---

[10] Similar in this respect to PoW consensus.

[11] For a similar argument in PoW consensus see Budish (2018).

A second important implication follows from this argument (Saleh, 2020): By restricting the access to the blockchain to sufficiently large stakeholders, an equilibrium can be induced that generates consensus (Fanti et al., 2019). As previously mentioned, the cost of updating the blockchain in a way that causes persistent disagreement increases with a validator's stake. A sufficiently high minimum stake requirement as a condition for gaining access to the validator function creates a situation in which the cost of persistent disagreement outweighs the benefits from adding "improper" blocks for all validators. The result is an equilibrium, in which all participants coordinate when updating the ledger to generate consensus (Saleh, 2020). Saleh concludes that using a PoS protocol for a blockchain not only avoids prohibitive energy consumption but also requires only a modest reward schedule, without endangering the viability of the consensus mechanism.

Of course, there is an ongoing discussion about whether the analysis of Saleh (2020) allows an appropriate implementation of PoS consensus. In the interest of brevity, we do not provide an overview here but refer in the footnote to the existing literature.[12] Instead, we want to point to one very interesting economic implication: Does the consensus protocol matters for scaling blockchains? John et al. (2020) investigate this question. On the basis of a model analysis, they indicate that it depends on the consensus protocol, i.e., either PoW or PoS, whether increasing the transaction rate has positive or negative effects on the security of the respective blockchain. In general, increasing the transaction rate (e.g., by extending the block size to process more transactions) mitigates congestion, resulting in decreasing transaction fees (Easley et al., 2019). The reason is that agents in equilibrium have to pay only proportionally smaller fees to obtain a comparable settlement speed when the processing capacity increases. In PoW blockchains, validators will consequently withdraw computational power from the network, as dictated by the incentive compatibility. In turn, a reduction of the computational power operated in the network lowers the cost of a successful attack (Budish, 2018) and therefore undermines the security of a PoW blockchain. It follows that increasing the scale of a PoW blockchain has a negative effect on network security.

In contrast, lower congestion leads to higher demand in a blockchain operated via a PoS protocol, which increases the market value of the native coin, i.e., the blockchain's cryptocurrency. This, in turn, increases the opportunity costs of an attack, given that the value of a validator's stake increases. Therefore, increasing the scale of a PoS blockchain improves its security (John et al., 2020). The results show that the design features of the PoS consensus mechanism are qualitatively very different from the PoW protocol. The computational power expended by validators of a PoS blockchain has no effect on its security. This feature makes the PoS consensus mechanism a particularly interesting alternative.

---

[12] E.g., Gans and Gandal (2019) and Halaburda et al. (2021). Savolainen and Ruiz-Ogarrio (2020) provide an interesting discussion of miners' incentives to attack and double spend in PoW blockchains, which is related to the concept of endogenous coin value in PoS consensus. By analyzing the occurrence of large mining pools, they argue that static costs (mining) are less important compared to dynamic incentives (revenue flows) to maintain honesty.

4 Conclusion

This paper gives an overview of the block building process and principles of different consensus protocols. We focused our descriptive analysis on the consensus protocol, which sets the rules for updating a given blockchain. Since consensus, i.e., the agreement on a unique ledger content, is key to the functionality of a decentralized record-keeping system, a more profound knowledge of these protocols provides a thorough understanding of the comparative advantages of different blockchain designs. Therefore, we analyzed the two most prominent economic protocols PoW and PoS, concerning the mechanisms under which the respective network achieves consensus. Of course, the public blockchain ecosystem consists also of many other alternatives, for instance, blockchains using hybrid PoW/PoS protocols and so-called Delegated PoS blockchains.[13] Since research on new consensus protocols is an active field, numerous other blockchain protocols were proposed.

A particularly interesting group are Byzantine consensus-based blockchains, such as Honeybadger, HotStuff or Tendermint.[14] Moreover, the Diem project proposed by Facebook, which claims "to build a trusted and innovative financial network that empowers people and businesses around the world", is based on a blockchain design using the Byzantine Fault Tolerant (BFT) consensus approach.[15] Amoussou-Guenou et al. (2020) offer a methodology to analyze Byzantine consensus-based blockchain protocols from a game-theoretic perspective. The protocols are set up as a committee coordination game between rational and Byzantine players. The authors specify conditions under which consensus properties are satisfied and show that coordination failures could be a big problem.

Trust in the record-keeper is the mechanism to establish a consensus in a traditional intermediary based centralized record-keeping system. As a fascinating decentralized alternative, the blockchain could revolutionize our traditional financial system. However, to live up to these expectations, further research on the viability of different consensus mechanisms is required. The results described in this paper prove that it is a worthwhile endeavor.

References

Al-kuwari, S., Davenport, J. H., & Bradford, R. J. (2011). Cryptographic hash functions: Recent design trends and security notions. *Eprint.Iacr.Org*, 1–36. Retrieved from http://eprint.iacr.org/2011/565.pdf

---

[13] Irresberger et al. (2020) provide an overview.

[14] A Byzantine fault tolerant system takes into account false messages provided by Byzantine players and allows for temporary disagreements among users (Halaburda et al., 2021). For more information on the practical implementation, see the whitepapers of Honeybadger, HotStuff and Tendermint.

[15] See Diem project homepage.

Amoussou-Guenou, Y., Biais, B., Potop-Butucaru, M., & Tucci-Piergiovanni, S. (2020). Rational behavior in committee-based blockchains. *IACR Cryptology EPrint Archive*, (2020/710), 1–22.

Berentsen, A., & Schär, F. (2018). A short introduction to the world of cryptocurrencies. *Federal Reserve Bank of St. Louis Review, 100*(1), 1–16. https://doi.org/10.20955/r.2018.1-16

Biais, B., Bisière, C., Bouvard, M., & Casamatta, C. (2019). Blockchains, coordination, and forks. *AEA Papers and Proceedings, 109*, 88–92. https://doi.org/10.1257/pandp.20191018

Böhme, R., Christin, N., Edelman, B., & Moore, T. (2015). Bitcoin: Economics, technology, and governance. *Journal of Economic Perspectives, 29*(2), 213–238.

Budish, E. B. (2018). The economic limits of bitcoin and the blockchain. *SSRN Electronic Journal*. https://doi.org/10.2139/ssrn.3197300

de Vries, A. (2018). Bitcoin's growing energy problem. *Joule*. https://doi.org/10.1016/j.joule.2018.04.016

Deutsche Bundesbank. (2017, September). Distributed ledger technologies in payments and securities settlement: Potential and risks. *Monthly Report*, pp. 35–49. Retrieved from https://www.bundesbank.de/Redaktion/EN/Downloads/Publications/Monthly_Report_Articles/2017/2017_09_distributed.pdf?__blob=publicationFile

Easley, D., O'Hara, M., & Basu, S. (2019). From mining to markets: The evolution of bitcoin transaction fees. *Journal of Financial Economics, 134*(1), 91–109. https://doi.org/10.1016/j.jfineco.2019.03.004

Eyal, I., & Sirer, E. G. (2014). Majority is not enough: Bitcoin mining is vulnerable. In N. Christin & R. Safavi-Naini (Eds.), *Financial cryptography and data security, FC 2014. Lecture Notes in Computer Science* (Vol. 8437, pp. 436–454). Springer. https://doi.org/10.1007/978-3-662-45472-5_28

Fanti, G., Kogan, L., Oh, S., Ruan, K., Viswanath, P., & Wang, G. (2019). Compounding of wealth in proof-of-stake cryptocurrencies. In I. Goldberg & T. Moore (Eds.), *Financial cryptography and data security. FC 2019. Lecture Notes in Computer Science* (Vol. 11598, pp. 42–61). Springer. https://doi.org/10.1007/978-3-030-32101-7_3

Gans, J. S., & Gandal, N. (2019). More (or less) economic limits of the blockchain. *SSRN Electronic Journal*. https://doi.org/10.2139/ssrn.3494434

Halaburda, H., Haeringer, G., Gans, J. S., & Gandal, N. (2021). The microeconomics of cryptocurrencies. *Journal of Economic Literature*, (forthcoming).

Hellman, M. E. (2002). An overview of public key cryptography. *IEEE Communications Magazine, 40*(5), 42–49. https://doi.org/10.1109/mcom.2002.1006971

Huberman, G., Leshno, J. D., & Moallemi, C. C. (2017). Monopoly without a monopolist: An economic analysis of the bitcoin payment system. *SSRN Electronic Journal*. https://doi.org/10.2139/ssrn.3025604

Irresberger, F., John, K., & Saleh, F. (2020). The public blockchain ecosystem: An empirical analysis. *SSRN Electronic Journal*. https://doi.org/10.2139/ssrn.3478264

John, K., Rivera, T., & Saleh, F. (2020). Economic implications of scaling blockchains : Why the consensus protocol matters. *SSRN Electronic Journal*. Retrieved from https://papers.ssrn.com/sol3/papers.cfm?abstract_id=3750467

Ma, J., Gans, J. S., & Tourky, R. (2018). Market structure in bitcoin mining. *SSRN Electronic Journal*. https://doi.org/10.2139/ssrn.3103104

Nakamoto, S. (2008). Bitcoin: A peer-to-peer electronic cash system. Www.Bitcoin.Org. Retrieved from https://bitcoin.org/bitcoin.pdf

Naor, M., & Yung, M. (1989). Universal one-way hash functions and their cryptographic applications. In *Proceedings of the Twenty-First Annual ACM Symposium on Theory of Computing* (pp. 33–43). https://doi.org/10.1145/73007.73011

Narayanan, A., Bonneau, J., Felten, E., Miller, A., & Goldfeder, S. (2016). *Bitcoin and cryptocurrency technologies: A comprehensive introduction*. Princeton University Press.

Rauchs, M., Blandin, A., Dek, A., & Wu, Y. (2021). Cambridge bitcoin electricity consumption index. Retrieved from Cambridge Center for Alternative Finance website: https://www.cbeci.org/cbeci/comparisons

Saleh, F. (2020). Blockchain without waste: Proof-of-Stake. *The Review of Financial Studies*, (forthcoming). https://doi.org/10.1093/rfs/hhaa075

Savolainen, V., & Ruiz-Ogarrio, J. (2020). Too big to cheat: Mining pools' incentives to double spend in blockchain based cryptocurrencies. *SSRN Electronic Journal*. https://doi.org/10.2139/ssrn.3506748

Schär, F., & Berentsen, A. (2020). *Bitcoin, blockchain, and cryptoassets—A comprehensive introduction*. MIT Press.

Blockchain to the Rescue—Tokenization of Residential Real Estate in the Emerging Token Economy

Piotr Kasprzak

1 Token Economics and Decentralized Finance

The coexistence of the Internet and social media with machine learning and artificial intelligence have led to substantial societal changes, represented by revolutionary and self-reinforcing platformization of the economy (Kasprzak, 2021). These new energy regimes (Ryfkin, 2011) have facilitated new economic activities and enhanced commercial exchange, thus unwinding new social relationships, which require redefined communication to organise and manage the new dynamics. This process is reflected in a new automated approach to collect and use of data and is changing the way market participants gather and exchange information (both internally and externally) including that on ownership. In the new reality, platformization has become more important than business processes alone. Finding a new, better solution for enhanced user experience is today's necessary way to success, which means further integration of businesses and a constant need for innovation. This paper is based not only on traditional sources: academic papers, technical reports, white papers, etc., but also extends the open discussion on internet platforms.

Development of cryptographic keys and shared ledgers incentivized users to redefine their interactions based on digital trust. The monopoly of financial institutions (serving as sole trusted third parties to process electronic payments in internet commerce) ended and a new element—blockchain entered the picture (Nakamoto, 2009). The blockchain, operated by independent servers (nodes), safely stores given transaction records on a widely distributed peer-to-peer computer network. It has enabled executing complex smart contracts, requiring multiple parties to approve

P. Kasprzak (✉)
pkasprzak.eu Strategy & Innovation, Alicante, Spain
e-mail: info@pkasprzak.eu

SGH Warsaw School of Economics, College of Business Administration, Innovative City Department, Warsaw, Poland

T. Herberger and J. Dötsch (eds.), *Digitalization, Digital Transformation and Sustainability in the Global Economy*, Springer Proceedings in Business and Economics, https://doi.org/10.1007/978-3-030-77340-3_3

transactions by introducing a multiple signature protocol and has given ground to another world-changing functionality-tokenization.

Tokenization can be defined as a process of digital storing and transferring cryptographed and digitally signed rights to any asset (or rights to access to any data or utility) on a distributed ledger where the ownership of these rights can be transferred via its protocol. In other words, it is a process of representing a given asset as a transferable unit on the blockchain infrastructure (Ross et al., 2019). It requires consensus algorithms to ensure replication of the information across nodes, but without central administration. Consequently, programable smart contracts are collectively managed by an unlimited network of computers running a designated software.

Almost any asset can be tokenized (Stefanoski et al., 2020). Tokens can have broad functionalities: from those inherent in money (medium of exchange, means of account and of storing value) to the representation of access to real assets, or digital and legal permissions to services and utilities.

Within the theoretical framework of the diffusion of innovations (Rogers, 2003) i.e. diffusion of technology, is justified to assume, that diffusion of blockchain—allowing tokenization of various types of assets is imminent as successive groups of its adopters are growing.

Tokenization may be strengthening expectations of the enhanced customer experience, intensified by platformization of social relations. The new energy of social media is contributing to the notion of personal liberation. It is leading to the emancipation of low-income opinion makers, which adds to the invention's spread in a vicious circle. The Bitcoin's popularity and its price boost, are the best examples. It is the next step in the history of the web-wise world, where "online" is not just an addition to computer functionality. Blockchain and tokenization have enabled the appearance of mass-mind blowing concepts, products and ideas, like thousands of different cryptocurrencies (CoinMarketCap, 2020) or the blockchain banking. They allowed users to hold digitalized financial assets in their digital wallets, not only on their computers but also on their mobile phones. Unlimited opportunities have appeared for new business models, ecosystems, legal frames and other fields of interest subject to issues of trust and value.

This process is supported by unlimited and freely available opportunities to analysis and scientific discourse, leading to an emergence of the token economy and the token economics. One can define it as *a combination of the modern definition of economics—the interdisciplinary social science concerned with description and analysis of individual human and social actions of production, distribution, exchange and consumption of goods and services (*Collins, 2005*), with tokenization, as the essential invention allowing digital representation of real assets on distributed ledgers (OECD,* 2020*), thus exchange and execution of contracts related practically to all of their physical and legal aspects.*

Blockchain technology and cryptocurrency offerings added new ways for people to create and exchange values within society. Fundamental definitions and rules governing societies and economic systems have been redefined by uncounted technological startups. Dynamic advances in technology opened a new field in the financial system—Decentralized Finance (DeFi).

Unlike within the conventional financial system, DeFi users can engage via decentralized software applications, where an internet connection is the only condition. It is an entirely digital alternative to banks, insurance companies, stock exchanges, etc., which exists without traditionally associated structure (offices, bankers, etc.) and is accessible to anyone with just a mobile device.

Decentralized platforms already allow not only trading digital tokens or currencies, but also lending, borrowing and swapping them, trading margins or yield farming. Automatization of market making by smart contracts permits matching of lenders and borrowers without intermediaries. DeFi creates unseen before innovative decentralized financial instruments, like synthetic assets (Synthetix) or prediction markets (Augur). It promotes on-chain exposure to practically any asset class, e.g. enabling protection against devaluation in the third-world countries (Airtm). It is giving a strong impulse to the emergence of the digital barter economy of the future.

On June 18, 2019, Facebook announced preparations of its stablecoin infrastructure. It aims at "modernizing payment infrastructure and creating a core transport layer for value, that is low-cost, interoperable, and compliant" (the Libra token). A group of stakeholders (from technology, venture capital, regulatory, telecommunication, online marketplace, payment and compliance) already works on the project.

This groundbreaking venture is taking place in our eyes. Interestingly, Facebook scaled the project down recently and renamed the coin to Diem. Reasons for the retreat remain unclear, but the giant's surrender to objections of the mainstream financial system seems highly plausible. Nevertheless, after the launch of Diem (predicted for 2021) and its potential reach to billions of Facebook users with a computer or a mobile phone, the world will not be the same. After reaching a critical size, such stablecoins could constrain monetary policy (Assenmacher, 2020). Free access to private money, of citizens from countries remaining outside monetary unions, might influence their government's control over the money supply and put pressure on their undercapitalized local currencies. Undoubtedly, the situation is serious, and the time pressure is high.

A tension between Facebook and regulators could cause unwanted administrative behaviours. It would be a poor prognostics for Bitcoin and the whole cryptocurrency concept. On the other hand, it might contribute to works around less concentrated stablecoins, as a widely accepted alternative.

Satoshi Nakamoto started the genesis block of Bitcoin (the first block forming the chain of connected data) on a small server located in Helsinki, Finland on Saturday, January 3, 2009, at precisely 1:15 p.m. Eastern Standard time. Most probably, to timestamp the birth of Bitcoin he has encrypted a message in the block, quoting this day's headline from The Times: "Chancellor on brink of the second bailout of banks".

This message to posterity is widely interpreted as Satoshi's warning of fractional-reserve banking instability and a mission statement for Bitcoin itself-being on the brink of the financial paradigm shift worldwide, and the end of the centralized banking (Fig. 1).

Fig. 1 Satoshi's hidden message. *Source* https://commons.wikimedia.org/wiki/File:Bitcoin-Genesis-block.jpg

Before the foreseen by its believers, Bitcoin's recognition as the world reserve currency, for the sake of this article's argument, one can read the message differently and form a thesis that: *"Bitcoin" and the blockchain can bailout the incumbent banking system, rather than replace it.*

The banking sector came out from the last financial crisis intertwined with the real estate sector (acquiring large troubled-property portfolios). Despite the global bailout of banks, financial intermediation remains expensive and the regulatory approach is subject to significant political economy and coordination costs, and thus unlikely to deliver much structural change (Philippon, 2013).

These observations indicate potential reserves existing at the junction of both sectors. Considering opportunities granted by tokenization, one can assume that real estate tokenization can capitalize on these reserves and contribute to the banking sector's development.

2 Stablecoins, Security Tokens and Oracles

The evolution of the crypto world generates new concepts of digital coins and tokens. In traditional finance, fiat currencies usually are not backed by any assets but are controlled by central banks. Typical cryptocurrencies neither have reserves backing their values, nor central authorities powering their prices, which results in extreme instabilities, damaging their function as means of payment.

Stablecoin is a cryptocurrency pegged to a specified asset (Arner et al., 2020) to curb its volatility. The following types of stablecoins can be distinguished (based on characteristics of assets backing them):

1. fiat currency collateralized, where a coin is partly or fully backed by a real-world currency and can be exchanged to it (e.g. Tether, USDC, PAX),
2. cryptocurrency collateralized (e.g. DAI, Synthetix),
3. tangible asset collateralized (coins backed by commodities, precious metals or non-fungible asset i.e. real estate, art, etc.),
4. non-tangible asset collateralized (coins backed by intellectual-property-related assets or royalty payments),
5. subject to the multi-asset-collateral model, in which a mix of different types of assets is packed and used to decrease their volatility (e.g. $RSV).

Stablecoins may also be backed by algorithmically programmed smart contracts to compensate for changes in their value, by influencing the coin's supply. Such algorithm stablecoins (e.g. AMPL) are not collateralized by any asset but adopt seigniorage-supply-control mechanism used by central banks.

The security token is a legal concept of a digital unit issued on the distributed ledger, which satisfies the applicable regulatory definition of a security or a financial instrument under local law (SIFMA, 2020) or digitally certificates an ownership interest in an underlying security or a financial instrument issued on a different platform (e.g. on a traditional register). In this context, it functions similarly to traditional securities, and the main difference between them is the distributed ledger listing. The security token can represent a share in traditional listed assets like equity or bonds and illiquid assets like close-end private placements, real estate, art, etc.

Security tokens are similar to equity shares backed by the blockchain and smart contracts, i.e. tokenized securities (Smith et al., 2019). Like traditional securities, they represent digital ownership, allow dividend or interest payments, etc. Unlike traditional securities, they are entirely programmable.

Security tokens represent the following key features of an underlying asset:

- the virtual description of the asset (or its tokenized attribute) and a fraction of ownership represented by the token,
- the identity chain of the token owners (allowing investors or third-parties to view the flow of funds and tokens on a public blockchain),
- rules of legal compliance concerning ownership and transactions (e.g. investor eligibility or risk profile).

The security token technology significantly improves drafting, issuance, trading and management of ownership. Security tokens can be programmed not only to fulfil regulatory requirements. Expanded and redefined fractionalization of ownership allows raising and trading capital through new and innovative financial products, combining different aspects of a given enterprise. Security Tokens can be divided and defined in ways traditional securities cannot (e. g. dividend payment can be related to preferences of their owner).

Characteristics of different tokens can be joined and traded. They can match their issuer's current and future ideas and evolve with them. For example, liquidity benefits of digital rights expanded by artificial intelligence and machine learning protocols could allow fractional ownership of combinations of financial returns with environmental, societal or cultural impact factors.

Utility tokens, providing digital access to a good or a service (EC, 2020), may serve as tools to support a specific business solution, platform or application. They give their holders rights to use the service and to influence its platform by voting.

Any security token solution requires a connection to the real world, either to validate the collateral or to deliver the required information. Usually, it is realized by a third-party service within the ecosystem—the blockchain oracle connecting the outside world with the network, by providing smart contracts with off-chain external data (Beniiche, 2020). It plays the most significant role in the system, as the information quality and relevance are crucial to the contract execution.

Oracles connect to the blockchain by application programming interfaces (APIs), i.e. by programs allowing two applications to share information. Different oracle types are necessary to fulfil a given smart contract requirement. For example, the information provided by software oracles can be obtained from various databases and transmitted in real-time. Hardware oracles validate, translate and standardize physical information into digital data. They can be centralized or decentralized in so-called trustless solutions, which grant trust without a reliable third party.

Unlike digital signatures, real-world data can be faked or manipulated. As trustless execution depends on oracles, secure and trustworthy mechanisms and their immutability are fundamental to such an ecosystem's systematic risk. But yet, they receive few literature contributions, leaving theoretical implications highly questionable, and a significant research effort is needed (Caldarelli, 2020).

3 Tokenized Real Estate

Globally, real estate (including residential, office, commercial, health, leisure and industrial properties) is the second-largest asset class after the global debt. In 2017, the world's real estate totalled USD228 trillion (Savills, 2016). Though professionally managed real estate investment market constitutes only a small fraction of this value, new DeFi solutions and tokenization of real estate assets could narrow the gap.

Real estate tokenization is a process of creating a digital asset (or an asset structure), which represents a property or a portfolio of properties, on a trading system within the distributed ledger. Principles of royalty finance and revenue-based investing (capitalizing on cash flows from lease contracts, resale of the property or revenues generated by it) base its business model.

This concept offers numerous benefits:

- possibility of high fractionalization of ownership, limiting entry barriers and allowing to target new types of investors and developers to reduce the cost of financing,
- liquidity management of a given property by partial tokenization,
- inclusion of low-income private investors into projects unavailable for them before, e.g. large commercial real estate projects around the world,
- globalization of offering and marketing, removing geographical barriers in fundraising,
- peer-to-peer contracts with instant settlements and the blockchain security, effecting in a lower cost of trading tokens and faster transactions,
- diversification of small investor portfolios in a manner reserved for institutional investors,
- improved transparency, traceability of transactions and identification of particular assets or investors,
- uncurbed programmability of smart contracts, allowing implementation of more complex dynamics of risk balancing.

Nevertheless, the potential of real estate tokenization remains still unrealized for a larger scale. It also rarely associates with residential properties, which may be caused by unique characteristics of this segment of the real estate market. It is:

1. Local and unique, as each property is different. Residential real estate is highly inhomogeneous, which makes it difficult to compare and to standardize data. Currency movements are important to valuations and comparisons. Single properties hold characteristics of non-fungibility, which limits their liquidity and makes the price definition process difficult.
2. Inelastic and imperfect. The elasticity of supply is limited (e.g. due to spatial constraints) and abrupt (for long investment cycle). The functioning of the law of supply and demand is limited (especially in imbalances of the market). The sector is exposed to the asymmetry of information. It is subject to common government interventions, various restrictions and monopolization of land supply and trade.
3. Informal, unorganized and non-transparent. Despite the existing formal requirements for concluding transactions of transferring ownership rights, their real value and official price can differ significantly. Access to information about transaction prices is difficult. Frequent price misrepresentations in concluded transactions may result from money laundering, lowering stamp duties, balance sheet manipulation, corruption, etc.
4. Expensive and difficult to trade. A real estate project is still a slow, mostly paper-based, expensive process of setting up its financing and management. It requires the physical presence of stakeholders, appraisers, signatures, notaries, etc. Entry barriers are high, as the unit price of real estate is high. Investors are locked exceptionally long. Direct and indirect investment options are limited, while banks usually finance residential projects. All of this translates into not

very sophisticated investment patterns of individual retail investors, who either buy residential or leisure single real estate or invest in REITs at best.

5. This market is driven by behavioural factors, where collective conservatism is dominating. Its participants tend to stick to established patterns, even if new possibilities arise. Pluralistic ignorance (Thaler & Sunstein, 2008) is significant and herding effects can be observed (Shiller, 2016). Owner-occupied residential real estate is misinterpreted as an investment. Moral hazard is inherent in indebted households, the banking sector and the political class (Kasprzak, 2018).

These features are essential to further discussion of real estate tokenization with the participation of traditional banks. Aside from the benefits of disintermediation in collaborative housing, free movement of persons and capital due to cross-border transactions, the blockchain technology will have a significant effect in making traditional business models obsolete (Nasarre-Aznar, 2018). This article is focused on the tokenization of single-asset residential property because it can offer the economic system-wide benefits unless realized outside the banking sector or against it.

4 The Oracle Bank Concept

Even though dedicated platforms already provide tokenization of single-property projects, large-scale approach towards tokenization of residential property is still a novelty. The presented concept reflects the synergies and comparative advantages of tokenization and traditional retail banking.

Besides broad access to financial markets, retail banks hold a privileged and trusted position in the society, assuring comparative advantages against newcomers to the retail client business (e.g. by reduced effects of frauds or regulatory fines). Their bloated branch networks, full of skilled workforce, offer the potential of knowledge of the local environment. Verification and implementation of the following assumptions of the Oracle Bank concept could redefine retail banking in the economy. It should unfold in the spirit of decentralization, but within the system providing the physical presence of experts and understanding of unique characteristics of the residential property market.

- Retail banks acting as the blockchain oracles in residential real estate tokenization can assure that real-world data is accurate and valuable.

In preparations for tokenization of a single property, it is essential to check its legal status, physically confirm its state and prepare a professional appraisal.

Blockchain only protects data within the chain, so the quality of information entering is essential to execute present and future smart contracts. It can only be accessed and modified by authorized parties. Although highly accurate statistical and machine learning single-property appraisal algorithms are already available, a real estate agent's expertise, local market analysis and a professional appraisal are still recommended. Banking professionals could fill up this gap, as they operate locally and can give reliable estimates. This further integration of the housing finance business would require only a slight adjustment of their qualifications.

Such information should not be limited to visual confirmation and filing legal or financial reports, but it should embrace complex data on material, economic, political and social factors. Most importantly, in a feedback function of the system, it would include evaluations of their reception by market participants. Furthermore, such a service would have a repeatable and long-term character.

- The Oracle Bank can act as a trusted partner within the necessary SPV structure, audit and feedback solutions.

Proper structuring of a given real estate token solution should provide control over the subject property management and minority interest protection. A simple example: ownership of a single property is transferred to an entity—the special purpose vehicle (SPV), by an entry in the land and mortgage register, to allow indirect trading of its tokens. Another SPV manages the property, maintains its standard, collect rents, pays local duties, etc. Statutory solutions for both SPVs guarantee the Oracle Bank's privileged position of a trusted partner for all stakeholders. Its experts appear not only as property validators but also auditors of property managers. They contribute to creating and verifying assessment data to be further digitalized (e.g. by adopting IoT technologies). Furthermore, basing the system on a distributed in-house network reduces the chances of data tampering or fraud with a motivational solution (based on utility tokens).

- The Oracle Bank can perform whitelisting of potential investors, set up the primary marketplace and the secondary trading.

A traditional banking group is already an ecosystem. It can offer licensed and experienced marketplace structure to property owners and investors.

Such a centralized exchange could adopt functionalities towards transparent accessibility, by adding mechanisms and solutions specific to decentralized autonomic organizations (DAOs) however drafted for an inner solution.

Security Token Offerings (STOs) organized by the Oracle Bank would combine a reach of Initial Coin Offerings (ICOs) with the regulatory transparency of Initial Public Offerings (IPOs), and banks know how to do them.

Single property tokenization promotes the participation of non-professional investors. Banks are already doing client risk classification, are involved in central programs, verification for electronic signatures and have enormous customer databases in the disposal.

The Oracle Bank could act as a market maker for its tokens and also provide custody services.

Furthermore, concluding from the dynamic development of cryptocurrency trading, the idealistically postulated disintermediation of financial services remains a myth. In reality, due to a high risk of losing privately-stored blockchain keys, large numbers of crypto assets are stored with crypto exchanges and custodians. There are hundreds of crypto trading platforms, but a bulk of trading happens in a few of them (CoinGecko, 2020). This apparent disintermediation creates significant risks and trust issues, associated with the custody of tokens. They could be limited if recognisable financial institutions backed particular solutions.

Assuring high-end trusted assistance in the tokenization process does not only mean adding new functionalities to existing bank services. Given the mass adoption of different oracle-bank-certified tokens, highly-trusted barter exchange network would emerge, giving ground to a whole range of businesses related to the real estate tokenization. Assuming unlimited swapping opportunities for different tokens certified by oracle banks in their ecosystems (or on higher-level markets) the whole scheme could be radically more efficient.

5 Potential Hazards of Residential Property Tokenization

Apart from inadequate token backing, unreliable valuations and audit controversies, which can be easily overpassed by the Oracle Bank, other selected potential hazards of crypto solutions and residential property tokens can be specified. They refer to the technical side (structural, legal) and qualitative socio-political constraints, specific to the residential real estate market. The Oracle Bank concept portrayed in this essay addresses most of them by offering trust and a systematic, institutional approach.

- Technological flaws, DeFi hacks, scams, smart contract vulnerabilities, and forks.

Even though there are significantly fewer flaws in the blockchain, the ability for anyone to duplicate open source codes (which dominate the ecosystem) remains a risk factor. Such an independent development of the source code, with its improved mathematical model or a smart contract, may generate a competitive solution to the original and steal its users, creating a so-called fork. It is a threat leading to fragmentation of cryptomarkets and liquidity dumping. Oracle banks trusted by regulators more than any other participant in the market could play an important role in standing to the issue.

- Lack of clear terminology and universal legal structure.

Tokenization still gives rise to concerns from various codes of law and national legal systems. Clear rules to deal with insolvency risks of crypto custodians are missing (Haentjens et al., 2020).

Particular solutions for residential property tokenization should be based on internationally agreed standards, with provisions on public offerings and trading of financial instruments and securities as a reference. The process requires the cooperation of national regulators, international standard-setting bodies and courts. As major banking groups operate across borders, oracle banks would intensify discussions on residential property tokenization influencing local and political monoliths.

- Unclear and non-universal local standards and concepts of the Internet which may cause unfair competition.

There is no common concept of world-wide-web. Essential differences exist between the decentralized and the authoritarian model of internet governance, hacking and misinformation, or protection for privacy from trolling and data manipulation (O'Hara & Hall, 2018). The United States and its private sector retain a disproportionate influence over internet technologies, and their commercial interests may be promoting technological advances motivated by rent-seeking behaviours. These discrepancies are visible not only between countries, but they also regard different groups of interest. They can have critical repercussions to tokenization, as it also can be subject to free riding, exploitation of regulatory loopholes or political pressure of such groups. The emergence of the Oracle Bank would add ferment to the existing mix of interests, groups and institutions.

- The asymmetry of information, embezzlement and moral hazard behaviours.

Residential property tokens remind shares of small-cap companies listed on OTC markets, making them particularly exposed to insider trading issues and asymmetry of information (e.g. about tenants' plans or local community initiatives). Untransparent assumptions of particular projects can intentionally be asymmetric. Although transparency lies in foundations of the very concept of asset tokenization, if unsupervised, bears huge risks of intentional fraud and manipulation or moral hazard behaviours. Mass tokenization of real estate seems little probable, without large-scale involvement of the banking sector with its internal regulations, control mechanisms and certifications. The Oracle Bank acting as a blockchain oracle, auditor, or the market maker, would guarantee enlarged transparency of information, certified by its utility tokens. It seems safe to assume that within this recognized financial group, fraudulent actions would be limited.

- Mass client participation in easily available investment activity may incur an increase in the systematic risk.

Investment patterns of retail investors can be risky, and susceptible to manipulation, trend creation and herd behaviours. Some researchers connect the last financial crash with the introduction of REITs and CMBS structures, and promote illiquidity, as a defensive force necessary to stabilize real estate prices (Baum, 2020).

One can hardly share this opinion. On the contrary, reasons for bubble-originated crises lie in progressing concentration, lack of competition and moral hazard behaviours throughout the system (Kasprzak, 2018). Numerous potential small-cap deals, being subject to standardized protocols and procedures, would lead to an explosion of automated brokerage solutions, where qualified retail investors could draft their risk/return preferences and yet unimaginable income scenarios. The Oracle Bank qualifying retail investors and educating them would lower the systematic risk. Additionally, hybrid solutions might allow pegging residential real estate tokens to qualitative features of a particular property owner, as a bank client. Such an approach could redefine the very concept of retail financing and client relations with the banking system.

- Operation on a living organism can hurt the very concept.

To implement changes to the existing economic system it is necessary to limit variables, without losing the key idea behind the blockchain revolution. Undoubtedly, enhanced legitimacy of the tokenization is needed, and the current unconstrained decentralization will have to be channelled. But, as the direction is not clear, it can happen at the cost of innovation. Higher pressure is necessary from the private sector and within governments and various groups of interest. It requires universal awareness of necessity and inevitability of the ongoing change.

Fierce competition between the financial system and DeFi will only delay and complicate the transition and should evolve into competition within the financial system—e.g. between different oracle banks.

Difficult integration of authorities into the transition can provoke enforcement actions dangerous to the very process and pushing it sideways. Different dynamics of regulation adjustments in particular countries can cause regulatory arbitrage between regulated and unregulated DeFi projects. The Oracle Back concept could be an international bridge of communication, founded by stakeholders being aware of the necessity of revaluation and redefinition of the housing finance.

Different characteristics of tokens, their role and impact on society still need to be explored and defined. Undoubtedly, this is and will be a painful learning process, volatile and based on errors. Shock waves originated by realized hazards across the whole crypto industry can provoke "bank runs" and massive pullouts of wallets, hurting solutions unrelated to the troubling case. Nevertheless, their probability seems lower within the innovation-integrated financial system- promoting competition, but protecting the blockchain idea itself and its numerous stakeholders.

6 Concluding Remarks

Modern societies face a never-ending and hardly controlled process of imminent change, where dominant values obtain a new shape, and knowledge and technology are the major social powers and sources of their dynamism (Bell, 1973). The educated and technical class dominates such a society, and service industries contribute to the economy more than manufacturing. Technological innovation is there a function of time, and the very process is unstoppable. Tokenization of the economy is such a process, and one day, ownership rights of all digital and physical assets will be tokenized, recorded and exchanged via blockchain protocols. Traditional middlemen will be dismissed, ownership guaranteed, and markets will work smoothly and effectively. But as of today, two obstacles remain -dim trust in apparently disintermediated trading and the irreplaceable necessity for oracle competence.

The Oracle Bank can provide solutions to both issues. Existing hazards are an excellent starting point for drafting formulas needed by issuers and investors furthermore required and understood by regulators and institutions.

As the blockchain has already allowed mass inclusion of mobile phone owners to financial services, the real estate tokenization should encourage institutional inclusion in the revolution. The cost of the transition is not the issue. Massive reserves in profit margins within the present model of real estate financing and trading can convert into the long-term income of entire societies. The real challenge is convincing institutional stakeholders to shift from unsophisticated and costly but a fully-fledged system to the redefined-intermediary involvement. Their retail clients will follow.

Real estate tokens can potentially unlock trillions of dollars in investable asset value backed by individual property or debt, bringing secondary liquidity to traditionally illiquid markets, allowing automatic operations and setting new paths to alter the financial landscape. Residential property tokens certified by the Oracle Bank could drive the irreversible process of the financial paradigm shift but within more predictable and secure frames. Ability to issue and safely trade such tokens with fiat currencies, cryptocurrencies and stablecoins or barter with other tokens would open unlimited options for further innovation, allowing capitalization of hidden reserves, particular skills, different incentives, anticipated benefits and unthinkable yet opportunities. In such a scenario, the importance of the banking sector would not decrease but grow.

In the face of private giant internet platforms' efforts towards crypto innovation, the urgent action is necessary, with little time remaining, counted in years or even months.

The new legal framework is already in preparation. The European Commission has been working on a single regulation regime for the token ecosystem-Markets in Crypto-Assets, (MiCA) since 2018. It already is a highly advanced process (as on September 24, 2020, the EC published this proposition within Digital Finance Package) even though its implementation by member states is due in 2024. The single legal framework will not only protect consumers but assure the integrity of previously unregulated services and markets in crypto-assets. It will encourage both regulators and companies to apply it in practice and will enable further innovation. As long as the definitions used will still be relevant and newly emerging hazards addressed.

There can be institutional resistance, as such tokenization of individual residential assets meddles with a silent bargain within the economic system. With tokenization of residential assets, popular understanding of safe investing could shift from tangible-but-illiquid of the past to intangible-but-liquid of the future. It could contradict traditional bank bias and politically motivated monetary policy. Mass tokenization of real estate could create alternatives to world currencies and change savings and investment paradigms because it relates to the largest transitive component of savings for generations.

Yet unobvious sociological effects of disconnecting social tissue from the tangible property can also be significant, as the feedback wheel will keep on turning, further changing modern societies. Open-minded and creative discussion of the concept is necessary. Postulates to focus on tokenization of indirect investments, i.e. funds or REITs (Baum, 2020) represent different logic and may only slow this process down.

Even though the blockchain revolution might seemingly be undermining the importance of central governance and funding, it could be an opportunity for smaller countries and their central institutions. It may positively contribute to their global competitiveness, by fast adoption to the unstoppable processes.

It will be captivating to see how governments and central banks align with the private sector to ensure a consistent and cohesive approach to the forthcoming paradigm shift.

Finally, as crypto ideas are strongly associated with the Internet community, innovating primus financial institutions will build their market position in the number-one segment of the future- belonging to young innovators, with oracle banks as their redefined, but wanted financial partners.

References

Arner, D., Auer, R., & Frost, J. (2020). *Stablecoins: Risks, potential and regulation.* BIS Working Papers No 905.

Assenmacher, K. (2020). *Monetary policy implications of digital currencies.* ECB SUERF Policy Note No 165.

Baum, A. (2020). *Tokenisation-the future of real estate investment?* University of Oxford Research.

Bell, D. (1973) *The coming of post-industrial society. A venture in social forecasting.* Basic Books.

Beniiche, A. (2020). Study of blockchain oracles. INRS, Montreal.

Caldarelli, G. (2020). *Understanding the blockchain oracle problem: A call for action.* University of Verona.

CoinGecko. (2020). Yearly report 2020. https://www.coingecko.com/en/exchanges. Accessed December 21, 2020

CoinMarketCap. (2020). All cryptocurrencies. https://coinmarketcap.com/all/views/all/. Accessed December 21, 2020.

Collins. (2005). *Dictionary of economics* (4th ed). https://financialdictionary.thefreedictionary.com/Modern+economics. Accessed December 21, 2020.

EC. (2020). Proposal for a regulation of the European Parliament and of the Council on markets in crypto-assets, and amending directive (EU) 2019/1937 (MiCA).

Haentjens, M., de Graaf, T., & Kokorin, I. (2020). *The failed hopes of disintermediation: crypto-custodian insolvency, legal risks and how to avoid them.* Hazelhoff Research Paper Series No. 9

Kasprzak, P. (2018). Moral hazard of indebted households as a potential threat to macroeconomic stability-observations from the Spanish real estate bubble. In J. Laszek, et al. (Eds.), *Recent trends in the real estate market and its analysis.* SGH Warsaw.

Kasprzak, P. (2021). The fourth industrial revolution and the real estate. In J. Laszek, et al. (Eds.)*Recent trends in the real estate market and its analysis.* SGH Warsaw.

Nakamoto, S. (2009). Bitcoin: A peer-to-peer electronic cash system. https://bitcoin.org/bitcoin.pdf. Accessed December 21, 2020.

Nasarre-Aznar, S. (2018). Collaborative housing and blockchain. *Administration, 66*(2), 59–82.

O'Hara, K., & Hall, W. (2018). *Four internets: The geopolitics of digital governance.* CIGI Papers No. 206.

OECD. (2020). The tokenisation of assets and potential implications for financial markets. OECD Blockchain Policy Series.

Philippon, T. (2013). *The fintech opportunity*. BIS Working Papers No 655.

Rogers, E. M. (2003). *Diffusion of innovations* (5th ed., p. 12). Free Press.

Ross, O., Jensen, J., & Asheim, T. (2019). Assets under tokenization: Can blockchain technology improve post-trade processing? https://ssrn.com/abstract=3488344. Accessed December 21, 2020.

Ryfkin, J. (2011). *The third industrial revolution: how lateral power is transforming energy, the economy, and the world* (p. 2). Palgrave Macmillan.

Savills. (2016). Around the world, Savills World Research. https://www.savills.com/blog/article/216300/residential-property/how-much-is-the-world-worth.aspx#article. Accessed December 21, 2020.

Shiller, R. J. (2016). *Irrational exuberance revised and expanded* (3rd ed., p. 175). Princeton University Press.

SIFMA. (2020). *Security tokens: Current regulatory and operational considerations for broker-dealers and a look towards the future*. SIMFA.

Smith, J., Manasi, V., Benedetti, H., Yoshida, K., & Vogel, Z. (2019). *Tokenized securities & commercial real estate*. MIT Digital Currency Initiative Working Group Research Paper.

Stefanoski, D., et al. (2020) Tokenization of assets. Decentralized finance (DeFi) volume 1. Spot on: Fundraising & stablecoins in Switzerland. Ernst & Young Ltd.

Thaler, R. H., & Sunstein, C. R. (2008). *Nudge: Improving decisions about health, wealth, and happiness*. Yale University Press.

The Impact of ICT on Policies, Politics, and Polities—An Evolutionary Economics Approach to Information and Communication Technologies (ICT)

Martina Eckardt

1 Introduction

Information and communication technologies (ICT) are not new. For some decades now, they have been shaping our everyday lives both as consumers as well as in the work place. ICT provided us—and are still doing so—with new goods and services as well as with new ways of producing them. But it is of a rather recent date that ICT also show a more than trivial impact on the political sphere which is characterized not by market relations, but by political and that is, collective decision-making.

During the so-called "Arab Spring" in 2011, Twitter proved very prominent in mobilizing people in autocratic regimes, thus furthering processes of democratization in the Arab world. It raised a lot of hopes and fuelled a lot of optimism as to the direct democratic potential of applying ICT in politics. But since then, a lot happened. For example, the widespread collection of information by secret services from democratic states like the UK and the US on other democracies like Germany, France and the EU show quite the opposite face of ICT. ICT open up new ways of endangering data privacy, thus also putting civil liberties at risk. In this way, eventually, it also jeopardizes political rights and thus the basis of democracy.

Assessing the potential influence of ICT on policies, politics and polities is a complex endeavour because ICT are not a set of uniform technologies, but consist of a number of separate technological components. To make things even more complicated, these single components are still also in a process of ongoing modifications. ICT are still not mature technologies, but such that are characterized by ongoing innovations. Since such innovation processes are in turn shaped by economic factors, any attempt to make a prediction of the overall impact of ICT on politics is doomed to failure.

M. Eckardt (✉)
Andrássy University Budapest, Pollack Mihály tér 3, Budapest 1088, Hungary
e-mail: martina.eckardt@andrassyuni.hu

T. Herberger and J. Dötsch (eds.), *Digitalization, Digital Transformation and Sustainability in the Global Economy*, Springer Proceedings in Business and Economics, https://doi.org/10.1007/978-3-030-77340-3_4

Said that, how then can we proceed? Of course, there is an obvious need to assess the potential impact of ICT on the political system. Therefore, this paper provides a clear conceptual approach that assists in analysing and evaluating the on-going processes of change at the different levels ICT bring about. To this end, we apply an evolutionary economics approach which enables one to deal with open-ended innovation processes. Section 2 introduces this approach and applies it to ICT. In Sect. 3 we discuss ICT in more detail in regard to policies, politics and polities. We firstly ask what impact ICT have in this respect on policies as the outcome of the policy-making process under given political institutions. Secondly, we analyse what influence ICT have on the policy-making process itself, again assuming given political institutions defining this process. Finally, we also touch the question what impact ICT have on the underlying constitutional institutions, defining the polity. Section 4 summarizes and provides an outlook on further research questions.

2 ICT from an Evolutionary Economics Perspective

Evolutionary Economics explicitly deals with the generation and diffusion of innovations (Fagerberg, 2005; Nelson, 1995). As Schumpeter (1952) stated, innovations include both novel or improved *products* and *services,* novel or improved *production processes* (incl. technologies/material), novel or improved forms of *organization* and novel *markets.* Carrying out any of such kind of innovation is part of entrepreneurial activity. This is not confined to "entrepreneurs" as leaders or managers of companies, but takes place whenever someone (re-)combines known elements in a novel way. This might be the outcome of a deliberative process, but can also result from chance—due to the creativity inherent in any human action. Accordingly, innovations are ubiquitous, leading to the permanent generation of new varieties of products and services in the economic sphere, but also to new varieties of policies and even to the permanent generation of novel legal rules generated, for example, in the course of jurisdiction. Besides this permanent stream of gradual change, there are also more radical innovations leading to breaks with traditional paths. However, evolutionary economics shows that even with a radical new technology it takes time until people have learned how to utilize its potential to its fullest.

In evolutionary economics, often a variation-selection-retention approach is applied (Fagerberg, 2005; Metcalfe, 1998). It enables one to make statements about the potential results of such on-going innovation processes, which are characterized both by chance and intention. With respect to the underlying variation processes one analyses what impact different forms of innovation systems, for example, have on generating innovations. But not all innovations are viable. Whether they are adopted depends on the relevant selection environment. The selection mechanisms in place decide on which novel varieties "survive". However, the latter are not superior in any absolute sense, but only relatively that is, with respect to the selection mechanisms in place at a given time and for a given selection environment. But even for such a "successful" innovation to be replicated over time, some kind of retention mechanism must be in place preventing that its characteristics are "forgotten".

When applying this approach to markets, companies are the actors generating innovations in the form stated above by competing for consumers' buying power. The relevant market delimits the selection environment, with the kind and intensity of competition defining the selection mechanism. Depending on the market cycle, market structure and the respective goods and services supplied, competition can take different forms, like for example competition for price, quantity or quality, with different outcomes on monopolistic or oligopolistic markets. Consumers finally decide which goods and services are successful by at the same time rewarding and punishing companies by (not) purchasing their products. Successful products "survive" over time in markets, because companies react to the incentives set by consumers. Companies which make money with their products keep on offering them over time. In contrast to that, less successful companies change their behaviour. They might either adopt a variant of the successful products, thus imitating other companies, or generate novel types themselves. In this way, a process of innovation and imitation takes place, leading to a steady change in the composition of the products, but also of the companies in the relevant market.

Technological change proved most important for economic development over the last 200 years. According to Dosi (1982, 151f.), a technology consists of "a set of pieces of knowledge, both directly 'practical' (related to concrete problems and devices) and 'theoretical' (but practically applicable although not necessarily already applied), know-how, methods, procedures, experience of successes and failures and also … physical devices and equipment. … (T)echnology, in this view, includes the 'perception' of a limited set of possible technological alternatives and of notional future developments." The different forms a technology can take are, however, not arbitrary, but constrained by the underlying technological paradigm (Dosi & Nelson, 2020). It "embodies strong prescriptions on the directions of technical change to pursue and those to neglect" (Dosi, 1982, 152). Within a given technological paradigm the actually realized technical solutions constitute a trajectory as time passes. This is "the pattern of 'normal' problem solving activity … on the ground of a paradigm" (ibid.). This whole evolutionary process again is characterized by innovations where "(a)n innovation is typically one step in a sequence of innovations within a particular technological regime. Post-innovative improvements play a vital role in increasing the rate of diffusion within existing applications, and extending the technology to new applications "(Metcalfe, 1988, 562).

When analysing in more detail such processes of technological change, one finds that there are a lot of different actors and institutions which cooperate (Cimoli et al., 2020). Complex technologies are the outcome of national systems of innovation (Chaminade et al., 2018). These are "(t)he network of institutions in the public- and private-sectors whose activities and interactions initiate, import, modify and diffuse new technologies" (Freeman, 1987 according to OECD 1997, 10). As a consequence, there are strong interdependences between technological, economic and political/institutional change over time.

Such co-evolution also plays an important role in regard to information and communication technologies (ICT) (Freeman & Louca, 2002). Fransman (2010, 21ff.), perceives the whole ICT sector as an ecosystem, thus allowing for complex interactions between a number of heterogeneous agents. According to him, reference to six functional layers are best suited to describe the current structure of the ICT sector (see Table 1). The basic layer consists of networked elements which provide telecommunication equipment as well as computer hard- and software. They feed into the networks of layer 2 which are increasingly substitutable. With the Transmission Control Protocol/Internet Protocol (*TCP/IP*) connection between hitherto separate networks became possible, leading to the emergence of new firms offering new services (layer 3–5). But only with the supply of easy to navigate software (browsers) (layer 4) the possibility to use different networks over the TCP/IP-interface became widespread. There is still no sign that the potential of ICT are exhausted, with an ongoing dynamic generating innovations at each layer on and on. Currently, they relate to the speed of data processing, innovations in storing and accessing data (cloud computing and blockchain technologies), novel ways of analysing data (Big Data, machine learning, artificial intelligence) or gaining and using data (Internet of Things), to name just a few of the more recent developments. The actors on all these layers differ. However, there is permanent interaction between them, with market processes and thus economic incentives dominating.

Although the origin of the ICT system goes back to the emergence of the telegraph and telephone in the late nineteenth century, it was not until after the Second World War that important innovations in a number of quite different and back then separate industries were made. This shaped the ICT trajectory that we experience these days. But only from 1995 on, a new era started characterized by the widespread use of the internet (see Appendix 1 in Fransman (2010) for a concise overview of the main

Table 1 The six-layer ICT system

Layer	Function with selected sectors
Layer 1	Networked elements (1) Devices: microprocessors, memories; others (2) Systems: telecoms equipment incl. routers and servers, computer hardware and system software, consumer electronics incl. mobile phones, etc.
Layer 2	Network operating (1) Core network operators: telecom operators (fixed and mobile), TV cable operators, broadcasters (terrestrial, satellite), others (electricity firms, e.g.) (2) Access network operators: fixed, cellular mobile, other wireless
TCP/IP	*Layer*
Layer 3	Internet connectivity: internet access and service providers
Layer 4	Middleware, navigation (browsers), search and innovation platforms
Layer 5	Content, applications and services
Layer 6	Final consumption

Source Own composition according to Fransman (2010, 32, exhibit 2.4)

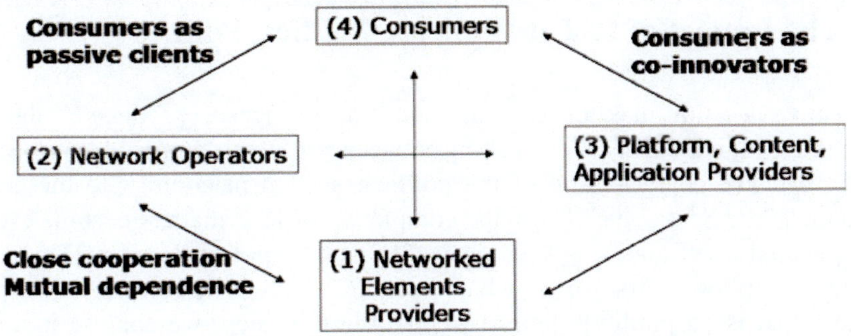

Fig. 1 Consumers' role in the ICT system. *Source* Own composition according to Fransman (2010, 39, exhibit 3.4)

technological innovations underlying the ICT sector). In addition, in the current period consumers acquire a new function as "co-evolving innovators" with respect to content, applications and services (Fransman, 2010, 50 and Fig. 1). This is quite in contrast to the traditional role of consumers as passive clients (Fransman, 2010, 50f.).

Traditionally, consumers are primarily a source of revenue for companies, finally deciding on the success of firms through their decisions on which goods and services to buy. With ICT consumers assume more and more additional functions. They become co-producers by providing knowledge and information to suppliers and finally even assume the function as co-innovators by creating content (see Table 2). "Through its aggregative and interactive properties, its widespread availability and its low cost and ease of use, the internet has incorporated final consumers as never before into the innovation process, not only in the ICT ecosystem but in the economy as a whole" (Fransman, 2010, 51). In the following section we take a closer look what implications these developments have in regard to the application of ICT in the political system.

Table 2 The changing role of final consumers

1	As sources of revenue
2	As **user-feedback providers** (e.g. von Hippel, 1998)
3	As **sources of knowledge** (e.g. open source software, Wikipedia)
4	As **sources of information** (e.g. Web 2.0)
5	As **content creators**
6	As **conversers** (e.g. social networking, blogging)
7	As **activist citizens**

Source Fransman (2010, 51, exhibit 3.7) (original emphasis)

3 The Impact of ICT on Policies, Politics, Polities

Collective decision-making on what goods and services to produce by the state as opposed to individual decision-making between consumers and producers on markets is the decisive characteristic of the political system in contrast to the economic system. While Sect. 2 has shown the complexity of ICT, matters become even more complicated when analysing the impact of ICT on the political system. Therefore, we proceed as follows. First we ask what impact ICT has on the outcome of the political system that is on public policies (3.1). In the next step, we analyse its influence on the political decision-making process, while still taking the underlying political institutions as given (3.2). Finally, we take a short look also at its potential impact on the constitutional dimension that is, on the polity (3.3).

3.1 ICT and Policies—From eGovernment to Smart Government

The public provision of goods and services including regulations (= policies) is the main output of the political decision-making process. As in regard to goods and services produced by private companies (eCommerce), ICT are also used by public bureaucracies. Over the last years the term eGovernment came in use to characterize this (Promberger et al., 2010). With the ongoing digitalization it is now also referred to as "digital government" or as "smart government" taking into account the latest developments (Breier et al., 2017; Kneuer, 2019; World Bank, n.d.); in regard to the by now widespread use of mobile devices one also finds the term "mGovernment" (OECD/International Telecommunications Union, 2011).

There exist numerous definitions of eGovernment. According to the EU Commission (2003, 7) it "is defined (…) as the use of information and communication technologies in public administrations combined with organisational change and new skills in order to improve public services and democratic processes and strengthen support to public policies." A more recent definition by the World Bank (2015) states that it "refers to the use by government agencies of information technologies (such as Wide Area Networks, the Internet, and mobile computing) that have the ability to transform relations with citizens, businesses, and other arms of government."

As in the economic sphere, ICT are applied to the interaction between government agencies (G2G) as well as between government agencies and the citizens (G2C), or government agencies and businesses (G2B). ICT assist in supplying public goods and services and regulations. (One way-) *Information* is provided, for example, by websites of cities or public agencies. (Two way-) C*ommunication* enables citizens or business to use email or other online communication services for directly interacting with public bureaucracies. Finally, ICT can be used for *transactions*, too, that is for complete *services delivery* (Promberger et al., 2010, 10ff.). A necessary prerequisite for this is investment in both adequate hardware and software by public administrations. This entails the adaptation of given ICT solutions provided by the industry to the special needs of public actors as compared to private businesses. As a consequence, innovations are generated which encompass not only content, applications and services but also require adaptations in the other layers as stated in Table 1. Besides, to successfully implement new technologies in an organization, complementary organizational changes must take place. Accordingly, organizational change and skill development are a necessary supplement. Such innovation processes are not freely available; they consume resources and take time. As with all innovation, there is no guarantee for them of being successfully implemented.

Moreover, there is co-evolution of ICT applications in public administrations and its impact on the public service provision. In the course of implementing ICT to provide public goods and services, the special needs and restrictions given by public administrations and their tasks have to be taken into account. Since the same holds for the technical restrictions provided by ICT, their implementation also has feedback effects on how to carry out public policies in the future. Accordingly, by adopting ICT both the technology evolves as well as the way in which public goods and services are provided. In addition, ICT also enable to provide new ways of how the public goods and services are supplied. Thus, innovation occurs both in the production process as well as in regard to the public goods and services. The trajectory of ICT application in public administration is characterized by four stages (Table 3).

Like in the private sphere, ICT in public services also evolves from a more supply-side perspective to one focussing more and more on the needs and preferences of the demand-side. Anderson et al. (2015, 30–34) classify this path as going from government-centric to a fully citizen-centric use of ICT (for more on this see Saeed et al., 2019).

What impact has ICT when applied to the supply of public goods and services? One of the main effects of ICT is the resulting strong reduction in information and transaction costs. This also holds in applying it to public policies. As a consequence, ICT enables the provision of tailor-made public goods and services which better match the preferences of the citizens. However, to assess the impact of ICT on public goods and services, additional criteria both from economics and political sciences are available. The former refer to the costs for and the quality of producing public goods with the help of ICT as well as to the rate of innovations generated by adopting ICT. In regard to the latter, access to the goods and services thus provided ('digital divide'), accountability and legitimacy are most important. Implementing ICT in public policies entail both positive and negative effects, which differ among different

Table 3 Stages of implementing ICT in public administrations

1	Billboard stage
2	Partial service-delivery stage
3	Portal stage with fully executable and integrated service delivery
4	Interactive democracy stage

Source Own composition according to West (2005, 8f.)

policies, but also for the same policy over the short- and the long-term. Therefore, no clear-cut overall assessment is possible (For a recent analysis see Stember et al., 2018).

So far, ICT in public administrations is still mainly used to realize efficiency effects by substituting analogous modes of providing public goods and services. However, the newest technological developments like the blockchain technology, the availability of "big data" for evaluating public policies and artificial intelligence (including machine learning and cognitive computing) may enable a quite novel way of producing public goods. It has the potential to fundamentally overhaul the way public administration works. This includes also a number of profound challenges not only in regard to data security, privacy issues, but also for how democracy will work in the future (Demaj, 2018; Guckelberger, 2019; Szostek, 2019).

While these latest technological developments open up the possibility of radically changing the way public administration works in the future, the application of eGovernment still shows a very slow rate of diffusion. The current COVID-19 pandemia gives a very pointed picture on the working of ICT applications in Europe (EU Commission, 2019; United Nations, 2020). Therefore, in the near future, we will find a simultaneity of efforts to catch-up with mainstream ICT solutions in public bureaucracies and of experiments with the latest ICT-based developments, like Open Government Data (Charalabidis et al., 2018). As a result, the unsolved problems regarding data security, privacy aspects etc. will come to the foreground showing how interlinked the technological, economic and political evolution of ICT is (Dwyer, 2020). In developing countries, eGovernment poses additional challenges, but opens also further opportunities to increase transparency, strengthen accountability and reduce corruption, for example (see the contributions in Alcaide Muñoz & Rodríguez Bolívar, 2018).

3.2 ICT and Politics—From eGovernance to eDemocarcy to eParticipation

ICT not only affects public policies, which are one of the main outcomes of the political process, but this very process of policy-making itself. Governments elected by the public for a limited time period are the main agent in putting forward legislation in representative democracies. Accordingly, getting elected is one of the main goals of political parties.

However, politics cannot be reduced to regular election campaigns. According to Fig. 2, politics is a process of policy formation in which individual preferences are aggregated by means of collective decision-making. Only after successfully mobilizing for one's individually perceived problem, this enters the legislative level. There it competes with other issues for attention in parliament. Only if its supporters are

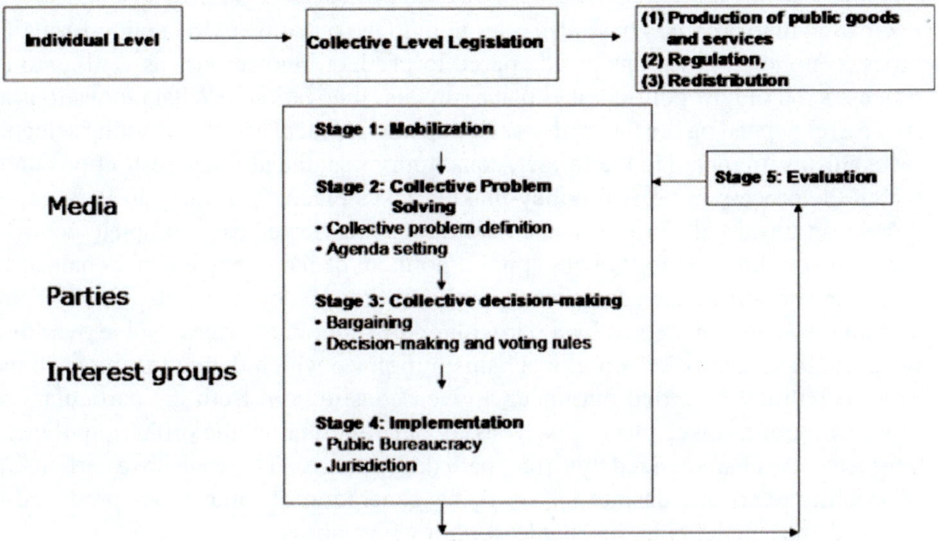

Fig. 2 The process of policy formation. *Source* Own composition according to Meier and Slembeck (1998)

successful in putting it on the collective agenda, legislation will be enacted and implemented eventually. For this to happen, not only political parties, but interest groups and the media play a decisive role, too.

Collective problems differ in regard to the number of people affected and the degree to which they might raise concerns among voters and/ or the public. When taking these two dimensions into account, the—simplified—classification in Table 4 holds. Chances are best to be successful in the policy formation process for interest-group problems with only a rather small group of people being affected, however, to a high degree, like e.g. trade unions. In contrast to that, chances are poorest for structural problems where a huge number of people are affected, but only to a low degree, like e.g. consumer protection or environmental issues.

To analyse innovation and change in politics, the evolutionary economics approach is useful, too. Like in markets, political entrepreneurs play an important role

Table 4 Classification of collective problems

	Degree of concern	
Number of people affected	Low	High
Few	Elite problem	**Interest-group problem**
Many	**Structural problem**	Crisis problem

Source According to Meier and Slembeck (1998, 74) (emphasis added by the author, M.E.)

in creating innovations. These also refer both to the outcome of the policy-formation process (policy innovations as compared to product innovations) as well as to the process itself of how politics takes place (process innovations). What innovations are successful depend on the respective selection environment and the resulting selection mechanisms. In regard to the former, constitutions set the ultimate restrictions under which the process of normal policy-making takes place. According to Persson and Tabellini (2002, 481), "(p)olitical constitutions are viewed as incomplete contracts laying down the rules for how to appoint political decision makers on behalf of the voters and how to allocate decision-making authority, or control rights, among them." Within the scope thus given by a particular constitution, the rules evolve over time, resulting in the set of selection mechanism in place which define the outer bounds on how politics is carried out under a given constitution. Both the particular way in which politics takes place as well as its outcome that is, the different policies it generates, are characterized by strong path dependences. These ensure a certain kind of stability over time despite the on-going generation of innovations produced by political entrepreneurs in the course of policy formation.

Terms like eGovernance or eDemocracy are in use in regard to the impact of ICT on politics, referring to different effects of ICT on collective decision-making. According to the UNESCO, eGovernance is characterized by "the public sector's use of information and communication technologies with the aim of improving information and service delivery, encouraging citizen participation in the decision-making process and making government more accountable, transparent and effective" (UNESCO, 2013). Following Lindner and Aichholzer (2020, 18) eDemocracy is "the practice of democracy with the support of digital media in political communication and participation", while eParticipation "encompasses all forms of political participation, making use of digital media, including both formally institutionalised mechanisms and informal civic engagement".

ICT affect politics in different ways over its whole cycle (Frissen et al., 2007). For one thing, ICT are used by already established political parties, interest groups, or media to support their activities. Thus, ICT are just another means to communicate with supporters and potential voters to increase mobilization (for the evolving views on how ICT affects political communication see Coleman, 2009; Neumayer, 2020; Wei, 2020). To this end applications, content and services are developed to fulfil the respective tasks in the policy formation process. In this way, ICT is used by parties also to reach additional voters (i.e. usually younger voters with higher educational background). Twitter and Facebook, along with the websites of party candidates and politicians are well-known examples. Besides, electoral campaigns also rely increasingly on ICT assistance, thus supplementing advertising campaigns in the traditional print as well as radio and television media. There are some signs that ICT are favourable for oppositional parties in election campaigns since it is a low cost instrument for reaching large groups of the electorate. This also seems to hold in regard to more extremist parties, which are rather at the margin of the political spectrum. While access to print and TV media seems to be more restricted for them, ICT provide a low cost alternative for disseminating their points of view (see for example Barlai, 2013 on the use of the internet by the extremist right-wing Austrian FPÖ and Hungarian Jobbik).

In addition to that, ICT also give way of new actors entering the political arena. The most prominent example are the Pirate parties. Currently Pirate parties are active in more than 40 countries, the first was founded in Sweden in 2006 (Wikipedia, 2013a). Pirate parties' programmes focus on issues directly linked to ICT like "civil rights, direct democracy and participation, reform of copyright and patent law, free sharing of knowledge (open content), information privacy, transparency, freedom of information and network neutrality" (Wikipedia, 2013b). Besides, Pirate parties not only apply ICT for externally mobilizing support (i.e. voters) for their subjects, but for internal collective decision-making as well. To this end "Liquid feedback" has been developed, which provides a tool to combine direct and representative democracy in novel ways for decision-making within the party (Interaktive Demokratie, 2013). Although Pirate parties had been very successful in some countries and elections, they realized a sharp decline in popularity among voters, resulting in a loss of representation in parliaments as well as active party members (for Germany see Biselli, 2017). The problems they encounter on their way to party formation are a good example of the limitations of ICT when applied to policy-making.

Many representative democracies also know direct democratic elements, often at different jurisdictional levels. ICT also lead to a decrease of the costs for mobilizing people to take part in such activities, like direct democratic referenda or initiatives. Through the impact on reducing information costs, ICT are, again, a means to improve transparency and the knowledge base for people taking part in such votes. By this, ICT do not have a different effect in regard to direct democratic activities when compared with representative democratic activities. Aichholzer and Rose (2020) provide a profound discussion of the different options, ICT tools and digitalization opens for eParticipation, along the following three functions of political participation: monitoring, agenda-setting and decision-making. They find that eParticipation is still most successful regarding monitoring and agenda-setting activities, while less important in the final decision-making stage (for a prescriptive analysis of eGovernance see Suri & Sushil, 2017). All in all, the former utopian hopes according to which ICT should enable more comprehensive participation of citizens in politics has now given way to a more differentiated view both at the opportunities as well as challenges and risks associated with it (Hintz, 2020; Kneuer & Datts, 2020; Ronchi, 2019; Schradie, 2019; Smith et al. 2019).

3.3 ICT, Polities and Regime Shifts

So far, we have assumed the underlying constitution, which defines the basic rules under which policy-making takes place, both to be democratic and given. However, in 2021, Freedom House reported the 15th year in series a decline in political rights and civil liberties including also Western democracies like the U.S. (Freedom

House, 2021). Shifts between different political systems are a widespread experience. Usually they entail also changes in the underlying constitutional rules. This holds in particular when there is a shift from authoritarian to democratic regimes and vice versa.

With the so-called Arab Spring a wave of protest and a number of regime shifts took place in the Arab region from the end of 2010 on. The online communication service 'Twitter' gained particular importance in the protests in Moldavia (2009), Iran (2009/20), Tunisia (2010/11) and Egypt (2011). We are far from fully understanding the dynamics of revolutionary regime shifts. However, ICT played an important role in mobilizing the opposition and feeding the resulting dynamics (for an interesting analysis see Lang and de Sterck 2014). Again, the properties of ICT in reducing information costs and in providing low-cost communication made it so effective. However, 10 years later, the outcome of these protests are more than disillusioning regarding the liberating effects and the potential of ICT to help establish a stable democratic polity.

In addition to its effects on regime shifts, ICT allow more profound changes in policy-making in democratic political systems, too. For example, ICT makes available a much broader set of direct democratic elements. Instead of applying a (qualified) majority rule in referenda or initiatives, more sophisticated decision rules could be used at low costs. They could capture individual preferences much better than it is the case with the rules currently in place. Again, creating such genuinely new democratic regime variants requires modifications of the underlying constitutional rules. While the Pirate parties had been agents aiming for such a change, so far, there are no majorities for such profound constitutional reforms in sight.

Finally, one has to keep in mind that ICT also entail risks for both political rights and civil liberties. Due to the decrease in information costs, ICT also reduce the costs of collecting large volumes of information. This, in turn, increases the risk that some form of authoritarian states might develop or persist, leading to the generation of novel dependencies and a reduction of civic freedom and liberties. In addition to questions of data privacy already addressed above, the issue of state surveillance comes on the agenda. In particular China's Social Credit Rating program seems to be an example of the possibilities of how to restrict personal freedom by ICT led tools (for an overview see von Bloomberg, 2020 as well as the contributions in Everling, 2020; see Dencik et al., 2019 who analyse the working of data-driven governance for the UK).

4 Conclusion

The main feature of ICT is to provide information and to communicate it at much higher speed and at much lower costs over time and space than it was possible with mere analogous modes of communication. Accordingly, the resulting information and communication costs decrease enormously in the areas where ICT are used, leading to a decrease in search and transaction costs. Besides, with ICT digital production technologies can be used substituting analogous technologies, both manual work as well as brain-work. Thus, like in the economic sphere, the use of ICT in providing public goods and services reduces production and transaction costs which may lead to efficiency gains. Moreover, ICT also influence the political transaction costs of public policy-making. In addition, ICT could also result in changing the underlying institutions shaping the political process so as to make further improvements possible.

As Sect. 2 shows, the development of ICT is a complex one, including a number of different technologies. The exploration of the underlying technological paradigm seems to be far from being exhausted. Therefore, also in the near future further innovations are to be expected which might change the current state of ICT completely, adding additional services and applications to the already existing ones. Accordingly, it would be misleading to speak about a "digital revolution". The developments we experience are the result of an on-going process of gradual modifications and changes ('recombinations of already known elements' in the Schumpeterian sense), while at the same time being of a very profound nature, too.

The same holds when it comes to the application of ICT in the political system. Both in regard to policies, politics and polities the application of ICT lags behind its use for commercial purposes. This is not surprising when taking into account that in markets competition between large numbers of companies for consumers' purchasing power pushes companies' efforts to use ICT for generating product and process innovations. In contrast to that, a state has a monopoly when it comes to supplying public goods and services to its citizens. This is the more so, as there are only few substitutes available for citizens. Accordingly, the lower rate of innovations generated by ICT which are applied in the public sphere is not surprising. But since further innovations in ICT are driven mainly by economic incentives resulting from its application in the commercial sphere, the resulting spill-overs to ICT application in the political system ensure an on-going evolution there, too.

References

Aichholzer, G., & Rose, G. (2020). Experience with digital tools in different types of e-Participation. In L. Hennen, et al. (Eds.), *European E-democracy in practice* (pp. 93–140). Cham/Switzerland.

Alcaide Muñoz, L., & Rodríguez Bolívar, M. P. (Eds.). (2018). *International E-government development*. Cham/Switzerland.

Anderson, D., et al. (2015). *E-Government strategy, ICT and innovation for citizen engagement*, New York.

Barlai, M. (2013). Politischer Extremismus und Populismus in Europa - Fester Bestandteil einer E-Öffentlichkeit? FPÖ und Jobbik im Web, In P. Filzmaier, et al. (Eds.), *Wir sind EU-ropa. Von vielen Eu-Öffentlichkeiten zu einer europäischen Öffentlichkeit*. Edition netPOL. Politische Kommunikation, Vol. 4 (pp. 60–72). Wien.

Biselli, A. (2017). Lieber auf zu neuen Ufern: Über den Zustand der Piratenpartei. Netzpolitik.org. September 18, 2017, https://netzpolitik.org/2017/lieber-auf-zu-neuen-ufern-ueber-den-zustand-der-piratenpartei/. Last access March 08, 2021.

Breier, C., Meyer, M., & Baumann, M. (2017). Smart Government: Was macht eine smarte Verwaltung aus? Eine Literaturanalyse. *Yearbook of Swiss Administrative Sciences, 8*, 168–184. https://doi.org/10.5334/ssas.113

Chaminade, C., Lundvall, B.-Å., & Haneef, S. (2018). *Advanced introduction to national innovation systems*. Cheltenham.

Charalabidis, Y., et al. (2018). *The world of open data*. Cham/Switzerland.

Cimoli, M., Dosi, G., & Yu, X. (2020). Industrial policies, patterns of learning, and development. In A. Oqubay, et al. (Eds.), *The Oxford handbook of industrial policy* (pp. 92–124).

Coleman, S. (2009). E-democracy: The history and future of an idea. In R. Mansell (Ed.), *The Oxford handbook of information and communication technologies* (pp. 362–382).

Demaj, L. (2018). Smart Government: Die Verwaltung und den Staat der Zukunft denken. *Informatik Spektrum, 41*, 123–137. https://doi.org/10.1007/s00287-018-1098-x.

Dencik, L., et al. (2019). The 'golden view': Data-driven governance in the scoring society. *Internet Policy Review* [online], *8*. https://doi.org/10.14763/2019.2.1413.

Dosi, G. (1982). Technological paradigms and technological trajectories. A suggested interpretation of the determinants and directions of technical change. *Research Policy, 11*, 147–162. https://doi.org/10.1016/0048-7333(82)90016-6.

Dosi, G., & Nelson, R. R. (2020). Technological paradigms and technological trajectories. In M. Augier & D. V. Teece (Eds.), *The Palgrave encyclopedia of strategic management* (pp. 1–12). https://doi.org/10.1057/978-1-349-94848-2_733-1.

Dwyer, T. (2020). Privacy from your mobile devices? In R. Ling, et al. (Eds.), *The Oxford handbook of mobile communication and society* (pp. 546–562).

EU Commission. (2003). *The role of eGovernment for Europe's future*. Communication {SEC(2003) 1038}, Brussels, 26.9.2003 COM(2003) 567 final. http://eur-lex.europa.eu/LexUriServ/LexUriServ.do?uri=COM:2003:0567:FIN:EN:PDF. Last access March 08, 2021.

EU Commission. (2019). Digital economy and society index report 2019, digital public services, DESI Report EU 2019, https://ec.europa.eu/digital-single-market/en/news/digital-economy-and-society-index-desi-2019. Last access March 03, 2021.

Everling, O. (Ed.). (2020). *Social Credit Rating. Reputation und Vertrauen beurteilen*. Wiesbaden.

Fagerberg, J. (2005). Innovation. A guide to the literature. In J. Fagerberg, D. C., Mowery, & R. R. Nelson (Eds.), *The Oxford handbook of innovation* (pp. 1–28).

Fagerberg, J., Mowery, D. C., & Nelson, R. R. (Eds.). (2005). *The Oxford handbook of innovation*, Oxford et al.

Fransman, M. (2010). *The new ICT ecosystem: Implications for policy and regulation*, Cambridge et al.

Freedom House. (2021). New report: The global decline in democracy has accelerated. *Press Release*, March 3, 2021, https://freedomhouse.org/article/new-report-global-decline-democracy-has-accelerated. Last access March 08, 2021.

Freeman, C. (1987). *Technology policy and economic performance*. Lessons from Japan. London.

Freeman, C., & Louca, F. (2002). *As time goes by: From the industrial revolution to the information revolution*. Oxford, New York.

Frissen, V., et al. (2007). *The future of eGovernment. An exploration of ICT-driven models of eGovernment for the EU in 2020*, European Commission, Joint Research Centre, Institute for Prospective Technological Studies, Luxembourg, http://ftp.jrc.es/EURdoc/eur22897en.pdf. Last access July 11, 2013.

Guckelberger, A. (2019). *Öffentliche Verwaltung im Zeitalter der Digitalisierung. Analysen und Strategien zur Verbesserung des E-Governments aus rechtlicher Sicht*, Baden-Baden.

Hintz, A. (2020). Digital citizenship in the age of datafication. In S. J. Yates, & R. E. Rice (Eds.), *The Oxford handbook of digital technology and society* (pp. 525–546).

Interaktive Demokratie. (2013). *Liquid feedback. Interactive democracy*, http://liquidfeedback.org/. Last access March 08, 2021.

Kneuer, M. (2019). E-government im internationalen Vergleich. In J. Hofmann, et al. (Eds.), *Politik in der digitalen Gesellschaft*, Bielefeld (pp. 189–204).

Kneuer, M., & Datts, M. (2020). E-democracy and the matter of scale revisiting the democratic promises of the internet in terms of the spatial dimension. *Politische Vierteljahresschrift, 61*, 285–308. https://doi.org/10.1007/s11615-020-00250-6.

Lang, J., & de Sterck, H. (2014). The Arab spring: A simple compartmental model for the dynamics of a revolution. *Mathematical Social Science, 69*, 12–21. https://doi.org/10.1016/j.mathsocsci.2014.01.004

Lindner, R., & Aichholzer, G. (2020). E-Democracy: Conceptual Foundations and Recent Trends. In L. Hennen, et al. (Eds.), *European E-democracy in practice*, Cham/Switzerland, (pp. 11–45).

Meier, A., & Slembeck, T. (1998). Wirtschaftspolitik. Ein kognitiv-evolutionärer Ansatz, München, Wien, 2.ed.

Metcalfe, S. J. (1988). The diffusion of innovations: An interpretative survey. In G. Dosi, et al. (Eds.), *Technical change and economic theory*, London (pp. 560–590).

Metcalfe, S. J. (1998). On rival concepts of competition and the evolutionary connection. In S. J. Metcalfe (Ed.), *Evolutionary economcis and creative destruction*, London et al. (pp. 10–39).

Nelson, R. R. (1995). Recent evolutionary theorizing about economic change. *Journal of Economic Literature, 33*, 48–90.

Neumayer, C. (2020). Political protest and mobile communication. In R. Ling, et al. (Eds.), *The Oxford handbook of mobile communication and society* (pp. 243–256).

OECD. (1997). *National systems of innovation*, http://www.oecd.org/science/inno/2101733.pdf. Last access March 08, 2021.

OECD/International Telecommunications Union. (2011). *M-Government: mobile technologies for responsive governments and connected societies*. https://doi.org/10.1787/9789264118706-en.

Persson, T., & Tabellin, G. (2002). Political economics: Explaining economic policy, Vol. 1, Cambridge/MA.

Promberger, K., Bernhart, J., & Früh, G. (2010). E-Government. In K. Promberger, J. Bernhart, & G. Früh (Eds.), *E-Government. Konzepte, Modelle und Erfahrungen*, Wien (pp. 1–35).

Ronchi, A. M. (2019). *e-Democracy*. Cham/Switzerland.

Saeed, S., Ramayah, T., & Mahmood, Z. (2019). *User centric E-government*. Cham/Switzerland.

Schradie, J. (2019). *The revolution that wasn't. How digital activism favors conservatives*. Cambridge/MA.

Schumpeter, J. A. (1952). *Theorie der wirtschaftlichen Entwicklung. Eine Untersuchung über Unternehmergewinn, Kapital, Kredit, Zins und den Konjunkturzyklus*, Berlin, 5.ed.

Smith, A., et al. (2019). *Publics in emerging economies worry social media sow division, even as they offer new chances for political engagement*, pew research center, May 2019, https://www.pewresearch.org. Last access March 08, 2021.

Stember, J., Eixelsberger, W., & Spichiger, A. (2018). *Wirkungen von E-Government*. Wiesbaden.

Suri, P. K., & Sushil. (2017). *Strategic planning and implementation of E-governance*. Singapore.

Szostek, D. (2019). *Blockchain and the law*. Baden-Baden.

UNESCO. (2013). art. E-Governance, http://portal.unesco.org/ci/en/ev.php-URL_ID=3038&URL_DO=DO_TOPIC&URL_SECTION=201.html. Last access March 08, 2021.

United Nations. (2020). *2020 United Nations E-government survey. Digital government in the decade of action for sustainable development. With addendum on COVID-19 response*, https://www.un.org/development/desa/publications/publication/2020-united-nations-e-government-survey. Last access March 03, 2021.

von Bloomberg, M. (2020). The social credit system and china's rule of law. In O. Everling (Ed.), *Social credit rating*. Reputation und Vertrauen beurteilen. Wiesbaden (pp. 111–137).

von Hippel, E. (1998). *The source of innovation*. Oxford.

Wei, R. (2020). Mobile media and political communication. In R. Ling, et al. (Eds.), *The Oxford handbook of mobile communication and society* (pp. 228–243).

West, D. M. (2005). *Digital government: Technology and public sector performance*. Princeton.

Wikipedia. (2013a). Art. List of Pirate Parties, http://en.wikipedia.org/wiki/List_of_Pirate_Parties. Last access July 11, 2013.

Wikipedia. (2013b). Art. Pirate Party, online *http://en.wikipedia.org/wiki/Pirate_Party*. Last access July 11, 2013.

World Bank. (n.d.). BRIEF Digital Government for Development, *https://www.worldbank.org/en/topic/digitaldevelopment/brief/digital-government-for-development*. Last access March 03, 2021.

World Bank. (2015). BRIEF e-Government, May 19, 2015 https://www.worldbank.org/en/topic/digitaldevelopment/brief/e-government. Last access March 03, 2021.

Sustainable Upscaling: The Role of Digitalization in Providing Health Care and Health Insurance Coverage in Developing Countries

Jens Geissler

1 Sustainability and Increasing Demand in the Health Sector

In a report published by the World Commission on Environment and Development in 1987, sustainable development is defined as 'development that meets the needs of the present without compromising the ability of future generations to meet their own needs.'[1] The document stresses need, but also acknowledges limitations posed by such environmental issues as climate change, loss of biodiversity, and pollution. In the health sector the term 'sustainability' is often applied in the very narrow sense of financial sustainability,[2] but the relation between environmental challenges and health[3] and waste produced in the medical sector are also factors.[4] Conservation of energy[5] and recycling of materials like personal protection equipment[6] are only slowly catching on in the health sector.

In 2015 the United Nations General Assembly agreed upon a set of Sustainable Development Goals.[7] Goal 3 (good health and well-being) focuses on basic health

1 See United Nations (1987).

2 See, for example, Hardcastle et al. (2017).

3 See, for example, van der Vliet et al. (2018).

4 See Carnero (2015). For a literature review on sustainability in the health sector, see Marimuthu and Paulose (2016). A more recent aspect appears to be the sustainability of the supply chains in the health sector. See Subramanian et al. (2020).

5 There is currently one hospital in Germany which aims to become a 'Zero Emissions Hospital' by 2030. See, for example, KMA-Online (2020).

6 See, for example, Kimberly-Clark (n.d.).

7 See UN (2015).

J. Geissler (✉)
FOM University of Applied Sciences, Hamburg, Germany
e-mail: jens.geissler@fom.de

T. Herberger and J. Dötsch (eds.), *Digitalization, Digital Transformation and Sustainability in the Global Economy*, Springer Proceedings in Business and Economics, https://doi.org/10.1007/978-3-030-77340-3_5

needs like reducing the maternal mortality rate, preventable deaths of newborns and children under five, as well as combating diseases such as AIDS, tuberculosis, and malaria. One target is to 'achieve universal health coverage, including financial risk protection, access to quality essential health care services and access to safe, effective, quality and affordable essential medicines and vaccines for all."[8] Currently there is no indication this target will be reached.[9]

Researchers estimated as early as 2018 that half the world population can be considered as middle class.[10] For this section of the world population—at that time some 3.8 billion—the question is not only to meet basic health needs, but to benefit from advanced health services and technologies. While some may argue for limiting consumerism to achieve sustainability—there is no human right to own an SUV or to go on long-distance holiday trips—it is difficult to argue that the global middle class should not have access to the same health services and technologies as people in industrialized countries. And it is equally difficult to argue that people in industrialized countries should reduce their access to high-standard health services in order to redistribute resources. So how can sustainability be achieved in a situation where the poor (rightly) demand access to basic health services, the growing global middle class (rightly) demand the right to spend more of their resources on health services, and people in industrialized countries (rightly) demand continued access to high-quality health care?

There is no simple remedy, only a *combination* of different measures will help. Focusing on one of these, I will argue for the role of digitalization in meeting increasing demand without a corresponding increase in resources.[11] IT systems are often difficult and expensive to design and implement, but the marginal costs of providing additional services are negligible. This is what makes digital health services so powerful in achieving universal health coverage. Digitalization can improve access to health care services, and it can support health insurances in processing large numbers of claims and payments. Both are essential to upscaling health services especially in developing countries.

The following section provides a brief discussion of the general role of IT in the health sector, specifically in relation to quality, access, and efficiency of health care and services. Section 3 gives examples of IT in the health sector, both in relation to health care services (e.g., electronic patient records and digital health services), and in relation to health insurances (e.g. business process automation and self-services used by insurees). In Sect. 4 I discuss different risks which may prevent digitalization from supporting health sector sustainability, like lack of digital literacy and access which may prevent patients from utilising services, as may nonacceptance by medical doctors acting as gatekeepers to these services; technical risks which

[8] See UNDP (2015).

[9] World Bank (n.d.), for example, indicates that out-of-pocket health expenditures have increased in many regions of the world.

[10] See Kharas and Hamel (2018).

[11] For a broader discussion on the relation between innovation and sustainable development, see McGahan et al. (2014).

are especially large in the design and implementation of large-scale data-exchange platforms, while financial risks may result from changing regulatory requirements. Sections 5 and 6 explain how international collaboration can support health sector digitalisation, and what role governments have in setting the regulatory framework. In the concluding Sect. 7 I argue for an approach to digitalization in the health sector based on organisational needs and capabilities. This will ensure that digitalisation can actually fulfill its role in supporting the sustainability of health sectors especially in developing countries.

2 The Role of IT in Satisfying the Demand for Health Care

IT systems are usually characterised by rather high initial costs, resulting from the initial development and from setting up the infrastructure to run them. There are also considerable costs in maintaining and running the systems, as well as adapting them to changing needs. The actual number of users, however, is a minor cost factor because of scalable cloud infrastructure services which make it easy and rather inexpensive to 'grow' the infrastructure in line with the number of users. Once the system has been set up, expanding the user base is inexpensive. This is important in terms of both the availability of staff and the costs of running a health care system.

Practically all areas of the health sector, including health insurance, are highly labour intensive. Lack of staff or the lack of financial resources to pay for staff are major obstacles in meeting health care demand. The health care demands of the poor and the growing middle classes cannot be met by simply hiring as many staff as in industrialized countries. Even in industrialized countries there is strong pressure to increase the efficiency of health care systems.

IT in the health sector includes a wide variety of technologies and systems. Broadly speaking, these fall into three areas. All three are relevant for health care services, as well as the administrative services provided by health insurances.

- Quality of care/services (e.g., higher level of accuracy in diagnostics)
- Access to care/services (e.g., video consultations or online service centers)
- Efficiency of care/services (e.g., through automation of procedures).

There is a certain interdependence between the three. For example, better diagnostics of (potential) tumors not only constitutes an improvement in the quality of care but will also increase efficiency in terms of treatment resources well spent. Likewise, improved access to specialist care through video consultations will also increase the quality of care provided.

It is quite challenging to assess and compare the status of health sector digitalization in different countries. In its Smart Health Systems project, the German Bertelsmann Foundation developed an index that takes into account not only the political system and digital health governance but also digital health infrastructure and the actual implementation of digital health services. The benchmarking of 17 primarily European countries (as well as Canada, Israel, and Australia) shows Estonia, Canada, and Denmark in the top spots, while France, Germany, and Poland received the lowest score.[12] A similar approach is the Global Digital Health Index (GDHI), a tool which helps countries benchmark and monitor their investments in digital health. In the first GDHI annual report, the 22 participating countries are ranged in five digital health maturity phases. Only Malaysia is ranked in the highest maturity level 5, while Sierra Leone, Uganda, Afghanistan, Pakistan, and Lao PRD have reached level 2.[13]

In the context of sustainability, the focus is on digital health systems which either fully replace human resources or through which human resources can be used in a much more economical way. Examples for this are illustrated in the following section of this text, without attempting to give a full overview of health-related IT. Most examples are from Germany, complemented by some from other, especially developing, countries.

3 Examples of IT in the Health Sector

3.1 Access to Information by Patients

People turn to available and trusted sources when they need information about medical issues. This information (often based on personal experience or coming from a family member) is used to decide if professional support is needed. Today, the internet has become a major source of this information, and especially 'Dr. Google' plays an important role.[14] But the main criterion for presenting content at the top of the Google list is not necessarily the quality of the content. Additionally, there is usually too much information rather than too little,[15] and much of it is directed more to health care professional than to patients. To address this gap, the German Ministry of Health launched and funds the 'National Health Portal' website, populated with patient-oriented content created by a team of independent health care professionals.[16]

This kind of information can improve the efficiency of health care systems. Patients can make an informed decision to seek professional care, thus reducing the number of unnecessary consultations and saving resources for the necessary ones. And it can reduce the risk of seeking professional care too late which may lead to complications and much higher demand for medical care.

The challenges in setting up such systems are less related to technology than to content and marketing. Establishing the professional consensus for treatment options is notoriously difficult, although this may be easier in the case of basic everyday medical needs. Secondly, the information must be presented in a way which is easily

[12] See Thiel et al. (2018).

[13] See Mechael and Edelman (2019), p. 12.

[14] See Waschinski (2019)

[15] For a list, albeit incomplete, of English-language sources, see HCF (n.d.).

[16] See Nationales Gesundheitsportal (n.d.).

understandable for nonprofessionals without compromising the quality of content. And thirdly, the information must be easy to find considering the vast number of sources on the internet. To address this, the German Ministry of Health has only recently begun to collaborate with Google. The material from the National Health Portal is presented in separate 'Knowledge Panels' which are visually separated from the usual search results.[17] In this way, the National Health Portal can use Google's large user base to reach its target audience. In terms of sustainable upscaling this means that the number of users may grow exponentially without a corresponding increase in the costs of running the portal.

3.2 Digital Health Services

Providing better access to information is certainly a positive step, but its impact on the resources needed for treatment is limited. It would be quite different if digitalization could be used not only to inform about diseases, but to treat them. Advances in artificial intelligence (AI) are rapidly increasing the treatment options of such digital health applications. Germany was—to my knowledge—the first country to establish a standard process for the accreditation of digital health apps—and their reimbursement through health insurance. Previously, reimbursement had been through individual health insurances for individual applications. Now, all insurees of the social health insurance system have access to an increasing number of applications which health care providers can prescribe and their insurance will reimburse. Inclusion in the benefit package depends on proof of medical benefits (similar to pharmaceuticals) or benefits in terms of patient empowerment and self-management, for example. Since early 2020, the start of the new process, 43 companies have sought approval for their digital health applications.[18] As of December 2020, six have been approved, covering tinnitus, insomnia, obesity, arthritis, and different types of phobias.[19]

It remains to be seen which range of diseases will at some point be treatable by digital health applications. The new approval and reimbursement process in Germany currently acts as a stimulus for the development of new applications, offering the prospect of access to a fully funded market of about 75 million potential customers. Indications from the approval process suggest that digital health apps are not focused on a small number of use cases but cover an extensive range of diseases. Digital health services will not replace the traditional health care system. But they may offer additional treatment options for an increasing number of diseases. And since they are digital, they can be offered to increasing numbers of patients without increasing the need for additional health care staff.

---

[17] See BMG (2020). Currently, there are Knowledge Panels for more than 160 diseases covered by the National Health Portal.

[18] See BfArM (n.d. a).

[19] See BfArM (n.d. b).

3.3 Access to Information by Health Care Provider/Insurance

Data plays an important role in the health sector. Data is generated and stored in the process of diagnosis and treatment: to document services provided, to determine the patient's insurance status and eligibility to receive certain services, and to verify claims either by patients or health care providers. Much of this data is generated at one point by one institution and used at a later point by another. With increasing digitalization of the health sector, more data is generated (e.g., by diagnostic imaging systems), must be stored, transferred, and made available to a user at the right point in a specific business process. Electronic records management systems are used to achieve this. Depending on the specific situation and data, the health care providers, the patients, or a health insurance—or all of them—could use electronic records.

In the context of sustainable upscaling, electronic patient records management systems serve different functions. For diagnosis and treatment, for example, the timely access to all available information prevents duplication of diagnostic activities, thus saving physical and human resources. For patients, they support patient empowerment and informed decision-making by giving them real-time access to all their health records. For health insurances, they save labour otherwise used for storage and retrieval of files and they are the basis for automating business processes. Digitalization can also be important in training health care staff. Digitalized training materials can be made available to larger numbers of training participants, including those in remote locations.

The data stored in electronic patient records also supports the further development of digital health services based on AI. The more data available in a digital and ideally well-structured form, the better the prospects of using AI-based systems to detect patterns in the data. Today, AI is successfully used in highly specific tasks like dermoscopic melanoma image classification.[20] But with more data stored in digital form and with further advances in AI technologies, AI-base solutions will become more available in a wider range of complex tasks in diagnostics and treatment.

3.4 Automation of Business Processes

When health insurance coverage increases, it increases both the number of insurees and the number of health care services covered. The result is an exponential increase in the workload for health insurance. A simple calculation may serve to illustrate this:

[20] See Brinker et al. (2019).

Insurees	1 million	2 million	3 million
Claims per insuree	1 per year	2 per year	3 per year
Workload of health insurance	1 million claims	4 million claims	9 million claims

Each claim must be verified by the health insurance. The following graph shows what this includes.

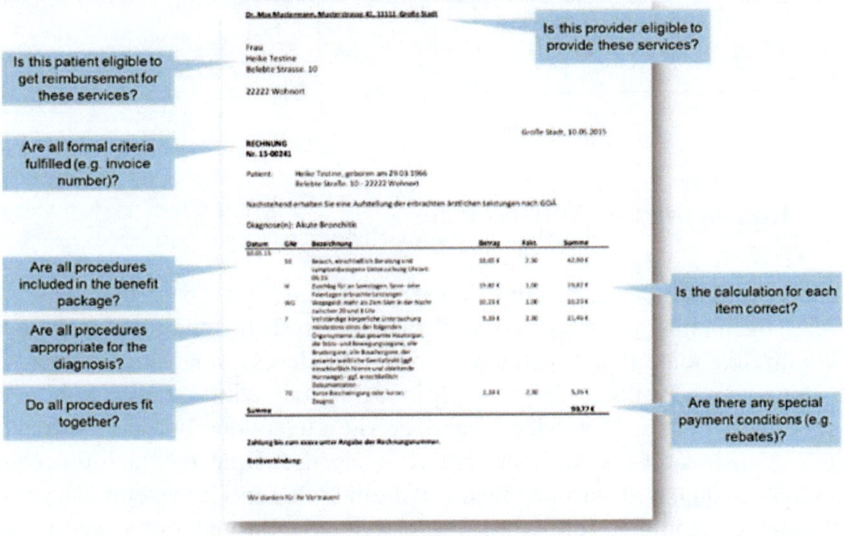

The time and skill required to verify the claim depend on the number and complexity of procedures involved. They may be very simple (an outpatient visit) or extremely complex (major surgery). Quite likely, as the benefit package increases, the number of complex procedures will increase as well. In any case, the administrative burden on health insurance will be immense. Covering this purely by increasing the number and qualifications of the workforce will not be viable. This is where the automation of business processes comes in: an IT system can electronically check data the providers submit electronically. This can be any individual or all aspects of the verification process indicated above. It can also be either for all claims of a certain type or only for selected ones. The systems are typically built up over time, i.e., starting with simple claims and/or only selected verification steps, all the way to a more or less completely automatic verification process. There will always be a certain number of claims which cannot be verified automatically. These are routed to staff members for manual verification.[21]

There are no standard figures to indicate what degree of automation is possible. Practical experience shows it depends very much on the complexity of the verification process and on the organizational capacities of the health insurance. But very generally speaking, automation rates between 65 and 95% are possible. Looking at the example above, one can calculate which automation rate would be required to manage increased coverage with the same number of staff (assuming that the original workload was handled without automation).

Workload of health insurance	1 million claims	4 million claims	9 million claims
Automation rate (%)	0	75	88.9

3.5 *Administrative Self-services*

The increased number of health care users and health insurance members will also increase the number of routine administrative requests hospitals and insurance must deal with, like making appointments, changing addresses, storing payment data or questions about available services. Without digitalization, staff members answer these requests, either in service centers or via a telephone hotline; both are rather labour intensive. Of course, there are very specific requests which do require the attention of a qualified staff member. But digital self-service systems can cover most of the above-mentioned routine issues, for example, through online service centers. Essentially, these are password-protected websites which registered users can access to update personal information or submit data relating to claims or other services. This not only saves resources for the hospital or health insurance, it can be a service to insurees or patients who don't have to travel to service centers or write letters.

Chat bots are currently less commonly used in the health care and health insurance sector but are certainly a way to augment call center staff in the future. Like online service centers, they are not meant to fully replace human staff at call centers but primarily to handle routine activities. Both online service centers and chat bots can play an important role in the sustainable upscaling of health care systems. Both are examples of digital systems which—once set up—can handle large volumes of transactions without an increase in staffing.[22]

[21] See Geissler (2017) for a detailed discussion on the automation of business processes in health insurances. In Geissler (2018) I argue that (almost) fully automated health insurances are generally possible.

[22] See Geissler (2018) for a more detailed discussion of changes and strategic challenges for health insurances by digitalization.

3.6 *Robotics*

Robotics is the replacement of physical labour by machines. The more complex the activity, and the less standardized the sequence of movement, the bigger the difficulties in implementing robotics solutions. In health care—in a hospital, for example—most activities involving the patient's body have a high level of complexity and a low level of standardization. After all, all patients have special medical needs and specific physical characteristics. For this reason, examples of robotics at the point of patient care are rare. And even some systems which are usually called 'robotics' are more accurately speaking systems to support and guide the physical movement of the surgeon, without actually replacing the movement.[23] The surgery system DaVinci is one example. There are pilot projects to replace nursing staff by robots in order to meet increasing demand. But there is very little evidence that existing robots can perform nursing activities. Only in support activities like transporting food, linen, or medication from service areas to the wards do robots currently play a larger role. In an example from a German university hospital, autonomous systems replace the labour of about a hundred staff members.[24]

These examples illustrate that robotics is certainly no solution to shortages of nursing or medical staff. This is due not only to the lack of available systems, but also to the extremely high costs and liability issues in case of malfunction. Even so, there are some areas in the health sector where robotics does play a role, as the current Corona pandemic shows. The upscaling of test capacities could only be achieved by using automated lab systems.[25] And the production of hundreds of millions of vaccine doses likewise depends on the automation of production processes.[26]

4 Risks and Risk Management

4.1 *Digital Literacy and Digital Access*

There are numerous hurdles preventing patients from using digital health services, especially in developing countries. For this paper, only a short summary of these hurdles is possible. The key point is that all the obstacles must be overcome—even one is enough to prevent the utilization of digital health services.[27]

- Literacy: Most digital health services are based on written language. However, especially in areas with low literacy, it would be possible to put more emphasis on pictures, speech or videos.

[23] See Intuitive Surgical, Inc. (n.d.).

[24] See Fuest (2018).

[25] See Wiener Zeitung (2020).

[26] See Macdonald (2020).

[27] See van Deursen and van Dijk (2015), p. 380f for a more general discussion of the digital divide.

- Access to hardware: Generally, a simple smartphone is sufficient to access digital health services. Without one, access would be severely limited.
- Access to electricity: Power outages may be a problem in remote locations, but smartphones have batteries which should be able to cover the periods without electricity.
- Network access: Most digital health services will require internet access. For very simple services (e.g., those based on text messaging) very limited internet access would be sufficient. But for more advanced services (e.g., video consultations or tutorials) much more data and better connectivity would be needed.
- Digital literacy: Users will most likely have to choose between different digital services. Making informed decisions requires a good understanding of how digital services work and how data is used.

All aspects (except, perhaps, basic literacy) are equally relevant for health care practitioners and for patients.

One should certainly be careful in trying to apply the findings about the digital divide drawn from studies done in industrialised countries to the situation in developing countries. Nonetheless, one should certainly consider the work of van Deursen and van Dijk who found that in the Netherlands, younger men with higher educational levels and higher income are, over all, most likely to have better digital access.[28] If this is the case in developing countries—and there is little to suggest that it would be different—then there is a great risk that investment in digitalization of the health sector would actually increase disparity in access to and use of health services. This is not an argument against digital health services but more of a call to consider program design as a way to explicitly address the causes for the digital divide.

4.2 Nonacceptance by Health Care Providers

Health care providers act as gatekeepers in terms of market access of health care innovations. With pharmaceuticals, for example, even if regulators and the insurance have approved them, a medical doctor still needs to prescribe them. The same is true with innovative diagnostic or other treatment options. Digital innovations in the health sector face the same hurdle. Even if they are technically available and have regulatory approval, they may still not gain widespread use if health care providers do not accept them.

Health care providers will probably not integrate digital solutions into their treatment if they perceive a given solution as increasing their administrative workload. For example, when health care providers are required to upload documents into a patient's digital health records, rather than just storing them in their own IT system or on paper. Only a high degree of usability and integration in existing systems and workflows will ensure acceptance. Ideally, digital systems should even reduce the

[28] See van Deursen and van Dijk (2015), p. 388.

administrative workload. A problem-based approach is the most likely option to lead to positive results: addressing the deficiencies health care providers deal with every day in managing their practice and caring for patients. IT systems will only be accepted if they help to solve real-life problems.

Another aspect to be considered is payment. If health care providers see the use of digital tools (e.g., providing video consultations) as additional workload, there must be a corresponding reimbursement. New activities like explaining the workings of a digital health application must also be included. After all it is quite likely that if health care providers prescribe digital health applications, they will also be asked by their patients when they need support.

4.3 Technical Challenges

The level of technical challenges depends on the type of application. In implementing (and perhaps adjusting) standardized applications with limited integration in digital data-exchange networks, the challenges are quite limited. Many applications such as video consultations have been around for a long time. The challenges are greater for customized systems in larger institutions like health insurances or hospitals where the IT systems are used not only to store and process data but also to manage work. Weaknesses in business process management (e.g., in terms of documentation and standardization of processes) will make it that much more challenging to implement adequate IT systems.

The greatest challenge—and risk—is the design and implementation of large-scale data-exchange platforms. The level of risk depends on the number and heterogeneity of users. The large number of users (hundreds of hospitals, thousands of health care providers, millions of patients/insurees) with very different technical capacities and professional expectations will make it very difficult to create a common understanding about what the system is supposed to do and how it should be set up. And this type of system can never be off-the-shelf. One can learn from the experiences of other countries, but it is not possible to simply implement an existing system.

4.4 Financial Risks

It is extremely difficult to estimate the costs of custom-made IT systems, and there is no direct relation between the costs of a system and the benefits it brings. The normal paradigm of 'pay more and get more' does not necessarily work, as the recent development of Corona tracing apps shows. The technical requirement was for an application which helps trace personal contacts and informs people at risk of having contact with a person infected by Covid-19. Based on media reports, actual development costs in Germany were €20 million, ten times as much as in Switzerland, Austria and Norway. In Iceland and Italy, companies and free-lance developers developed the apps for free. One IT consultant in Germany estimated potential development costs at €450,000 based on standard rates.[29] The UK spent about £35 million, including about £10 million for a version which was later abandoned.[30]

Clearly, very similar features can result in vastly different costs. One reason is that there are different requirements (e.g., in terms of data protection and interconnection with other systems), in addition to the contracts negotiated with the developers/service providers. Another factor is time: it will certainly cost considerably more to develop a system in a short time span. Changes in regulatory requirements, (e.g., in terms of data protection) will also lead to increases in costs.

5 International Collaboration

It is certainly more difficult to transfer digital health systems from one country to another than—say—use pharmaceutical products in another one. But considering the high initial costs of developing digital solutions and the low costs of extending the use to additional users, international collaboration can be especially beneficial. We can identify different types of collaboration in the digital health sector, ranging from exchange of information and experiences and adoption of international standards like SNOMED CT[31] to international collaborations in which tools are developed and shared. There are networks of digital health institutions at the global level and in different regions of the world. The WHO plays an important role in this regard and in 2019 established the Department for Digital Health and Innovation which has produced two guidelines on the topic: *Recommendations on Digital Interventions for Health System Strengthening*[32] and *Digital Implementation Investment Guide*.[33] One of the largest nongovernmental international networks is the International Society for Telemedicine and eHealth (ISfTeH) which aims to facilitate the international dissemination of knowledge and experiences in telemedicine and eHealth.[34] The mapping of regional and national associations in the field of digital health would be a subject for a separate paper. To mention only two very active regional initiatives, there is the Asia eHealth Information Network (AeHIN)[35] and the European Connected Health Alliance (ECAlliance).[36]

There are fewer international initiatives where actual digital solutions are jointly developed. This is due to the need for localized solutions in line with specific requirements, regulations and needs. The most remarkable and successful one is probably

[29] See Bott and Gill (2020).

[30] See Downey (2020).

[31] See SNOMED (n.d.).

[32] See WHO (2019).

[33] See WHO (2020).

[34] See ISfTeH (n.d.).

[35] See AeHIN (n.d.).

[36] See ECHA (n.d.).

the District Health Information Software 2 (DHIS2), an open-source, web-based health management information system platform which is in use in 73 low- and middle-income countries. The Health Information Systems Program (HISP) at the University of Oslo manages the development of the core DHIS2 software. HISP is a global network of 13 in-country and regional organizations, providing direct support to ministries and local implementers of DHIS2.[37] A similar although more recent and smaller collaboration is openIMIS, an open-source software for managing health-financing systems like health insurances. Features include enrollment of insurees, patient verification at the point of service and claims management.[38]

6 The Role of Governments

The successful use of digitalization in the health sector is never a bottom-up activity. It requires a strong regulatory framework and strong institutions. Setting up and maintaining digital health solutions require political leadership and legislative activities. To achieve data exchange between different institutions, there needs to be regulation on semantic and syntactic interoperability. For this reason, the German federal government recently acquired a license for the international SNOMED CT standard and passed legislation requiring the use of this standard in digital health activities.[39] But the need for legislation goes much further, including standards on data security, licensing of products/services, reimbursement for digital health services, and patient rights. Apart from legislation, there is also a need for governance structures—institutions bringing together the different players in the digital health sector. This can be public companies in charge of setting up and maintaining digital health systems at a national level,[40] or networks of experts and stakeholders to stimulate innovation.[41]

The political framework is critical to successful digitalization in the health sector, both in a positive and negative sense. Strong political leadership can boost developments. This is certainly the case with the German Minister of Health who has made digitalization one of his policy priorities from the very start of his tenure in 2018, stimulating a pace of progress so far unknown in Germany. Conversely, a lack of political leadership will most likely prevent much meaningful progress. Even worse, inconsistency in regulatory requirements or the selection of projects based on the possibility of political prestige rather than on the needs of the health sector will lead to large expenditures and little actual benefits for patients or providers.

---

[37] See DHIS2 (n.d.).

[38] See openIMIS (n.d.).

[39] See Krüger-Brand (2020).

[40] The German example would be the company gematik. See gematik (n.d.).

[41] In Germany, this function is performed nationally by the health innovation hub which was set up in 2019; see BMG (n.d.).

7 Conclusion and Best Practices

Covid-19 has been a catalyst for the digitalization in the health sector. The pandemic has stimulated the use of video consultations, electronic prescriptions, contact tracing, and monitoring of health care resources like hospital beds.[42] Not all innovations piloted during these special times will necessarily withstand the test of time. First experiences show that the use of video consultations will not remain at the level achieved during the height of the pandemic. But in a 'new normal,' digital health applications will certainly play a more important role than before. The crisis has also stimulated international networks in the digital health sector.[43] Without being cynical, the pandemic came at the right time as far as digitalization of the health sector is concerned: systems to help fight the pandemic were already available or rather easy to adjust in a short time.

Building on the extensive experience of health-sector digitalization before Corona, one can draw conclusions for the time after the pandemic. There should be a focus more on standards and interoperability of individual systems, rather than trying to cover large parts of health-sector needs in a few large-scale IT systems. This will reduce the complexity of the systems and provide more flexibility in adjusting to changing needs and technological developments. Modular systems are also more open to development and maintenance by local or regional IT ecosystems. They have the flexibility and knowledge of the local situation and needs to design, implement, and maintain acceptable solutions.

Taking a needs-based approach means starting from the real-life challenges in the health sector and developing solutions for these challenges. High-tech solutions will not be accepted if they are not in line with the actual operational needs. This is especially the case in the health sector where medical professionals will act as gatekeepers to digital innovations. If they do not see the benefit of the innovations, the new tools will most likely not gain widespread acceptance and use.

Existing institutions must take up and implement new digital solutions. It is important to consider the managerial capacities of these institutions. One should neither try to solve managerial problems through IT, nor should weak institutions be overwhelmed by large IT systems. The development of new IT systems (e.g., digitalization and automation in health insurance) may be a starting point to clarify business processes and procedures. But that will take time, and it will certainly delay the implementation of IT systems.

Digitalization in the health sector holds significant promise to delink the increase in health care demand from the poor and the growing middle classes around the world from the use of resources in the health sector. Better access to information and new digital treatment options will reduce needed resources in health care delivery, while the automation of business processes will support the upscaling of health insurances. Considering the limited application of robotics in the health sector, more health care

---

[42] See, for example, Deutsches Ärzteblatt (2020); GTAI (2020).

[43] See, for example, ISfTeH (2020) for a collection of Covid-19 information and resources.

users will always mean an increase in health care staff and resources. But IT will play an important role in achieving the sustainable upscaling of the health sector in order to achieve universal health coverage.

References

Asian eHealth Information Network (AeHIN). (n.d.). http://www.aehin.org/ (viewed 20 June 2020).

Bott, K., & Gill, C. (2020). Corona Warn-App: Ziemlich teuer, RBB – Kontraste, 25 June 2020, https://www.rbb-online.de/kontraste/archiv/kontraste-vom-25-06-2020/corona-warn-app-ziemlich-teuer.html (viewed 15 December 2020).

Brinker, T. J., et al. (2019). Deep learning outperformed 136 of 157 dermatologists in a head-to-head dermoscopic melanoma image classification task. *European Journal of Cancer, 113*, P47–54.

Bundesinstitut für Arzneimittel und Medizinprodukte (BfArM). (n.d. a). Digitale Gesundheitsanwendungen (DiGA), https://www.bfarm.de/DE/Medizinprodukte/DVG/_node.html (viewed 15 December 2020).

Bundesinstitut für Arzneimittel und Medizinprodukte (BfArM). (n.d. b). DiGA-Verzeichnis, https://diga.bfarm.de/de/verzeichnis (viewed 15 December 2020).

Bundesministerium für Gesundheit (BMG). (2020). Verlässliche Gesundheitsinfos leichter finden - BMG startet Zusammenarbeit mit Google, 10 November 2020, https://www.bundesgesundheitsministerium.de/presse/pressemitteilungen/2020/4-quartal/bmg-google.html (viewed 15 December 2020).

Bundesministerium für Gesundheit (BMG). (n.d.). health innovation hub, https://hih-2025.de/ (viewed 15 December 2020).

Carnero, M. C. (2015). Assessment of environmental sustainability in health care organizations. *Sustainability, 2015*(7), 8270–8291.

Deutsches Ärzteblatt. (2020). Coronakrise bringt Aufschwung bei Videosprechstunden, 9 July 2020, https://www.aerzteblatt.de/nachrichten/114528 (viewed 15 December 2020).

District Health Information Software 2 (DHIS2). (n.d.). About DHIS2, https://www.dhis2.org/about (viewed 15 December 2020).

Downey, A. (2020). Total cost of NHS contact-tracing app set to top £35 million, digital health, 22 September 2020, https://www.digitalhealth.net/2020/09/total-cost-of-nhs-contact-tracing-app-set-to-top-35-million/ (viewed 15 December 2020).

European Connected Health Alliance (ECHA). (n.d.). https://echalliance.com/ (viewed 15 December 2020).

Fuest, B. (2018). Keine Chance für Roboter, WELT, 7 July 2018, https://www.welt.de/print/die_welt/finanzen/article178943036/Keine-Chance-fuer-Roboter.html (viewed 15 December 2020).

Geissler, J. (2017). Die Digitalisierung von Geschäftsprozessen in der gesetzlichen Kranken- und Unfallversicherung als Herausforderung für das Management, in: Matusiewicz, D. / Cassens, M. (Hrsg.): ifgs Schriftenreihe der FOM Hochschule. Essen: MA Akademie Verlags- und Druck-Gesellschaft mbH.

Geissler, J. (2018). Die Zukunft der gesetzlichen Krankenversicherung jenseits von Digitalisierung und Automatisierung, in: Verwaltung und Management 1/2018, S. 3–16. Wiesbaden: Nomos.

Gematik. (n.d.). https://www.gematik.de/ (viewed 15 December 2020).

Germany Trade and Invest (GTAI). (2020). The Robots are Coming – Innovative Solutions for Covid-19 Crisis, 29 April 2020, https://www.gtai.de/gtai-en/invest/industries/the-robots-are-coming-innovative-solutions-for-covid-19-crisis-244106 (viewed 15 December 2020).

Hardcastle, L., Flood, C. M., & Ogbogu, U. (2017). The future role of health law and medicare: The holy grail of access, quality, and sustainability. *Alberta Law Review, 54*(3).

HCF. (n.d.). Ask Dr Google: Where should you go for health information? https://www.hcf.com.au/health-agenda/health-care/treatments-and-procedures/ask-dr-google-health-advice-websites (viewed 15 December 2020).

International Society for Telemedicine and eHealth. (ISfTeH 2020). ISfTeH COVID-19 information and resources, 16 April 2020, https://www.isfteh.org/news/isfteh_covid_19_information_and_resources (viewed 15 December 2020).

International Society for Telemedicine and eHealth. (ISfTeH n.d.). https://www.isfteh.org/ (viewed 15 December 2020).

Intuitive Surgical, Inc. (n.d.). About da Vinci Systems - Surgical robotics for minimally invasive surgery, https://www.davincisurgery.com/da-vinci-systems/about-da-vinci-systems (viewed 15 December 2020).

Kharas, H., & Hamel, K. (2018). A global tipping point: Half the world is now middle class or wealthier, published at Brookings on September 27, 2018, https://www.brookings.edu/blog/future-development/2018/09/27/a-global-tipping-point-half-the-world-is-now-middle-class-or-wealthier/ (viewed 20 June 2020).

Kimberly-Clark. (n.d.). RightCycle by Kimberly-Clark Professional, https://www.kcprofessional.com/en-us/solutions/rightcycle-by-kimberly-clark-professional (viewed 15 December 2020).

KMA-Online. (2020). Gemeinschaftskrankenhaus Havelhöhe - Erstes Zero Emission Hospital in Deutschland bis 2030, 20 November 2020, https://www.kma-online.de/aktuelles/klinik-news/detail/erstes-zero-emission-hospital-in-deutschland-bis-2030-a-44400 (viewed 15 December 2020).

Krüger-Brand, H. E. (2020). SNOMED CT: Meilenstein für die Standardisierung, Deutsches Ärzteblatt, 15/2020, https://www.aerzteblatt.de/archiv/213513/SNOMED-CT-Meilenstein-fuer-die-Standardisierung (viewed 15 December 2020).

Macdonald, G. J. (2020). Automation a Key Focus for Moderna's COVID-19 Vaccine Contractor, Genetic Engineering and Biotechnology News, September 15, 2020, https://www.genengnews.com/topics/bioprocessing/automation-a-key-focus-for-modernas-covid-19-vaccine-contractor/ (viewed 15 December 2020).

McGahan, A. M., Rezaie, R., & Cole, D. C. (2014). Embedded Innovation in Health. In J. Wong, D. Soman, & J. Stein (Eds.), *Innovating for the global south: Towards an inclusive innovation agenda*, University of Toronto Press.

Marimuthua, M., & Paulose, H. (2016). Emergence of sustainability based approaches in healthcare: Expanding research and practice. *Procedia—Social and Behavioral Sciences, 224*, 554–561.

Mechael, P., & Edelman, J. K. (2019). Global Digital Health Index. The State of Digital Health 2019. https://www.digitalhealthindex.org/stateofdigitalhealth19 (viewed 28 January 2021).

Nationales Gesundheitsportal. (n.d.). https://gesund.bund.de/ (viewed 15 December 2020).

openIMIS. (n.d.). https://www.openimis.org/ (viewed 20 June 2020).

SNOMED International. (SNOMED n.d.). https://www.snomed.org/ (viewed 15 December 2020).

Subramanian, L., Alexiou, C., Nellis, J., Steele, P., & Tolani, F. (2020). Developing a sustainability index for public health supply chains. In *Sustainable futures* (Vol. 2, p. 100019).

Thiel, R., et al. (2018). #SmartHealthSystems. Digitalisierungsstrategien im internationalen Vergleich. Bertelsmann Stiftung, Gütersloh, November 2018. https://www.bertelsmann-stiftung.de/de/publikationen/publikation/did/smarthealthsystems (viewed 28 January 2021).

United Nations (UN). (1987). Our common future: Report of the world commission on environment and development, Chapter 2: Towards sustainable development. http://www.un-documents.net/ocf-02.htm (viewed 20 June 2020).

United Nations (UN). (2015). Sustainable development goals, https://www.un.org/sustainabledevelopment/ (viewed 20 June 2020).

United Nations Development Programme (UNDP). (2015). Sustainable development goals, goal 3: Good health and well-being, targets http://www.undp.org/content/undp/en/home/sustainable-development-goals/goal-3-good-health-and-well-being.html (viewed 20 June 2020).

van der Vliet, N., et al. (2018). The INHERIT model: A tool to jointly improve health, environmental sustainability and health equity through behavior and lifestyle change. *International Journal of Environmental Research and Public Health, 15*(7).

van Deursen, A. J. A. M., & van Dijk, J. A. G. M. (2015). Toward a multifaceted model of internet access for understanding digital divides: An empirical investigation. *The Information Society, 31*(379–391), 2015.

Waschinski, G. (2019). Google, Apple und Amazon werden zur Gefahr für deutsche Krankenversicherer, Handelsblatt 03.03.2019, https://www.handelsblatt.com/unternehmen/it-medien/sxsw-2019/gesundheitspolitik-google-apple-und-amazon-werden-zur-gefahr-fuer-deutsche-krankenversicherer/24056698.html?ticket=ST-536897-e0H2mzSpgFt6ioZ6Alcu-ap2 (viewed 29 May 29 2020).

World Bank. (n.d.). World development indicators—Sustainable development goals, target 3.8, indicator: Proportion of population spending more than 25% of household consumption or income on out-of-pocket health expenditure, https://datatopics.worldbank.org/sdgs/ (viewed 16 December 2020).

World Health Organization (WHO). (2019). WHO guideline: recommendations on digital interventions for health system strengthening, https://www.who.int/reproductivehealth/publications/digital-interventions-health-system-strengthening/en/ (viewed 15 December 2020).

World Health Organization (WHO). (2020). Digital implementation investment guide (DIIG): Integrating digital interventions into health programmes, https://www.who.int/publications/i/item/9789240010567 (viewed 15 December 2020).

Zeitung, W. (2020). Coronavirus—automatisierte tests im Kommen, 16 March 2020, https://www.wienerzeitung.at/nachrichten/politik/oesterreich/2054464-Coronavirus-Automatisierte-Tests-im-Kommen.html (viewed 15 December 2020).

Corporate Digital Responsibility—Understanding and Applying

Erik Pelters

1 Introduction

In January 2020, German universities were rumored to be handling digitalization leisurely (Füller, 2020). Due to the corona pandemic, universities were forced to switch from classroom teaching to digital teaching in the 2020 summer semester in order to reduce the risk of infection. A lack of basic (technical) requirements, didactic gaps and legal uncertainty regarding the implementation of digital examination formats are examples of the challenges universities had to take on. However, the effort was worth it: In Germany, approximately 76% of the courses were offered despite the online semester (Stifterverband für die Deutsche Wissenschaft, 2020). The digitalization boost triggered by the pandemic shows what is possible when the need for digitalization meets the will of implementation. But digitalization in universities does not mean saying goodbye to classroom teaching. This would reduce the didactic added value gained through personal exchange. The teaching of the future is based on analog and digital hybrid forms—so called "blended learning approaches" (Auricchio & Káganer, 2015: 32).

Following the new institutional economics approach, universities—like other institutions—are subject to information asymmetries that must be taken into account when developing a holistic digital university strategy. A prerequisite for a solution that will continue to exist in the further course of the digitalization process is to combine considerations on digitalization with sustainable efforts. So far, there have hardly been any considerations in literature on the compatibility of digitalization, digital transformation and sustainability and the examination of their interdependencies. It is obvious that a triad of these areas has enormous potential to meet two of the

E. Pelters (✉)
Chair of Business Administration, specifically Corporate Management, Organization and Corporate Social Responsibility, Andrássy University Budapest, Budapest, Hungary
e-mail: erik.pelters@andrassyuni.hu

T. Herberger and J. Dötsch (eds.), *Digitalization, Digital Transformation and Sustainability in the Global Economy*, Springer Proceedings in Business and Economics, https://doi.org/10.1007/978-3-030-77340-3_6

driving changes in the world: the digital penetration of economy and society paired with an increasing understanding that we have to change our way of life to reduce negative impacts on our planet. To this end, the first research question examines how digitalization can be reconciled with an existing theoretical sustainability construct.

RQ1: *How can digitalization be integrated into an existing theoretical sustainability construct?*

On this basis, the scenario technique of the German Federal Ministry of Justice and Consumer Protection (BMJV) is presented to help individuals and organizations to independently develop and reflect on possible opportunities and risks of digital change. This particular scenario technique was chosen because of its simple but versatile application possibilities. Since the examples exclusively derive from the corporate context, the second research question examines whether the scenario technique can be transferred to other contexts. Using universities as an example in this article was chosen because the backlog that universities have with regard to digitalization is compounded due to the lack of concrete starting points for developing a sustainable digitalization strategy. The scenario technique provides this starting point. In advance, the transferability of the technique to the university context must be tested. Hence, the second research question is:

RQ2: *Can the BMJV's scenario technique be transferred to the university context?*

This article is structured as follows: First, digitalization and digital transformation is explained with reference to the university context. Second, an existing model of sustainability is introduced and further developed by integrating the challenges and responsibilities of the digital age. As a next step, the emerging model forms the basis for showing what is meant by CDR and how organizations can meet their digital responsibility in the future. For this purpose, with the help of the BMJV's scenario technique, a practical implementation instruction is provided, the universal applicability of which is proven by the transfer to the university context. After taking reference to the underlying limitations of this paper, it presents implications for further research in the CDR area and practical starting points not only for universities but any organization. The paper concludes with a brief outlook on the challenges CDR in general and universities in particular need to overcome in the future.

2 Digitalization and Digital Transformation of Universities

Digitalization no longer only refers to technologies that convert analog files into digital ones. Nowadays, digitalization mainly describes processes as well as the technologies and devices required to control these processes. Digitalization ensures that information can be used and processed digitally, whereby activities being converted or integrated into digital processes and being carried out completely or largely automatically (Hüther, 2020: 12). These processes are fueled by data that is fed by as large quantities as possible. Thereby, digital technologies lead to diverse potentials that can be used in new ways.

The continuous consequences and effects of digitalization control the digital transformation which is characterized as "the creation and resulting change in market offers, business processes or models that result from the use of digital technology" (Nambisan et al., 2017: 224).[1] Digital transformation is forcing companies to rethink the role and value of data in their business models (Brownlow et al., 2015). In most cases, a fundamental change in the organization's underlying mindsets, systems, and tools is required to reposition the organization partly or as a whole (Gupta, 2018). According to Oswald and Krcmar (2018: 7–9) digital transformation is: (1) inevitable: For some challenges of social and economic developments solutions can only be developed with the help of the innovative use of digital technologies; (2) irreversible: The cost–benefit ratio of new technologies is constantly improving and displacing existing technologies from the market; (3) fast: Continuous ongoing and new developments are essential in order not to be overtaken by other market participants; (4) insecure: The dynamics with which digital technologies are developing makes it difficult to predict which technologies will be built on in the future. Due to its characteristics, the digital transformation is changing the way in which organizational added value is created. Furthermore, the characteristics show that a rejection or an insufficient examination of digitalization will inevitably lead to organizational failure sooner or later. It is nearly impossible to resist the digital transformation process. On the contrary, as a continuous change process, digital transformation permeates all areas of society (Fig. 1).

The illustration shows that through the use of digital technologies, all interest groups benefit from the newly created exploitation potential and new technologies. They are developed by science institutions and companies to satisfy social needs. The state assumes a regulatory and promotional function depending on the expectations within society. Changes in expectations, in turn, force science institutions and companies to develop new solutions. This leads to a continuous and incessant advance of the digital transformation process (Arntz et al., 2020: 47) that is reshaping people's professional and private lives.

Universities—as bodies of science—are also affected by the digital transformation process, leading to changes in teaching, learning and research methods. The use of electronic data processing in universities has been common practice for years as it supports e.g. administrative processes or e-learning. As the transformation process progresses, new forms of use and application potentials for digital tools in the individual areas of the university system are constantly opening up, so that digital technologies permeate the entire university system.[2] As the switch from classroom to online teaching in the corona crisis illustrates, the boundaries between administrative processes and digitally supported teaching and learning techniques blend into one another. The blurring of this classic border leads to a change in the university as a place of learning, which harbors opportunities, risks and requirements for all actors

[1] A classic example is the change in the music and media industry due to the development from analog sound carriers to streaming portals.

[2] In the past the use of digital media was limited to the provision of lecture and exercise materials. Today, forms of self-determined, interactive, cooperative and action-oriented learning are available.

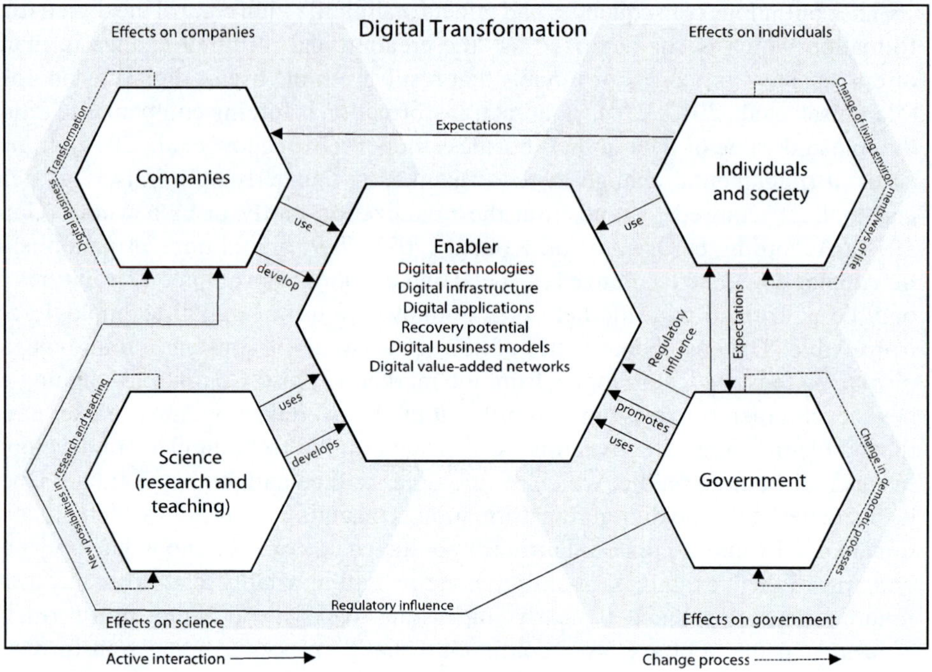

Fig. 1 Digital transformation (Reproduced from Kofler 2016)

within the university environment. The digitalization and networking of educational processes open up new access and dissemination possibilities for knowledge and thus potential for diversifying courses and tapping into new target groups.[3] This requires the establishment of a digital infrastructure with regard to the equipment including technical components and their service facilities as well as the infrastructure that enables the use of new digital media. At the same time, this transformation harbors the risk of shaking the very foundations that make up the quality of universities such as being a place for critical thinking, personal exchange and networking, as well as the transfer of scientifically substantiated knowledge. These are factors that live from physical presence and analog structures (e.g. lecture halls, libraries, shared workspaces). The didactic added value of physical exchange cannot be replaced by any form of online teaching. Consequently, a major challenge for university digitalization is to combine digital teaching and learning scenarios with analog infrastructures in a blended learning solution and to develop them evenly so that new potentials are linked with existing strengths (Kannenberg & May, 2014: 10). Digitalization is not limited to individual areas of application (e.g. studies and teaching), it requires an overall strategic consideration in the university system. This consideration goes far beyond the purely technological aspects, since the changed requirements for the university system not only affect the underlying processes but also the actors

[3] Due to the temporal, didactic and spatial diversity of digital formats, the compatibility of family, work and further education is improved.

who move within the university context. Consequently, in addition to economic and educational considerations, social and cultural perspectives should also be included into the strategic orientation. Coming back to Kofler's diagram (Fig. 1), clearly all actors (including universities) are an inevitable part of the digital transformation. Therefore, not only the desire, but also the demand for a responsible handling of innovations becomes evident. This requires digitalization and digital change to be developed with respect to the concepts of sustainability and responsibility.

3 Changes in the Concept of Sustainability and Responsibility in the Digital Age

The classic model of sustainability aims to use finite resources responsibly, so that current and future generations can lead a life in dignity and according to their needs (Hauff, 1987: 46–47). By now, the model has evolved into the three-pillar principle of sustainability according to which sustainable development can only be achieved if ecological, economic and social considerations are taken into account (Enquete-Kommission Schutz des Menschen und der Umwelt, 1998: 24).[4] (Fig. 2).

There is disagreement in literature about the arrangement and interdependencies of the individual pillars with one another, whether all three levels should be treated equally or if there is a priority model (Kleine & v. Hauff, 2009: 33).[5] For this, Pufé (2017: 110–115) compared several models with the sustainability triangle emerging

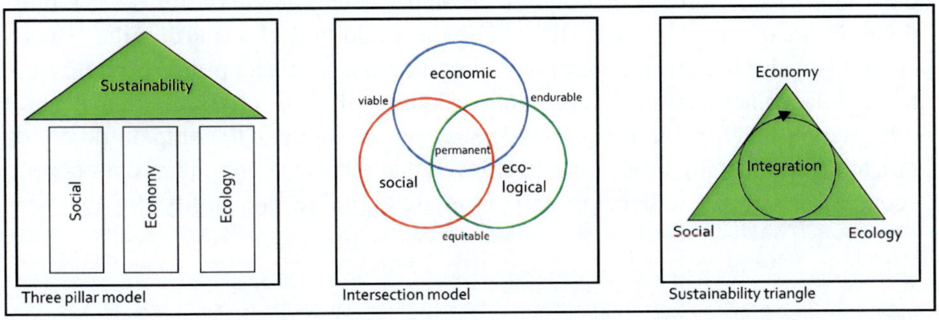

Fig. 2 Models of sustainability (Reproduced from Pufé, 2017: 110–115)

[4] **Ecological considerations** on the moderate use of natural resources (e.g. resource conservation, emission reduction, preservation of ecosystems, minimization of risks), **economic considerations** to ensure long-term company security (e.g. increase added value, efficient satisfaction of needs, high innovation potential, no accumulation of debts), **social considerations** to ensure the "good life" (e.g. cooperation, solidarity system, equal rights, job security).

[5] In the scientific discourse, a distinction is made between "weak sustainability" and "strong sustainability". In the case of "weak sustainability", ecology, economy and social affairs are treated equally, while "strong sustainability" sees ecology as a prerequisite for social affairs and social issues as a prerequisite for economy.

as the preferred model. The three-pillar model is subject to the criticism that the roof of sustainability could already be supported by two pillars, so one pillar could easily be omitted. The intersection model is popular but suggests that one pillar can be neglected if this deficit can be offset by corresponding added value within the other two pillars. The sustainability triangle basically corresponds to the middle of the intersection model, but does not allow any other solution than the equal integration of all three pillars in order to achieve sustainable development in the long term. Hence, the model of the sustainability triangle will be used in the further course. Regardless of any criticism, literature largely agrees that a society can never develop sustainably if it is based solely on one of these pillars.[6]

The concept of Corporate Social Responsibility (CSR) is also based on the pillars of sustainability. The classic CSR approach generally describes a company's responsibility for sustainable management in economic, ecological and social terms. It serves as a basis for companies to voluntarily bring social and ecological concerns into harmony with their economic value creation (European Commission, 2011: 7). With digitalization and the associated innovation dynamics as well as the networking of various new products and services, social phenomena arise that have not been taken into account in the previous concept of CSR. An example is the development of assistance systems in automobiles that use artificial intelligence to increasingly intervene on driving behavior and thus raise completely new questions regarding the responsibility dilemma when accidents can be traced back to technical malfunctions. It therefore makes sense to add a digital component to the model of sustainability, in order to answer the questions of what responsible corporate behavior looks like in a digital world and who takes responsibility for what and to whom. Moreover, the diagram by Kofler proves that digitalization permeates all areas of life—and thus all three pillars of sustainability. Hence, the mere addition of a fourth pillar is insufficient. Instead, a holistic integration of digitalization across all pillars is required. The three-pillar principle must be taken into account both in the physical and in the digital living environments. If this succeeds, a successful (theoretical) compatibility of digitalization and sustainability can be achieved that forms the prerequisite for corporate social responsibility to develop into corporate digital responsibility (Fig. 3).

[6] There is more of a tendency to expand the model to include other pillars (e.g. culture, politics). These extensions of the model have played a subordinate role in the literature so far.

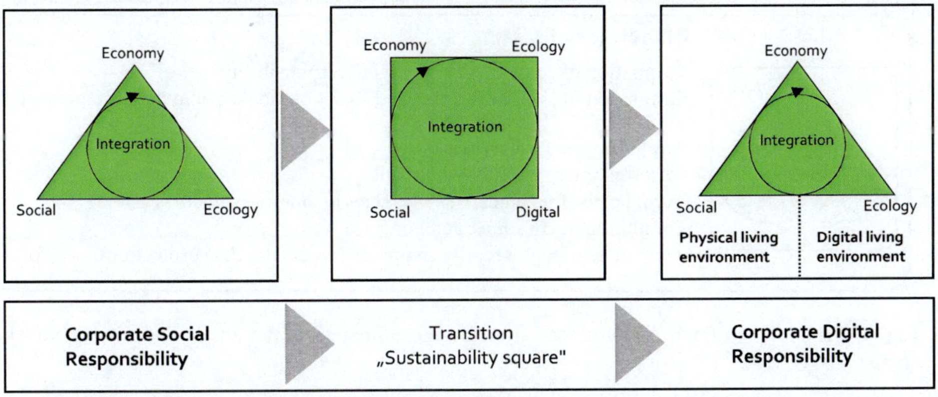

Fig. 3 From CSR to CDR (Own proposal for solution based on the sustainability triangle and the configuration concept of Dörr, 2020: 40)

4 Corporate Digital Responsibility

Corporate Digital Responsibility (CDR) complements corporate responsibility and partly rethinks it by describing principles of corporate responsibility in the digital transformation[7]. This refers to voluntary entrepreneurial activities that are intended to help shape the digital world for the benefit of society (Thorun, 2018: 176).[8] Like CSR, CDR is ahead of positive law and closes digital responsibility gaps where the legal basis ends or has not yet arrived.[9] This also includes "questioning technical developments and, if necessary, setting limits" (Deloitte GmbH Wirtschaftsprüfungsgesellschaft, 2020). In addition to paying attention to digital sustainability in the sense of the responsible use of data (Stuermer et al., 2017), CDR also considers the social, economic and ecological effects of digital corporate actions in the world (Esselmann & Brink, 2016: 38–41; Thorun, 2018). The driving force behind CDR is the sharpening of the sense of responsibility for the effects of digital transformation processes and the associated opportunities and risks for different interest groups (Gärtner & Heinrich, 2018: 176). Combining the interests of different actors is the basis for the existence and perception of CDR. A requirement for the compatibility of interests is to give all members of society the opportunity to actively participate in technological progress and in the process itself. This is the only way to meet the complex requirements of digitalization and the expectations of users—e.g. in terms of data protection and transparency. This can protect consumers in the digital world and improve their digital self-determination, creating trust so that innovative technological applications can successfully establish themselves and enrich our lives.

[7] For example, companies have to consider the social effects of digital products and services as early as their development and ensure that they are compatible with our value standards.

[8] As with corporate social responsibility, there is currently no standard definition of the term "CDR".

[9] Digitalization sometimes leads to disruptive technologies that require a completely different legal basis. This takes time. CDR can form a bridge here.

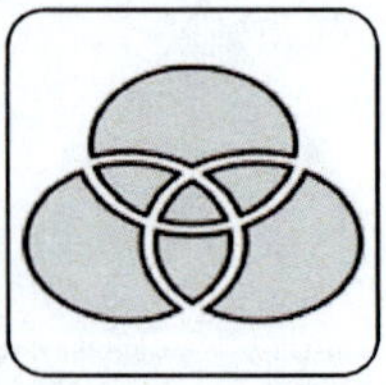

Principles of CDR

- Promotion of education about digital responsibility
- Promotion of social discourse and social participation in the development process
- Digitalization for everyone
- Offering interoperable technologies
- Avoidance of technical dependencies among consumers
- Promotion of consumer autonomy
- Guarantee of high security standards (especially data protection).

Fig. 4 Principles of CDR (Reproduced from Bundesministerium der Justiz und für Verbraucherschutz, 2019a: 10)

To this end, the German Federal Ministry of Justice and Consumer Protection (BMJV) launched the *CDR initiative* in 2018, in cooperation with representatives from business and politics (Bundesministerium der Justiz und für Verbraucherschutz, 2019b). The initiative develops solutions based on relevant scenarios of a digital future and makes them available to the public as an open source approach (Bundesministerium der Justiz und für Verbraucherschutz, 2020). This is combined with the invitation to analyze activities using the methodology to find answers to the question of what entrepreneurial digital responsibility can mean for one's own organization. The overarching goal of CDR is to turn digital responsibility into a matter of course for organizations in all areas and industries (Bundesministerium der Justiz und für Verbraucherschutz, 2019c: 5). Thereby, this should give consumers a better overview of how companies handle their data while responsible entrepreneurs should achieve a real market advantage by their conscious behavior.[10] This goal is to be achieved by following the principles of responsible action in the digital world (Fig. 4).

As part of a holistic approach, the working group of the CDR initiative is to be gradually expanded to include representatives from all areas of society in order to ensure that the debates also address their expectations.[11] A comparison of the list of members shows that the number has doubled since its founding (Bundesministerium der Justiz und für Verbraucherschutz, 2019c)[12]. However, the new members are all companies. Considering the holistic approach to handling digital responsibility envisaged by the CDR initiative, other interest groups must be involved in the process.[13]

[10] For example, through a gain in legitimacy on the part of society.

[11] This includes representatives from civil society, associations, science, investors, influencers and users.

[12] Overview of members of the CDR initiative: Allianz Germany, **Federal Ministry of Justice and Consumer Protection (BMJV)**, Cliqz MyOffrz GmbH, Daimler AG, **Deutsche Bahn AG**, Deutsche Telekom, IBM Germany, ING, **Miele**, **Otto Group**, Rewe Group, SAP, Siemens AG, **Telefónica**, Zalando SE, **ZEIT Online**; highlighted institutions are founding members.

[13] In particular, this includes representatives from science (e.g. universities).

5 Scenario Technique of the BMJV

Uncertainty about the consequences of a decision inhibits a responsible digital transformation process and provides an explanation as to why some institutions have progressed more significantly in the process than others. In order to work out possible consequences of the digital transformation in practical case studies, the scenario technique was developed as part of the CDR initiative (Bundesministerium der Justiz und für Verbraucherschutz, 2019a). In four successive steps, it offers a way to leave the abstract level and illuminate (hypothetical) everyday life situations of the individual organizational context against the background of responsibility. Those scenarios are examined regarding their changes, opportunities, risks and goals in order to develop recommendations for action. The application to many different situations provides a more precise picture of questions and possible answers in relation to generalizable principles for responsible digitalization (Fig. 5).

The presentation of the scenario technique is accompanied by concrete case examples including considerations on autonomous driving or networked refrigerators. What is striking is the focus on company-related case studies which could be an indicator of why all the members who have joined the initiative since introduction are companies.

The following self-chosen example from a university perspective shows that the scenario technique can be transferred to another context outside the corporate world,

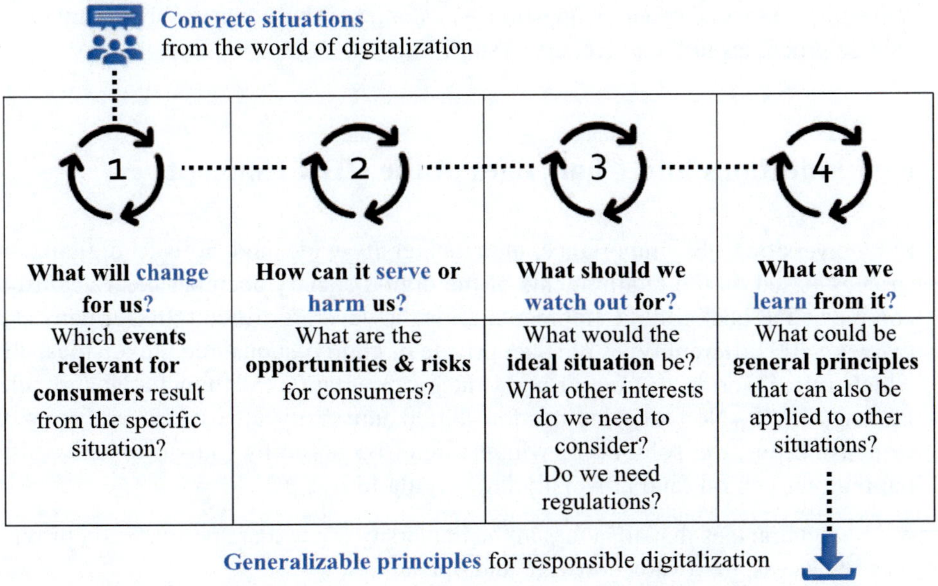

Fig. 5 Scenario technique step by step (Reproduced from Bundesministerium der Justiz und für Verbraucherschutz, 2019a: 6)

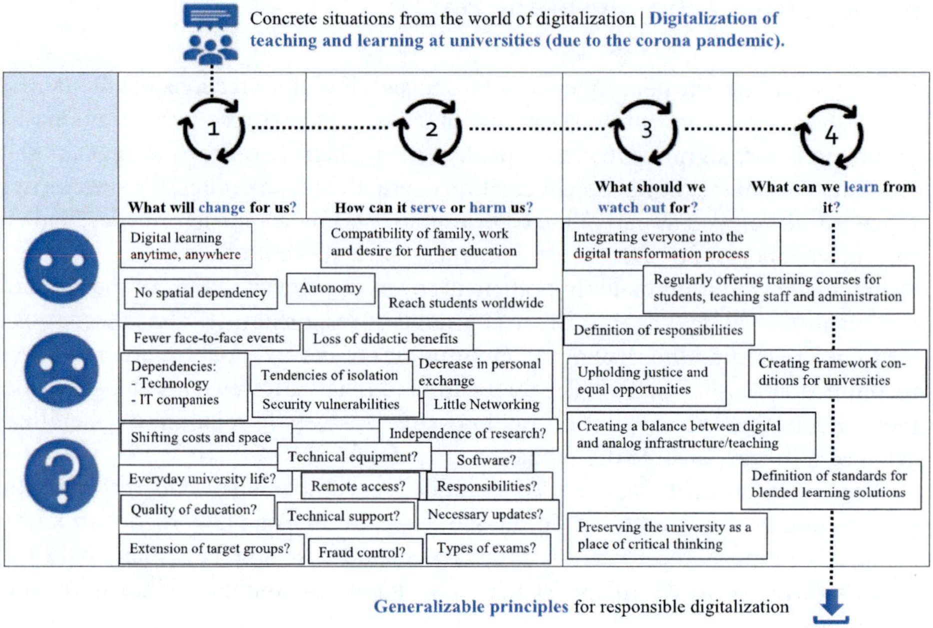

Fig. 6 Digitalization of teaching and learning at universities (Own scenario based on the BMJV's scenario technique 2019a: 6)

affirming the second research question. The content is based on the above-mentioned change processes in the university system (Fig. 6).

6 Limitations and Challenges of the CDR Concept

For universities, the importance of a university-wide and holistic digitalization strategy based on the requirements of the digital society becomes clear against the complex CDR background. Implementation, however, is difficult. In Germany alone there are 400 different types of state, private or church-sponsored universities, all of which differ in terms of structure and strategic orientation (Stiftung für Hochschulzulassung, 2020). Notwithstanding, the digital university also raises problems and responsibilities, the solution of which cannot be borne by individual universities, but requires central (and university law) regulations, e.g.:

- Who guarantees that all actors in the university context are permanently provided with access, hardware, software and updates?
- Who is responsible for technical support and security guarantee (e.g. data protection) if the digital requirements exceed the capacities of the local data center?
- Which authority guarantees equal opportunities in digital teaching?

- Who is responsible and to what extend if the cell phone of a student or employee is hacked in the public Wi-Fi and sensitive university data is stolen and/or misused?
- Who bears which costs?

Systemic implications and the resulting strategic challenges are seldomly taken into consideration in university strategy processes, neither by the universities themselves nor by politics. The problems that arise in the course of the digital transformation process cannot be tackled by universities on their own. They require reconsidering the relationship between science institutions and politics, which is currently not the case.[14] Central solutions through the joint creation of framework conditions require the involvement of the state. At the same time, interfaces must be identified and clear-cut (responsibility) boundaries must be set in order to guarantee the freedom of science. The commitment of politics as well as the support of activities of those who are keen to experiment is needed. "Politicians have to understand that universities are currently not in the process of implementing tried and tested solutions, but have to experience and research opportunities, potentials and dead ends on an individual and institutional level" (Dürkop & Ladwig, 2016: 8). In order to successfully master the increasing influence of digitalization on higher education in the future, universities should adopt a more comprehensive and cross-system perspective when evaluating decisions and actions.

Management consultancies and auditing companies such as Deloitte or PricewaterhouseCoopers have taken up the concept of CDR and are developing independent solution strategies for successfully designing the digital transformation process. In contrast to the results of the CDR initiative, these solutions are not openly accessible, but are sold as a lucrative consulting concept (Deloitte GmbH Wirtschaftsprüfungsgesellschaft, 2020; PricewaterhouseCoopers GmbH, 2020). This is not condemnable per se, but it illustrates the information advantage and the added value that comes with an early adoption of the CDR concept. At the same time, it underlines the importance of dealing with digital responsibility. Furthermore, it also shows that with regard to corporate digital responsibility—as the name suggests—companies are currently the only actors who have the (financial) capacities and the scope to live up to this responsibility.

7 Implications for Further Research in the CDR Area

Although the scenario technique is a methodology developed in Germany, it can easily be adapted and used across national borders, due to its transparent result management and its simple handling. Solutions could be developed internationally and on a common basis, for instance at EU level. This includes working on scenarios with identical questions across several countries in order to be able to filter and

[14] See Kofler's diagram (Fig. 1). A classic relationship between science (advisory function) and the state (regulatory function) has always existed, but in view of the independence of science it is often excluded from scientific presentations.

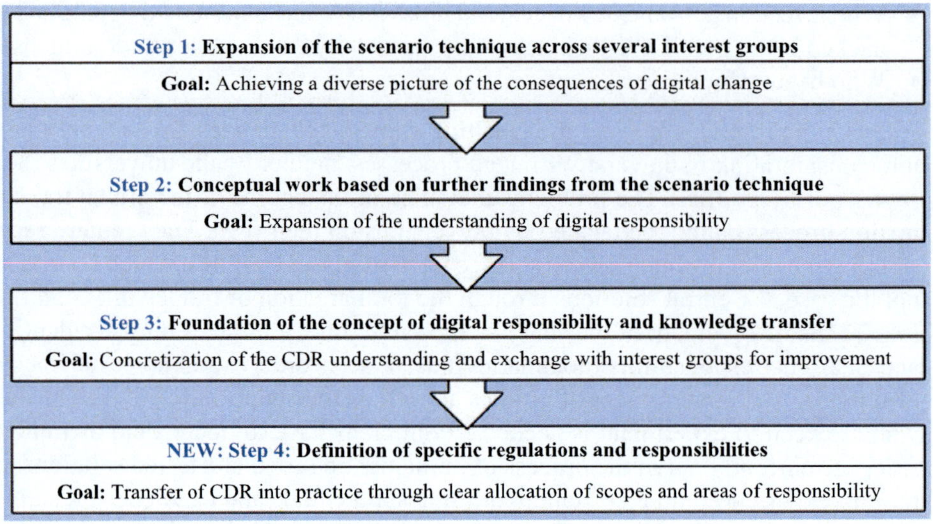

Fig. 7 Steps in future CDR research (Based on Bundesministerium der Justiz und für Verbraucherschutz 2019a: 12)

consider national differences. Thus, disputes within the European Union could be avoided, if a member state sees an individually created solution concept for an EU-wide problem as a model solution for the entire EU. Cross-linking several solution concepts from different member states and combining them into suitable clusters could prove to be an alternative strategy for success.

From a university perspective, the scenario technique offers universities the opportunity to develop strategic plans that are individually tailored to their needs. Consequently, parallels across all results could be summarized and create a reflow of knowledge into politics and higher education law. Future research in the CDR area can be based on the following steps (Fig. 7).

8 Conclusion

Digital transformation is inescapable, irreversible, proceeds extremely fast and is fraught with uncertainty. It is an ongoing trend that is constantly being renewed by new generations of digital technologies. Universities cannot escape this trend. The universities' quick reaction to the challenges of the corona crisis along with the rapid transition from classroom to online teaching was a success—albeit a short-term one. Preparing universities for the digital future on a long-term and sustainable basis requires an intensive examination of the opportunities and risks initiated by technological advances. For this purpose, the BMJV's scenario technique provides a useful starting point for universities to grasp their status quo and compare it with digital challenges of the future. In the competition with other universities for promising students, the ongoing evaluation of new, digital technologies with regard to their potential for the further development of existing processes is a decisive competitive advantage. Universities are therefore forced to see the possibilities of digitalization as a constant companion in everyday life and as an opportunity for progress without endangering their core competencies. This way it can be possible to combine responsible digital change with the university as a place of critical thinking and high-quality education.

References

Arntz, M., Gregory, T., & Zierahn, U. (2020). Digitalisierung und die Zukunft der Arbeit. *Wirtschaftsdienst, 100*, 41–47. https://doi.org/10.1007/s10273-020-2614-6

Auricchio, G., & Káganer, E. (2015). How digitalization is changing the way executives learn: The road to Omni-learning. *IESE Insight, 26*, 31–38. https://doi.org/10.15581/002.ART-2747

Brownlow, J., Zaki, M., Neely, A., & Urmetzer, F. (2015). Data-driven business models: A blueprint for innovation. https://doi.org/10.13140/RG.2.1.2233.2320

Bundesministerium der Justiz und für Verbraucherschutz. (2020). Corporate Digital Responsibility (CDR) – Initiative. https://www.bmjv.de/DE/Themen/FokusThemen/CDR_Initiative/CDR_Initiative_node.html. Accessed August 16, 2020.

Bundesministerium der Justiz und für Verbraucherschutz. (2019a). Szenarientechnik der CDR-Initiative: Die Methode erklärt. https://www.bmjv.de/DE/Themen/FokusThemen/CDR_Initiative/_downloads/cdr_szenarientechnik.pdf?__blob=publicationFile&v=1. Accessed August 10, 2020.

Bundesministerium der Justiz und für Verbraucherschutz. (2019b). CDR Initiative. Digitalisierung verantwortungsvoll gestalten: Corporate Digital Responsibility-Initiative in Brüssel vorgestellt. https://www.bmjv.de/SharedDocs/Artikel/DE/2019/051619_CDR_Bruessel.html. Accessed August 11, 2020.

Bundesministerium der Justiz und für Verbraucherschutz. (2019c). CDR-Initiative: Eine gemeinsame Plattform. https://www.bmjv.de/DE/Themen/FokusThemen/CDR_Initiative/_downloads/cdr_plattform.pdf?__blob=publicationFile&v=3. Accessed August 13, 2020.

Deloitte GmbH Wirtschaftsprüfungsgesellschaft. (2020). Corporate Digital Responsibility: Verantwortungsvolle Digitalisierung – Herausforderung und Chance für deutsche Unternehmen. https://www2.deloitte.com/de/de/pages/innovation/contents/corporate-digital-responsibility.html. Accessed August 23, 2020.

Dörr, S. (2020). *Praxisleitfaden Corporate Digital Responsibility: Unternehmerische Verantwortung und Nachhaltigkeitsmanagement im Digitalzeitalter*. Springer Gabler.

Dürkop, A., & Ladwig, T. (2016). Neue Formen der Koproduktion von Wissen durch Lehrende und Lernende. *Arbeitspapier 24 des Hochschulforums Digitalisierung, 24*, 1–60. https://doi.org/10.15480/882.1334

Enquete-Kommission Schutz des Menschen und der Umwelt. (1998). Abschlussbericht der Enquete-Kommission "Schutz des Menschen und der Umwelt – Ziele und Rahmenbedingungen einer nachhaltig zukunftsverträglichen Entwicklung". Konzept Nachhaltigkeit: Vom Leitbild zur Umsetzung. https://dserver.bundestag.de/btd/13/112/1311200.pdf. Accessed August 17, 2020.

Esselmann, F., & Brink, A. (2016). Corporate Digital Responsibility: Den digitalen Wandel von Unternehmen und Gesellschaft erfolgreich gestalten. *Spektrum, 12*, 38–41.

Europäische Kommission. (2011). Mitteilung der Kommission an das Europäische Parlament, den Rat, den Europäischen Wirtschafts- und Sozialausschuss und dem Ausschuss der Regionen: Eine neue EU-Strategie (2011–14) für die soziale Verantwortung der Unternehmen

(CSR). https://eur-lex.europa.eu/legal-content/DE/TXT/PDF/?uri=CELEX:52011DC0681&from=DE. Accessed September 25, 2020.

Füller, C. (2020). Digitalisierung der Hochschule: Zauberlehrling im Wartestand. In: FAZ.NET. https://www.faz.net/aktuell/karriere-hochschule/langsame-fortschritte-bei-der-digitalisierung-der-hochschulen-16568614.html. Accessed August 09, 2020.

Gärtner, C., & Heinrich, C. (Eds.). (2018). *Fallstudien zur Digitalen Transformation: Case Studies für die Lehre und praktische Anwendung*. Springer Gabler.

Gupta, S. (2018). *Driving Digital Strategy: A Guide to Reimagining Your Business*. Harvard Business Review Press.

Hauff, V. (Ed.). (1987). *Unsere gemeinsame Zukunft. Brundtland-Bericht der Weltkommission für Umwelt und Entwicklung*. Eggenkamp.

Hüther, M. (2020). Potenziale und Umsetzung der Digitalisierung auf Unternehmensebene. *Wirtschaftsdienst, 100*, 12–19. https://doi.org/10.1007/s10273-020-2610-x

Kannenberg, S., & May, A. (2014). Entgrenzung und Zusammenarbeit – die Notwendigkeit von Kooperationen im Lernraum. *ABI Technik, 34*, 9–19. https://doi.org/10.1515/abitech-2014-0003

Kleine, A., & v. Hauff, M. (2009). *Nachhaltige Entwicklung: Grundlagen Und Umsetzung*. https://doi.org/10.1524/9783486850949

Kofler, T. (2016). Digitale Transformation, CC-BY-SA 4.0. https://commons.wikimedia.org/w/index.php?curid=48399771. Accessed 12 Aug 2020

Nambisan, S., Lyytinen, K., Majchrzak, A., & Song, M. (2017). Digital Innovation Management: Reinventing Innovation Management Research in a Digital World. *MISQ, 41*, 223–238. https://doi.org/10.25300/MISQ/2017/41:1.03

Oswald, G., & Krcmar, H. (2018). *Digitale Transformation: Fallbeispiele und Branchenanalysen*. Springer Gabler.

Pufé, I. (2017). Nachhaltigkeit, 3rd rev. ed. UVK.

PricewaterhouseCoopers GmbH. (2020). Corporate Digital Responsibility (CDR). https://www.pwc.de/de/digitale-transformation/corporate-digital-responsibility-cdr.html. Accessed August 23, 2020.

Stifterverband für die Deutsche Wissenschaft e.V. (2020). Hochschulen sehen sich digital gut gerüstet für den Start ins Sommersemester. https://www.stifterverband.org/pressemitteilungen/2020_04_20_hochschul-barometer_corona-krise. Accessed August 12, 2020.

tiftung für Hochschulzulassung. (2020). Die Hochschultypen im Überblick. https://studienwahl.de/studieninfos/hochschultypen. Accessed August 20, Aug 2020.

Stuermer, M., Abu-Tayeh, G., & Myrach, T. (2017). Digital sustainability: Basic conditions for sustainable digital artifacts and their ecosystems. *Sustainability Science, 12*, 247–262.https://doi.org/10.1007/s11625-016-0412-2

Thorun, C. (2018). Corporate Digital Responsibility: Unternehmerische Verantwortung in der digitalen Welt. In C. Gärtner & C. Heinrich (Eds.), *Fallstudien zur Digitalen Transformation. Case Studies für die Lehre und praktische Anwendung* (pp. 173–191). Springer Fachmedien Wiesbaden.

The Transformation in the Public Administration—Status Quo Against the Background of COVID-19

Katja Posselt

1 Introduction

The outbreak of the COVID-19 pandemic led to global governmental and societal restrictions of unknown dimensions and required humanity and solidarity to implement major adjustments in nearly every aspect of daily life. State and nationwide curfews and contact bans were imposed and public life was mostly shut down. In order to protect citizens and employees from an infection with the COVID-19 virus, public institutions were partially closed and the provision of public services was reduced to essential requirements only.

Therefore, the COVID-19 pandemic also impacted the public administration, particularly local governments that provide direct services to local citizens. While the COVID-19 pandemic persists, the public administration must protect its citizens and its own employees from contracting the virus. At the same time the public administration must remain capable fulfilling its ordered tasks as it provides systemically relevant services. A significant percentage of the tasks of the public administration are part of the critical infrastructure, for example the fire department, the urban drainage company or parts of the youth welfare offices and job centres. This is because, for example, the payment of social benefits for services of general interest or the operation of shelters for the homeless must inevitably be performed also in times of crisis. The provision of such system-relevant tasks poses a major challenge to the public sector during the COVID-19 pandemic. At the same time, new tasks arise due to the pandemic, e.g. contact tracing or setting up service hotlines for citizens to provide further and Covid-19 tailored information. These tasks are pushing the public administration to their limit.

K. Posselt (✉)
Andrássy Universität Budapest, Budapest, Hungary
e-mail: katja.posselt@andrassyuni.hu

T. Herberger and J. Dötsch (eds.), *Digitalization, Digital Transformation and Sustainability in the Global Economy*, Springer Proceedings in Business and Economics, https://doi.org/10.1007/978-3-030-77340-3_7

The Corona crisis is still ongoing and yet, numerous papers and reviews are already addressing the impact of the COVID-19 pandemic on the public sector. The present paper looks at the impact of the COVID-19 pandemic on the public sector, particularly against the background of the digital transformation. It is intended to serve as a field report on the current state of the digital transformation and the problems and concerns this transformation poses for local governments in the Federal Republic of Germany. The changes brought about by the pandemic are described from the perspective of a local government official. This field report therefore provides an internal perspective on the impact of the COVID 19 pandemic on local governments and the challenges they face.

2 Digital Administration

The term 'digital transformation' stands for the automation of processes on the one hand and the change in behaviour on the other hand (Safar, 2020). In contrast to digitisation digital transformation is therefore a holistic approach.

Digital transformation and the digitisation of administrative procedures have been at the top of the public administration agenda for some time now. However, the public administration is facing the challenge of introducing new, digital solutions. In a European comparison the German public administration is lagging behind in regard to the progress in digitisation. In the European Commission's Digital and Economy Society Index, Germany ranks 22nd in terms of digital public services (European Commission, 2020).

Structured, reliable and familiar processes and workflows have a high priority in the public administration, so modernisation takes a lot of time. However, the digitisation of primarily classical administrative services, such as issuing a passport, or registering a residence, or motor vehicle offers considerable potential. Positive effects of a widespread digitisation arise, among other things, with regard to the reduction of processing times and waiting times (Schüür-Langkau, 2020). In addition, personnel or financial savings can be achieved or a contribution to sustainability can be made. Such as conserving resources like paper and eliminating the need for citizens to travel to and from the department. The reduction of waiting periods or the elimination of compulsory presence is very valuable, especially in times of this unique crisis. Nevertheless, the digital transformation poses a major challenge for public administration; local governments in particular often lack the financial resources and technical expertise (Schöppe, 2020).

Due to the effects of the COVID-19 pandemic the public service provision and the utilisation of these kinds of services is currently no longer possible on site and in person. As a result, interest in and demands for digitized administrative services are increasing on both sides (citizens and public administration) enormously. Nonetheless, innovation and progress regularly require a certain lead time in the public sector. In this context the question arises as to whether the COVID-19 pandemic has the potential to accelerate the digital transformation of the public administration.

3 Outbreak of the COVID-19 Pandemic

The measures associated with the pandemic response, for example the closure of public institutions or the observance of distance bans and contact restrictions, demonstrate to the public administration the urgency of a progressive digital transformation. Thus, in order to remain accessible and continue to execute services while maintaining infection control, improvisation was required following the COVID-19 pandemic outbreak (Müller, 2020).

The crisis initially revealed, to local governments in particular, the limits of their ability to uphold previously implemented work processes and provide services (Punz, 2020). As previously outlined the level of digitisation in local governments is in need of catching up. At the beginning of the Corona crisis, digital service offerings and a resilient IT infrastructure were lacking. Additionally, the technology equipment was outdated and there was a shortage of personnel in the area of services of general interest. The concerns of managers and employees regarding a new way of working are also problematic. On the one hand, managers have prejudices against leading at a distance and on the other hand, there is scepticism among employees towards new techniques and approaches.

That was the state of public administration before the crisis. Yet, crises can have a stimulating effect (Petersdorff, 2020). Managing such a crisis requires quick actions and agility. Crisis management ultimately increases the pressure to innovate, while improvisation tends to occur during the crisis itself (Petersdorff, 2020).

4 Effects of the COVID-19 Pandemic

Based on the assumption that crises can have a stimulating effect the following chapter presents examples of the dynamic use of digital technologies and modern ways of working to perform public service tasks during the Corona crisis. In this context, four essential categories are defined that underwent a process of change due to the outbreak of the COVID-19 pandemic.

Adding to the content of these categories, local governments had numerous ideas, some of them simple yet innovative, to maintain their service offering to citizens within the bounds of possibility. To communicate with their citizens the local governments set up video channels on their own websites as well as on new YouTube-Channels. Furthermore, live broadcasts were held via Facebook to provide information about crisis-related decisions. Additionally, municipal museums offered online tours of their exhibition spaces and municipal music schools taught digitally.[1]

---

[1] Here are a few examples of the innovative measures taken by local governments: video messages from the former Lord Mayor T. Geisel of Düsseldorf or Mayor C. Fleischhauer of Moers, digital music lessons at the municipal music schools in Düsseldorf and Hattingen and digital speed tours through the Cologne as well as the Düsseldorf City Museum.

4.1 Mode of Operation

Mobile work, teleworking and home office are terms that are gaining in importance in the public sector but have not yet been widely applied in practice. This was due, among other things, to a lack of IT equipment, data protection concerns and a lack of mentality for leading over spatial distance (Höhn, 2020). During the COVID-19 pandemic, on the contrary, great importance was attached to working from home because avoiding chains of infection and reducing the number of infections were mandatory. As a result many public administration workers were given the opportunity to work from home. This happened at a speed that would not have been conceivable without the crisis-related situation (Höhn, 2020). Around one third of municipal employees worked from their home desks during the pandemic. However, a lack of IT equipment and access to the office servers limited the work there. Only just under 70% of home office workers had access to documents and specialised procedures (Next:Public GmbH, 2020).

The short-term solutions worked during the crisis. Now it is important to remove the remaining obstacles in the long term. For instance increasing digitisation of paper files can counter concerns about data protection (Ebel, 2020). The experience gained with mobile working during the Corona crisis has the potential to take the wind out of the sails of critical voices against modern ways of working and can initiate a sustainable change in behaviour among public service employees and managers.

As well as the place of work the nature of work has changed. Local governments have switched from being open to the public (in physical presence) in many areas and have instead set-up an electronic exchange with their citizens. Applying for a registration certificate by mail or using an online form are just two of many ways that local governments have explored to offer services without going in person (Schrader, 2020). The Corona Bridging Grant from the German federal government for instance, could also be applied for in a purely digital process which shows the responsiveness of the public administration (Schleyer, 2020). Furthermore, the online application for unemployment benefits was completed in a fast-track procedure (Schüür-Langkau, 2020).

For the public administration, crisis management also meant a break with traditional hierarchical thinking. To manage the crisis a new approach was tested that works across hierarchies. Crisis teams have taken the lead in the administration and have shown that it is possible to work quickly, effectively and flexibly across departmental boundaries. In addition, many employees were assigned to areas that were unfamiliar to them in order to mitigate additional work. For example, new tasks occurred in the newly established service hotlines or in contact tracing (Bastians, 2020b). This demonstrates that the public administration showed increasing agility during their crisis management.

It is not only the hierarchical thinking that has changed. Applying for a mobile workplace and setting it up recently took a lot of time, as occupational health and safety regulations had to be met. In the crisis situation, exceptions to the strict occupational health and safety regulations were allowed, so that the employees were quickly able to work at home. Employees were allowed to dismantle their Desktop Personal Computer (PCs) and use them at home without first conducting a site inspection. A possibility that would have been unthinkable before the pandemic, but has proven itself in the crisis situation.

4.2 Hardware and Software Equipment

The changed conditions led to a change in the need for technical equipment. Since the beginning of the crisis, more and more portable devices, i.e. laptops and business mobile phones, have been procured. Due to the higher acquisition costs of portable devices, the standard before the Corona crisis was to procure a PC. At the beginning of the Corona crisis, it quickly became apparent that the basic IT equipment used so far was to the largest extent incompatible with mobile work.

Immediately after the outbreak of the COVID-19 pandemic, secure access to the office servers of the local governments was provided for thousands of employees enabling them to do their work in their home offices (Dreyer, 2020). Moreover video conferencing systems were procured at short notice (Dreyer, 2020). The professional use of video conferencing systems or messengers was still uncharted territory for many public sector employees until the beginning of 2020 (Next:Public GmbH, 2020). The use of such conferencing and messaging systems thus increased with the onset of the COVID-19 pandemic, bringing local governments a little closer to a modern way of working.

In order to provide services remotely, many local governments have introduced digital appointment booking systems to grant access for the citizens to various administrative services (Bastians, 2020b). The pioneers in digitalisation of the local governments were at an advantage because they could work with existing systems and didn't have to find quick solutions (Schleyer, 2020).

It might be a reasonably assumption that the software and hardware procured will prevail and further will pave the way for a modern way of working.

4.3 Investments

The COVID-19 pandemic resulted in considerable additional financial expenditure for local governments, as crisis management costs millions of Euros. Nonetheless, the digital transformation benefits from this short-term provision of funds because the acquisition of new soft- and hardware would otherwise not have been prioritised and would have cost much more time in advance.

In the context of the crisis, the focus on the added value of digital transformation led the German government to provide three billion Euros for digitisation of the public administration in the Economic and Crisis Management Package (Bastians, 2020a). The funds have to be used for digitisation projects and are intended to relieve local governments by providing them with digital administrative procedures instead of having to develop it themselves (Schüür-Langkau, 2020). This is a funding that local governments would probably not have received to this extent and speed without the disclosures of the COVID-19 pandemic (Schleyer, 2020).

4.4 External Perception of the Public Sector

The external perception of the public administration may not necessarily have anything to do with the digital transformation but it can promote the holistic change process. The COVID-19 pandemic highlighted the relevance of the public sector (Dreyer, 2020). Local governments in particular formed the backbone of the pandemic response, as they are responsible for multiple systemically relevant tasks such as the important work of the public health departments (Next:Public GmbH, 2020). Due to the high flexibility and commitment of the employees, it was also possible to refute prejudices about the supposed working mindset in the public sector (Bastians, 2020b). This has anchored the systemic relevance of the public sector in the public's consciousness (Karp, 2020). This in turn can lead to an increase in attractiveness as an employer and counteract the shortage of skilled workers (Karp, 2020) which has been prevalent in the public sector for years and is, inter alia, slowing down the digital transformation.

A holistic digital transformation requires not only the efforts of the public administration but also the use of digital offerings by the citizens. The pandemic-related shutdown has led to citizens becoming more aware of the available digital services and using them more (Bastians, 2020b). The increased user numbers, however, are the best argument for the necessity of digitisation and investments in digital citizen services (Schleyer, 2020).

5 Conclusion

The COVID-19 pandemic was and continues to be a stress test for the public sector. It revealed deficits and clearly demonstrated that public administration needs an acceleration boost in digitisation (Schöppe, 2020). However, as already explained, crises can have a stimulating effect and they always have a positive side as well (Petersdorff, 2020). The changes in relation to the above mentioned issues brought about by the COVID-19 pandemic are mostly positive and they are able to promote the holistic change process.

A successful digital transformation makes the public administration resilient and crisis-resistant, because it entails a modern way of working, digitised processes and improved technical equipment. By keeping the appropriate technology and hardware on hand, the public sector will be able to maintain service operations as far as possible, even in crisis situations (Ebel, 2020). The pandemic-related conversion to a largely digital administration shows that the public institutions not only gained a communication channel or increased efficiency but that the digital transformation provides a backstop for the administration to remain able to work even in times of crisis (Next:Public GmbH, 2020).

Maintaining service capability on the one hand and digital action capability on the other are a necessity (Bastians, 2020b). The COVID-19 pandemic underlined that digital transformation is not just nice to have, but a mandatory programme (Bastians, 2020a) and has clearly raised the importance of immediate digitisation of administrative procedures (Egyedy, 2020).

As part of the crisis management, numerous new systems and hardware were procured and new working methods were tested. The changeover to a new way of working has largely succeeded (Next:Public GmbH, 2020). Nonetheless, it remains questionable whether the short-term measures taken and ad-hoc processes installed will be sustainable. The practical experience gained during the COVID-19 pandemic is an ideal starting point for permanently implementing new digital solutions and ways of working (Höhn, 2020). Any provisional solutions must now be replaced by a targeted transformation strategy (Karp, 2020). Following the crisis management, the changes should be considered and a discussion should follow to what extent the processes can be continued in this way or ad hoc minimal variants introduced can be further developed. For the future and possible subsequent crises, it is desirable to be able to fall back on well-established processes and infrastructure (Schleyer, 2020).

The dominant view in local governments is that they do not want to return to the status quo before the outbreak of the COVID-19 pandemic, but rather use the push to benefit in a targeted and service-oriented way from the (technical) progress achieved in short term (Bastians, 2020b). In addition to technical possibilities, behavioural change will also play an essential role. Looking at the internal perspective of this paper, it becomes clear that innovations can also fail due to the mentality of local government employees. It is therefore to be hoped that there will be no relapse into old patterns of behaviour after the crisis. Provided that the new ways of working that have now been tested are continued, the mentality of the employees will also be able to change in long term.

At the beginning of the crisis, the public service had no choice but to improvise. The benefits of ad hoc measures will remain even after the crisis is over and will presumably change the way tasks are carried out in the future. The outbreak of the COVID-19 pandemic that has led to a stressful, unprecedented situation in the recent past thus has the potential to generate considerable added value and serve as a catalyst so that digital administration becomes more and more the norm (Schleyer, 2020).

References

Bastians, U. (2020a). Der „Wumms“ für die digitale Verwaltung kann kommen, in: Verwaltung der Zukunft, https://www.verwaltung-der-zukunft.org/digitale-verwaltung/der-wumms-fuer-die-digitale-verwaltung-kann-kommen (12.12.2020).

Bastians, U. (2020b). Digitalisierung ist kein Luxus, sondern unabdingbar, in: Verwaltung der Zukunft, https://www.verwaltung-der-zukunft.org/digitale-verwaltung/digitalisierung-ist-kein-luxus-sondern-unabdingbar (12.12.2020).

Dreyer, Malu, interviewed by Schaeff, Andreas. (2020). Resiliente Verwaltung, in: Kommune 21 (11/2020), p. 22.

Ebel, O. (2020). Nur ein frommer Wunsch? New Work im öffentlichen Sektor, in: Behördenspiegel (April 2020), Digitaler Staat.

Egyedy, S. (2020). Thesen zur Digitalisierung der Verwaltung, in: Tagesspiegel Background, https://background.tagesspiegel.de/digitalisierung/thesen-zur-digitalisierung-der-verwaltung (26.09.2020).

European Commission. (2020). Digital economy and society index report 2020. Digital Public Services, https://ec.europa.eu/digital-single-market/en/digital-economy-and-society-index-desi (10.12.2020).

Höhn, T. (2020). Digital unterstütztes Home-Office der Kommunalverwaltung, in: Verwaltung der Zukunft, https://www.verwaltung-der-zukunft.org/digitale-verwaltung/digital-unterstuetztes-home-office-der-kommunalverwaltung (12.12.2020).

Karp, T. (2020). Bloß keine Rückkehr zur alten Normalität. Der Öffentliche Dienst nach der Corona-Krise, in: Behörden Spiegel (September 2002), Bund.

Müller, V. (2020). Digitales Rathaus - Wie Kommunen in herausfordernden Zeiten ein verlässlicher Partner sein können, in: Behördenspiegel (April 2020), Digitaler Staat (p. 5).

Next:Public GmbH. (2020). Verwaltung in Krisenzeiten. Eine Bestandsaufnahme der Auswirkungen der Corona-Pandemie auf den Öffentlichen Dienst, https://nextpublic.de/studie-verwaltung-in-krisenzeiten (11.12.2020).

Petersdorff, T. (2020). Innovation in Zeiten von Corona. Wie COVID-19 dazu beiträgt, digitale Kreativkräfte freizusetzen, in: Behörden Spiegel. Digitaler Staat (April 2020), (p. 25).

Punz, M. (2020). Verwaltung unter Druck. Wie die Coronakrise das Land digitalisiert, https://www.tagesspiegel.de/wirtschaft/verwaltung-unter-druck-wie-die-coronakrise-das-land-digitalisiert/25667160.html (11.12.2020).

Safar, M. (2020). Was ist der Unterschied zwischen Digitalisierung & digitaler Transformation?, in: Weissenberg Solutions, https://weissenberg-solutions.de/digitalisierung-vs-digitale-transformation-was-ist-der-unterschied (26.09.2020).

Schöppe, D. (2020). Blitzumfrage „Auswirkungen der Corona-Pandemie in der Verwaltung", in: Verwaltung der Zukunft, https://www.verwaltung-der-zukunft.org/blitzumfrage-auswirkungen-der-corona-pandemie-der-verwaltung (12.12.2020).

Schleyer, R. (2020). Krise als Chance, in: Kommune 21 (11/2020), (p. 18).

Schrader, D. (2020). Düsseldorfer Ämter nehmen ihren Betrieb wieder auf, https://rp-online.de/nrw/staedte/duesseldorf/duesseldorf-buergerbueros-und-strassenverkehrsamt-nehmen-wieder-betrieb-auf_aid-51480917 (11.12.2020).

Schüür-Langkau, A. (2020). Digitale Prozesse sind nicht nur, nice to have. *Innovative Verwaltung, 42*(9), 14–17.

The Top Managerial Influence on Innovation: Development of a Comprehensive Framework

Sonja Sperber

1 Innovations in the Organizational Context

Change and adaptation as topics as well as the discussion regarding their significance for organizations have a long tradition in management research. Over a century ago, this concept has already been discussed by Davies (1900: 517), highlighting the omnipresence of change by indicating that "*[…] at present, all that we can say is that the universe manifests itself not as permanent and unchanging, but as a cosmic whole which unfolds according to a law which is autonomous.*" Change is recognized as a universal phenomenon, being one of the most fundamental principles of human life and affecting all parts of society, especially its cultural, political, social, as well as economic system (cf. Hagen, 1962). Organizations constantly must adapt to economic change occurring due to shifting social, technological, or political circumstances. It is the application to all changes of real being which points to the complexity and the dynamic nature of change processes. More precisely, the ubiquity of change affects business life in manifold ways, requiring distinct skills, abilities, and capabilities from leaders. This connection has, however, not been fully explored until today.

Within the last century, the management task of moderating renewal has been researched from manifold perspectives. Highly notable is the occurrence of change in its direct relation to innovation, appearing as both force to and result from innovation (e.g., Ruttan, 1959). This relation mainly derives from the fact that new developments provoke a constant alteration in business life and its associated operations to cope with the shifting environment, for instance and particularly through innovations. Consequently, the adaptation of organizations to their environment is essential for

S. Sperber (✉)
International Business & Strategy, MSc International Business Management, Newcastle University London, 102 Middlesex Street, London E1 7EZ, UK
e-mail: sonja.sperber@newcastle.ac.uk
URL: https://www.ncl.ac.uk/london

T. Herberger and J. Dötsch (eds.), *Digitalization, Digital Transformation and Sustainability in the Global Economy*, Springer Proceedings in Business and Economics, https://doi.org/10.1007/978-3-030-77340-3_8

their survival, while a firm's competitive advantage in a dynamic environment is the result of innovative and creative answers to technological changes (Mumford & Gustafson, 1988). Thus, the necessity of an organization's constant renewal for its long-term success has been accepted by scholars and practitioners. The adaptation to change by constantly abandoning past success and aiming at innovations hence is inevitable (Utterback, 1994). Because of this realization, the topic has continuously moved into focus, leading to nowadays' creed on innovation and change as the imperative and dogma of today's business life.

Schumpeter (1934) was among the first to address the aspect of innovation in the context of organizational life by referring to it as the implementation of new combinations. Since this first academic attention to innovation, research on this topic has experienced a great increase in popularity, leading to a high quantity of academic approaches for assessing it while being stretched to a broad variety of subjects, as for instance cultural aspects (e.g., the innovation culture), human resource-based aspects (e.g., innovative actors), product-based aspects (e.g., open innovation) and organizational aspects (e.g., business model innovation).

However, innovation is not naturally occurring by itself within the organizational context, but the firm's innovative power rather is the result of an effective management, which instantly also raises the question on the managerial role in renewal processes. It generally is proceeded on the assumption that organizational leaders represent the most decisive shapers of organizational operations, including strategy, culture, processes, and structure (e.g., Finkelstein & Hambrick, 1996; Hambrick & Mason, 1984; Shalley & Gilson, 2004; Sperber, 2017). As the member of the top management team (TMT) are the most powerful players due to their hierarchical position, a top manager (TM) can influence the organization in many ways. Past studies have outlined several positions, which crucially contribute to innovations, for instance referring to specific functions of employees or technical experts (Ettlie et al., 1984; Fennell, 1984). The TMs' position regarding its influence on innovation, however, has only rarely been addressed (Hueske & Guenther, 2015; Tierney et al., 1999), only starting to be receive attention in recent decades.

2 Influencing Factors on Firm Innovativeness

To later investigate the TMs' influence on firm innovations, their overall significance for organizations needs to be clarified. Only after this, the crucial influence of TMs on innovations in principle and their effectively executed impact becomes evident. Firm innovativeness, which alludes to all innovation activities of an organization (in relation to products, processes, and services), is vital for an organization for adapting to the perpetually changing market environment through the generation and the implementation of innovations, with the goal of continually retaining a competitive advantage and with this indirectly contributing to the firm's performance (Anderson et al., 2014; Read, 2000). Following Boso et al. (2013: 64), "*[f]irm innovativeness is [...] viewed as a strategic resource that may provide a firm with the ability to compete in target markets by offering customers products and services with added and/or different sources of value relative to competitors*".

Research on firm innovativeness in general addresses two major aspects: (1) The first stream of research focuses on *whether* and *how* firm innovativeness eventually effects firm performance respectively growth (e.g., Kraiczy et al., 2015), while (2) the second stream addresses the *factors* which influence the firm innovativeness and, in consequence, the performance. Regarding (1), broad agreement exists that innovation activities are highly important to ensure advancement and to foster the emergence and maintenance of a competitive advantage within the market sphere (e.g., Bowen et al., 2010; Damanpour & Evan, 1984; Howell, 2005; Smith et al., 2008). In times of accelerated market competition, the innovation needs to generate a distinctive position in the market place for the respective company (Porter, 1985). New—respectively innovative—ideas are therefore essential for the long-term performance of the organization (e.g., Anderson et al., 2014; De Massis et al., 2015), since these ideas allow the company to adapt to the changing market demand or to an overall change in the economic system (e.g., in technological standards or market conditions) (Dawson & Andriopoulos, 2014). Since innovations represent the most effective medium in adapting to occurring changes, the firms' dependency on innovations has accelerated over time (Smith & Tushman, 2005), which continually increases the overall need for an organization to generate and foster innovative ideas. As the innovation activities impact the firm performance and its growth, they are recognized to be highly relevant for the company's overall success (e.g., Bledow et al., 2009; Utterback, 1994). Regarding the (2) second stream of research, i.e. the antecedents of firm innovativeness, multifarious factors located in diverse areas within the organization as well as in its environment have been addressed. This paper specifically focuses on the factors of *management*, *culture*, *leadership,* and *network* as they have a significant influence on the TMs' impact on the firm innovativeness.

3 The Complex Relation Between the Top Management and Innovation

As it is the objective to assess the top managerial influence on innovations, the focus is exclusively on those factors located within their direct scope; further factors (e.g., market conditions and developments, competitors' behavior, environmental conditions) are not considered. Regarding those factors within their scope, Hult et al., (2004: 429) refer to the fact that still only little is known on the TMs as "*[…] the drivers of innovativeness and how those drivers operate* via*innovativeness to collectively influence performance*". The high relevance of their role for firm's innovations is, however, evident: the explanation can, among others, be approached from the resource-based view (e.g., Peteraf, 1993; Pfeffer & Salancik, 2003). From this perspective, firm innovativeness is viewed as a strategic resource (Boso et al., 2013), and it is the TMs' exertion of influence on firm competitiveness through firm innovativeness which distinguishes successful managers from less effective ones. This refers to a high probability that a firm with a greater level of innovativeness and, accordingly, more effective leaders is more likely to develop multiple types of innovative product portfolios. Regarding the factors via which the TMs execute direct influence, the following ones require special attention:

(a) *Organizational culture*: Due to its significant influence on innovativeness (e.g., Chua et al., 2015; Flynn & Chatman, 2001; Kitchell, 1995; Martins & Terblanche, 2003), the fruitful setup of the organizational culture for innovations is increasingly becoming a corporate mandate (Miller & Brankovic, 2011); it, among others, has a direct influence on organizational creativity (e.g., Tesluk et al., 1997) and accordingly on firm innovativeness. Regarding this prior research, the question on which actions managers must engage in to generate and/or support innovations within the organizational context has experienced consideration in theory and practice. Amabile (1998) addresses the importance of the individual or the team creativity as a necessary condition for innovation activities; she further points out that innovation mainly is about creating something that is appropriate to the goal at hand in terms of being applicable, valuable, or expressive of meaning (Amabile, 1996). Even if the pursuing of this objective depends on both internal as well as external information and knowledge, the internal fostering of creativity seems to be the essential task of leaders to support organizational innovativeness (Amabile, 1998; Amabile & Khaire, 2008). In this vein, numerous explanatory approaches of innovation allude to the aspect of creativity (e.g., De Sousa et al., 2012). One of them is Woodman et al., and and's (1993: 293) approach of referring to creativity as a necessary organizational element in describing it "*[…] as the creation of a valuable, useful new product, service, idea, procedure, or process by individuals working together in a complex social system*". For this, the organizational culture fostering innovativeness is inevitable.

(b) *Leadership*: In this vein, past research addressed the aspect of leadership as an approach for conceptualizing the direct and indirect links between TMs and workforce. Previous studies have referred to the assumption that not all TMs act as omnipotential leaders—as usually assumed—due to certain demographic characteristics and personality factors. Yet, leadership's impact on firm innovations (e.g., Adair, 2009; Woodman et al., 1993) as well as creativity (e.g., Shin & Zhou, 2003; Tierney et al., 1999) has been asserted multiple times, overall resulting in the concordant acceptance that their high impact (e.g., Hoffman & Hegarty, 1993; Howell & Avolio, 1993; Jung et al., 2003). This high level of impact predominantly is inferred from their leadership behavior (Elenkov et al., 2005).

(c) *Network ties*: The network previously has been acknowledged to influence firm innovativeness with regard to knowledge transfer (e.g., Ibarra & Hunter, 2007). In general, the transfer of knowledge between the single intraorganizational units and the respective TM's information delivering network is highly important for the stimulation of innovative ideas and creativity (e.g., Nonaka et al.,

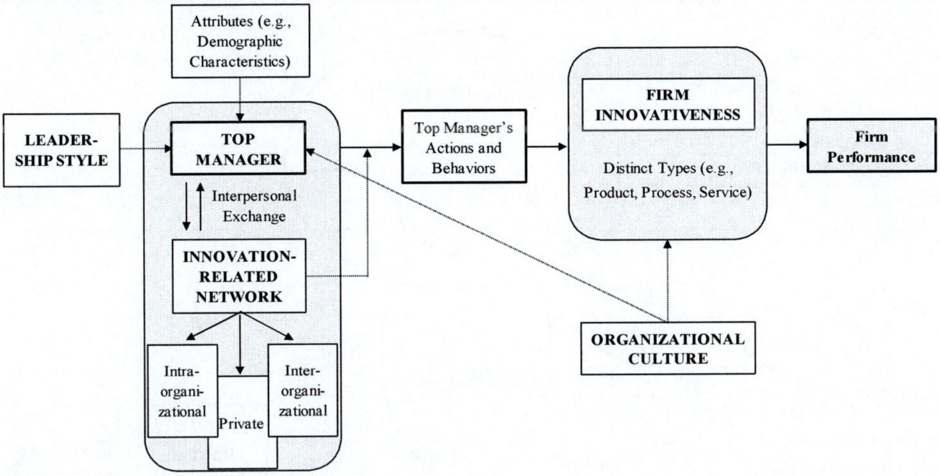

Fig. 1 Interrelation of the factors of investigation

1996; Tang, 2011; Wissema & Euser, 1991). Since the TM's leadership thus "*[…] is about enabling knowledge creation*" (Nonaka et al., 2006: 1192), the network ties inside but also outside the organization are essential for the organizational creativity and innovation process (e.g., Geletkanycz & Hambrick, 1997; Landsperger et al., 2012). Yet, not only the impact of leadership on innovations is of importance, but rather the influence from the network on the leadership behavior itself must be considered, as the knowledge ties contribute essential information to the respective TM and therefore expand the individual knowledge state.

In summary, the relation between TMs as organizational leaders and their impact on innovations appears to be complex and multidimensional, even though the highly important role of the TMs in fostering and managing a firm's innovation activities has in the past been widely acknowledged. Figure 1 outlines the overall interrelation of the single thematic components and directly refers to those factors, which have been identified as important elements.

4 The Central Perspectives for the Theoretical Foundation

To enlarge the understanding of the top managerial impact on innovations over the different factors of influence (cf. Elenkov et al., 2005; Li et al., 2013; Smith & Tushman, 2005; Yuan et al., 2014), four central perspectives are identified. It is referred to the overall perspective of *Management* from a holistic point of view by applying the *New St. Galler Management-Model* (Rüegg-Stürm, 2003). In addition, as prior research indicates, the perspectives of *Culture, Leadership,* and *Network* deliver a large explanatory power regarding firm performance: the conceptualization

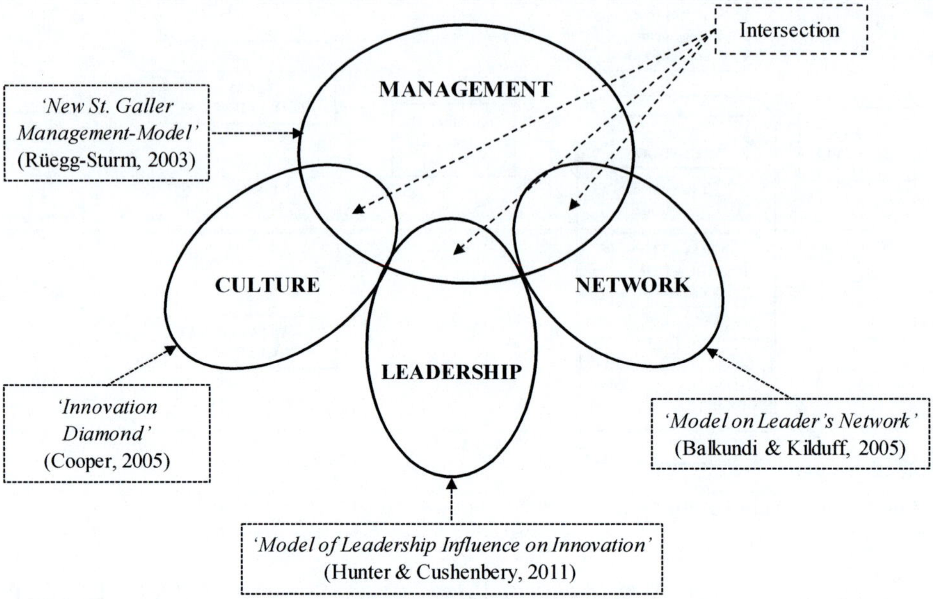

Fig. 2 Main theoretical perspectives and corresponding models

of *Culture* is based on the *Innovation Diamond* (Cooper, 2005), offering a systematization of innovation that exceeds the scope of the more universal management model. A modified version of Hunter and Cushenbery's (2011) *Model of Leadership Influence on Innovation* is applied for the *Leadership* perspective and Balkundi and Kilduff's (2005) *Model on Leader's Network* for the *Network* perspective. The following section displays the theoretical background of these models (Fig. 2).

4.1 The Management Perspective: New St. Galler Management-Model

The *New St. Galler Management-Model* by Rüegg-Sturm (2003) serves as a generic model for the management perspective, which has been developed over several generations, representing a holistic framework to encompass the top managerial actions while differentiating between internal and external sphere. The model itself does not focus on the process-related application within a certain context, but rather offers an integrated framework for embedding and observing specific problem statements from a more general view. The model's first generation by Ulrich and Krieg (1974) in its initial composition pursued the objective of delivering a holistically-oriented framework for management operations and consisted of three sections: the enterprise model, the leadership model, and the organization model. The model's second generation focused on the newly developed management direction in research during that

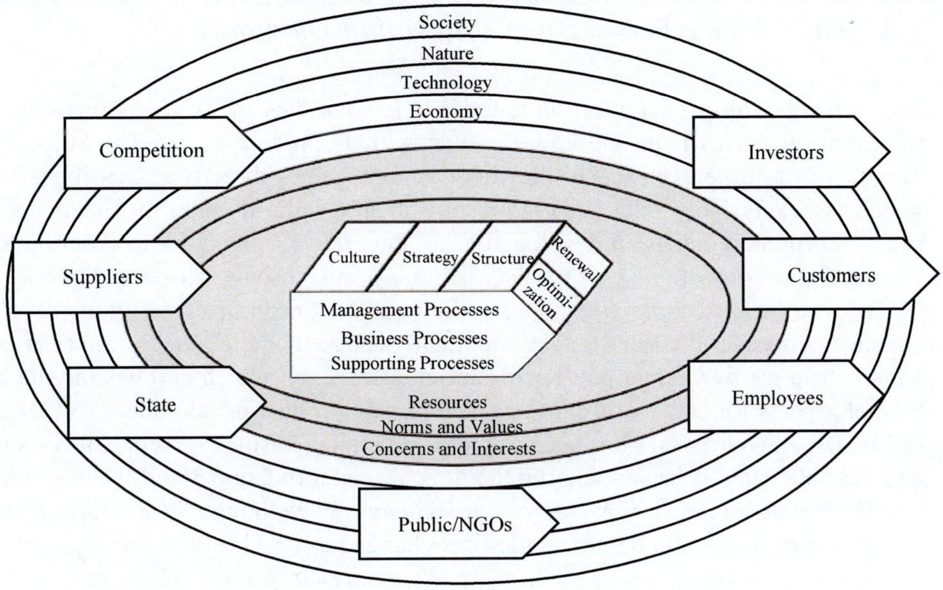

Fig. 3 New St. Galler Management-model (Rüegg-Sturm, 2003)

time by explicitly referring to the dimensions of strategy, culture, and management philosophy.

The model's third generation (Rüegg-Stürm, 2003) expands the initial model by two aspects: first, the differentiation into normative, strategic, and operative dimensions, introduced from the second generation finds consideration. Second, it overall contains six dimensions (Fig. 3): processes (management, business, and supporting ones), vertical aspects of integration (culture, strategy, structure), development modes (optimization, renewal), stakeholders (competition, customers, employees, etc.), environmental domains (society, nature, technology, economy), and the organizational area of interaction (resources, norms and values, concerns and interests). These dimensions are important for the general reflection of the corporate activities and require consideration within the scope of an integrated management approach.

This generation of the *New St. Galler Management-Model* by Rüegg-Stürm (2003) delivers the largest explanatory power as it presents an integrated view over all elements and puts emphasis on the integrated perception of elements and their correlation. Its most important features lie in the differentiation of the vertical integration as well as the environmental domains; the latter refer to the fact that managerial action is always embedded in a larger context. A fourth generation has later been developed, which investigates the aspects in several minor frameworks detached from each other; it hence is not beneficial for application in this context.

4.2 The Culture Perspective: Innovation Diamond

The value of Cooper's (2005) *Innovation Diamond* lies in its focus on innovation processes. This is in line with the management process of the *New St. Galler Management-Model* but exceeds the previous approach by directly addressing issues which are exclusively related to innovation as a specific domain of management tasks. It originally has been developed as an integrative framework to describe top managerial action with respect to success in innovative product development.

The *Innovation Diamond* as one key innovation concept has undergone several enhancements over the last decades and mainly is based on the *New Product Performance Triangle* by Cooper and Kleinschmidt (1995a, b), which outlines the fundamental aspects for successful performance in new product development (NPD). In the 1990s, this framework has been implemented in the business practice of 'Procter and Gamble' (P&G), advancing the theoretical model of Cooper and Kleinschmidt into the practical *Initiatives Management Diamond*. Even though the model contains a similar content, the fundamental idea has changed as P&G acts on the assumption "*[...] that there is no one key to success in product innovation*" (Cooper & Mills, 2005: 10). It focuses on a rather broad picture of the correlation between the single cornerstones of the model. For the enterprise P&G, the adjustment of the internal innovation process based on the developed model has significantly increased the company's NPD success and has often been referred to as best practice on product development (Cooper & Mills, 2005).

Cooper's (2005) *Innovation Diamond* (Fig. 4), has been established on the foundation of the P&G model and is mainly based on the insights of a study regarding the best practices that lead to high performance in NPD. Besides its reference to the strategy as first, the resources as second, and the idea-to-launch process as third cornerstone, this model includes one significant alteration, which takes place in the fourth cornerstone: here, the *Innovation Diamond* directly includes the element of 'People' by

Fig. 4 Innovation diamond (Cooper, 2005)

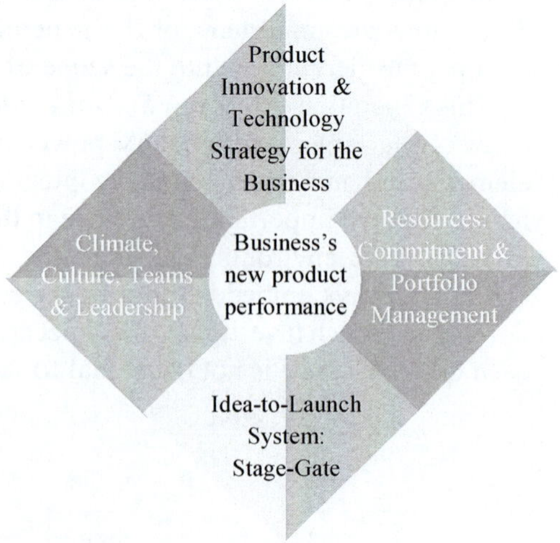

its denomination of 'Climate, Culture, Teams & Leadership', often referred to as the 'soft' element. Cooper and Mills (2005: 9) define this aspect as "*[…] having the right climate and culture, effective cross-functional teams, and senior management commitment to New Product Development*". Accordingly, this model directly addresses the importance of a positive and fruitful culture and climate for the internal collaboration and the overall innovation activities by referring to it as "*[…] the fourth driver of performance*" (Cooper & Mills, 2005: 12). Further, this fourth cornerstone addresses leadership as a vital element, since the TMT members have to lead all innovation efforts and needs to be strongly committed to product innovativeness (Cooper, 2005). This outlines the essential importance of the top managerial support for innovation activities in order to be successful.

Even though the *Innovation Diamond* primarily addresses product innovations, it demonstrates the overall importance of innovations in the organizational context by highlighting general success factors, such as cultural aspects and leadership (cf. Kahn et al., 2012). It enables the understanding of TMs' influence from a rather technical perspective by identifying tasks and action fields that promise a competitive advantage if executed properly. The TMs' task is to develop the strategic roadmap, to engage people ('team') into this vision, and to support it by building a corresponding culture.

4.3 The Leadership Perspective: Model of Leadership Influence on Innovation

Although the *Innovation Diamond* takes 'soft' elements into consideration, it is not fine-grained enough to investigate leadership in depth as it jointly focuses on the factors of climate, culture, teams, and leadership as interconnected elements. Accordingly, a distinct approach is required. In the past, diverse approaches to investigate the influence of the top managerial leadership on innovations were developed (e.g., Elenkov & Manev, 2005; Jung et al., 2003; Li et al., 2016; Makri & Scandura, 2010). Yet, most studies on the leader's impact hereby outline the fact that the influence mainly addresses the facilitation of creativity (e.g., Cheung & Wong, 2011; Jaussi & Dionne, 2003; Shin & Zhou, 2003), which in turn supports innovation (Howell & Avolio, 1993). In this regard, distinct leadership styles have been investigated in a long tradition of research regarding their levels of influence on innovations, resulting in concordant evidence that the transformational leadership style is beneficial for supporting innovation (e.g., Bass, 1990; Yukl, 2012), as it is the transformational leaders' main potential to inspire the employees to be creative and innovative (Howell & Avolio, 1993).

In this respect, Hunter and Cushenbery (2011: 248) propose a model which directly builds on the assumption "*[…] that leaders are one of the primary driving forces in increasing innovative output*". This approach focuses on detecting the leaders' direct and indirect influence of leadership on innovation; the model establishes a multilevel-process perspective, which highlights the fact that the leaders' efforts regarding creativity and innovation require the investigation within a larger context (e.g., including teams, departments, or entire organizations), as they do not function as detached entities within the organization. Even though the model delivers an important approach for assessing leadership, its original version yet holds some severe shortcomings, for which it requires modification. Hunter and Cushenbery (2011) have examined the direct leadership influence (e.g., the allocation of resources, the decision making on a specific idea) as well as the indirect influence (e.g., the establishment of an internal climate for fostering creativity, the rewards and recognition of employees' innovative ideas) (cf. Jung et al., 2008). However, even though the leadership effects exert their impact both via direct and indirect paths, past research has acknowledged the fact that the boundary between the two is floating. Hence, an adapted version based on the new theoretical insights is shown in Fig. 5.

The modified version emphasizes the fact that leadership upholds several ways of influencing innovation; it hence is not possible to specify the leader's precise impact on one single aspect. Rather, "*[...] there is a system of activities, actions, and behaviors needed that often operate in concert with one another*" (Hunter & Cushenbery, 2011: 259). The model's reference to diverse factors of influence thus provides a broad and multilateral approach for investigating the leadership influence on innovations.

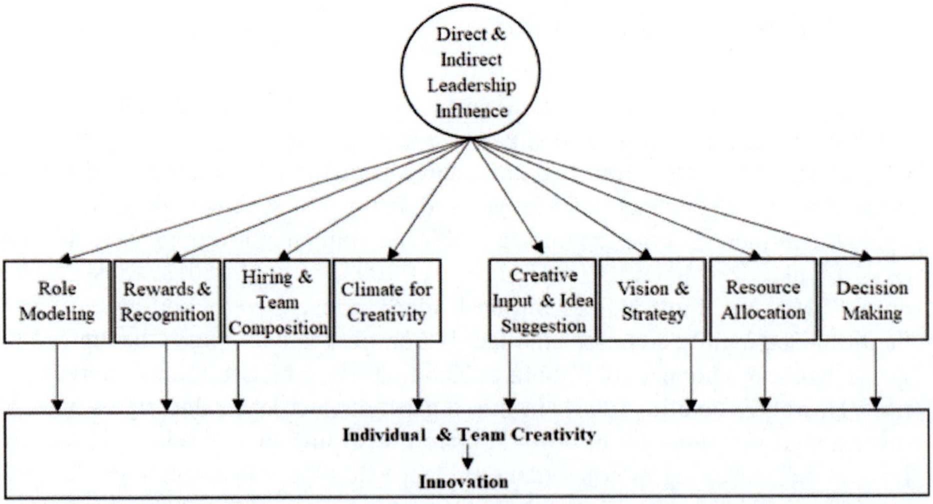

Fig. 5 Model of leadership influence on innovation (Hunter & Cushenbery, 2011; modified)

4.4 The Network Perspective: Model on Leader's Network

According to Balkundi and Kilduff (2005), leadership is a social process and as any other behavior is subject to manifold influences, among others the TMs' social network ties. Social network theory hereby serves as a substantial source, since it characterizes networks "*[…] as both cognitive structures in the minds of organizational members and opportunity structures that facilitate and constrain action*" (Balkundi & Kilduff, 2005: 941). Accordingly, the facilitation of action—as for instance for innovation—is considerably contingent on networks. With focus on the individual level, special emphasis is put on the significance of the TMs' relationships regarding the network collaboration for the firm innovativeness (Elenkov & Manev, 2005; Elenkov et al., 2005). However, the direct effect of dyadic tie collaborations—referring to pairwise direct ties—on innovation has mostly been neglected in past research (Fliaster & Schloderer, 2010); the dyadic ties yet are important for the TMs' obtaining and exchange of knowledge.

In the context of the ties' origin, the structural holes theory (Burt, 1997) proposes that the organizational members are predominantly connected to those actors within the organization who share common foci of activities (Feld, 1981). Thus, "*[t]he lack of direct connections among a firm's partners, […] indicates that these partners operate in distinct parts of the network, increasing the likelihood that they carry heterogeneous information.*" (Frankort, 2008: 1). This yet indicates that managers, who span structural holes and establish a connection to other organizational parts, gain access to new information (Burt, 1997); empirical evidence has been found for the positive impact of the structural holes on innovation through the access to new information. However, the TMs' networks are not limited to the organizational boundaries, but rather also include ties outside the internal sphere (e.g., Collins & Clark, 2003). Regarding the network differences between (top) managers and nonmanagers, Carroll and Teo (1996: 433) indicated: "*Managers belong to more clubs and societies than nonmanagers […]. In terms of core discussion networks, managers […] have large networks, and also have a greater number of close ties with network members*". Further, their ties are to a larger extent located outside the organizational boundaries compared to colleagues from lower hierarchical levels (Michael & Yukl, 1993). As the TMs' network collaboration inside as well as outside the firm hence can be seen as essential source of knowledge, it accordingly directly affects their influence on innovations. This relation further is highlighted in Balkundi and Kilduff's (2005) *Model on Leader's Network* in Fig. 6, differentiating between types of network ties and the leader effectiveness.

The model represents a tentative approach to leadership effectiveness from a network perspective and exclusively addresses the extent of leaders' influence in the ego, the organizational and the interorganizational network; further types of ties, as for instance private ties, are not considered. The model yet highlights the important insight that leaders' ego networks are affected by the individual cognition on networks, leading to the assumption that social ties are shaped in accordance with

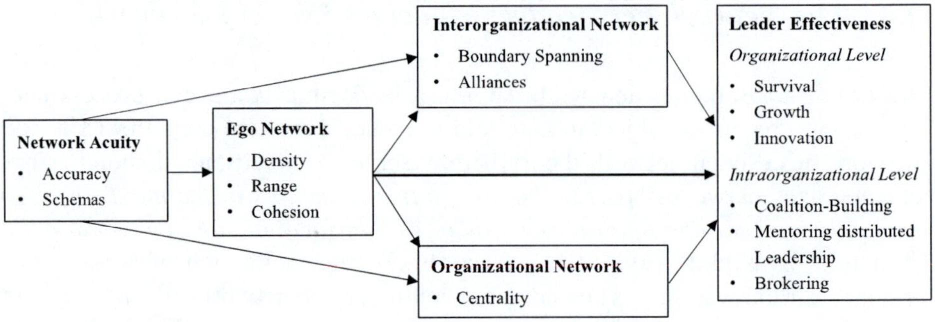

Fig. 6 Model on leader's network (Balkundi & Kilduff, 2005)

one's expectations on the network setup. Further, network accuracy improves the extent to which a strategic position is occupied by a leader within the network.

In summary, the network perspective proposes that the effectiveness of TMs' networks on organizational and intraorganizational level significantly influences the firm innovativeness, yet in a distinct manner: while a central position in the organizational network positively contributes to internal effectiveness, the latter focuses on the formation of important external partnerships. It therefore is seen as an important source of information, which directly contributes to innovation (Balkundi & Kilduff, 2005).

5 The Development of a Comprehensive Framework

The four perspectives discussed provide a rich basis to comprehend the TMs' influence on innovation in the organizational context. They offer an access for investigation, which contributes to the enlargement of the topic's understanding in multiple ways. Combining the different perspectives, however, appears to be more profitable than the detached examination of the single influence areas. Due to several shortcomings of the previous models from today's point of view in explaining the top managerial impact on innovation and the so far missing combination of the distinct areas of influence into one framework, this paper aims at closing the prevailing gap.

5.1 Shortcomings of the Current Models

The most important shortcoming of the discussed models refers to their generic nature and in consequence the possible gaps of explanation of the models' single elements. They exclusively focus on a macro-level rather than allowing the framing of micro-oriented perspectives, leading to the fact that the precise circumstances are insufficiently taken into consideration and that in-depth information is not available.

This fact limits the understanding of top managerial influence in multiple ways: first, only little is known on the precise actions successful leaders take to moderate innovation processes. Leadership models which apply a macro-perspective can express the relation between different dimensions, yet are they blind for understanding the meaning and sense of interaction between leader and follower in complex networks.

Second, broad concepts of efficacy, effectiveness, and performance regarding innovation processes claim universal validity. This, however, neglects the fact that the particular context can let one action appear adequate in one situation, while in another situation the same action is not. Such models assume causal linearity of the phenomenon under research, while instead the value of their application can increase by taking on a micro-perspective. Addressing the micro-perspective also provides an opportunity for advancing the understanding of innovativeness in a general view on the macro-level. To explore the social mechanisms and to illuminate the multifaceted micro-foundations of top management influence on innovation, an in-depth analysis of the distinct areas of influence in combination can provide important insights.

Third, a managerial perspective of cognition and behavior comprehends managers' cognitive framing as underpinning basis for their decision making and their manifested behaviors (Hodgkinson & Healey, 2008). If leaders try to navigate through complex innovation-related issues with multiple interdependencies to economical, technological, and social aspects, it is valuable to apply the network perspective for analysis of this issue. The question *whether* networks represent an important aspect in shaping cognitive patterns appears to be sufficiently answered by the previously discussed models. However, the questions on *how* this occurs, what the meaning of network embeddedness for decision making is, as well as which specific information, emotions, and values are exchanged, so far remains open.

Fourth, social exchange relationships and behaviors can affect creativity and, accordingly, innovation (Khazanchi & Masterson, 2011). The mentioned models do neither consider nor assume side-effects from the industry focused on, but rather claim general validity. This is astounding as this implicitly supposes that social exchange relationships are of the same quality in any industry. As this in sum highlights, the prevailing models generally focus on the macro-perspective and derive their explanations from a generic view. Accordingly, they mostly disregard the micro-perspective and pay insufficient attention to the precise context at hand. This is taken into account when developing the comprehensive framework.

5.2 Framework

In summary, the setup of the comprehensive framework in Fig. 7 derives from the basic assumption that the TMs are one of most decisive shapers of all innovation concerns within the organizational context (Daellenbach et al., 1999; Hoffman & Hegarty, 1993; Wong, 2013). However, numerous factors affect the top managerial impact on innovations: some of these factors are based on the individual level—among them the demographic characteristics (e.g., age), the functional background, and the personal experience (e.g., Boeker, 1997; Hambrick & Mason, 1984)—whole some other factors are based on the group level—as for instance the composition of the TMT in which they operate (e.g., Carpenter et al., 2004). These factors therefore necessarily require attention in a holistic framework on TM's innovation influence.

Regarding the previously discussed four perspectives of management, culture, leadership and networks, their already addressed high importance is recognized by the incorporation in the conjoint model's setup: in practice, the TM's network ties determine the leadership style applied, which in turn influences the leader's impact on the innovation culture. In conclusion, the direct impact of the TM effects innovativeness, yet via different paths of indirect influence.

Complementary to the perspectives considered, it is further argued that leadership is never independent of the context it is executed in and therefore the industry focus is incorporated within the conceptual framework. Numerous past studies have indicated its special relevance, especially for studies regarding TMs: most importantly, this is because a long top managerial career within a certain industry enhances the TM's knowledge on industry specificities and trends, and thus enlarges the personal openness towards innovations in reacting to new trends and changes (Daellenbach et al., 1999). Hayes and Abernathy (1980: 77) accordingly state that TMs "*[...] who are less informed about their industry [...] are likely to exhibit a noninnovative bias in their choices*". Further, the long industry tenure increases the likelihood that the network ties are embedded in the same industry, as the exchange of information takes place specifically regarding these industry factors, predominantly with other (top) managers of the same industry.

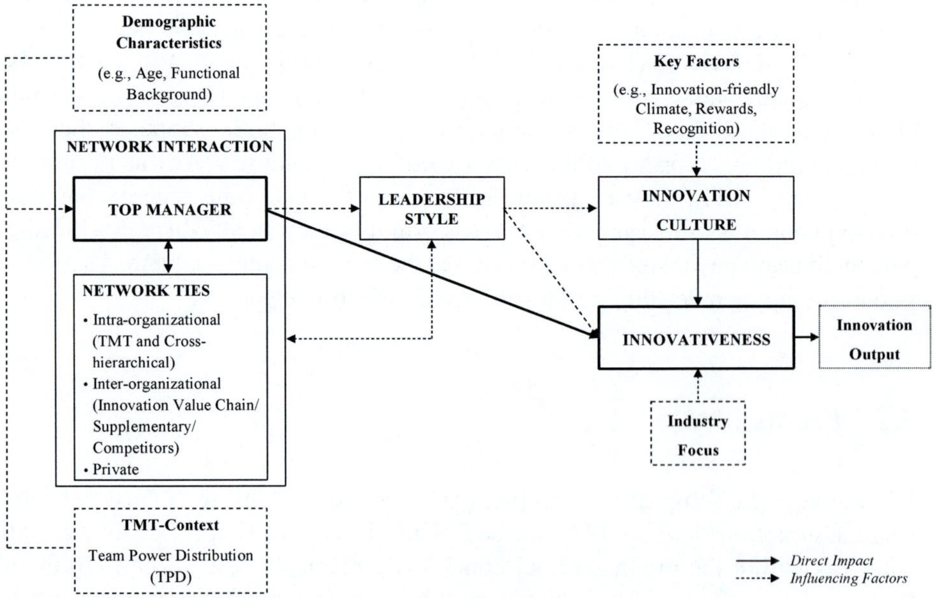

Fig. 7 The comprehensive framework on the top managerial influence on innovation

Therefore, long-term experience and respective knowledge gained within a certain industry overall increase the tendency towards innovative behavior of TMs. However, numerous past studies have mentioned that research on innovation altogether lacks findings with focus on specific industry settings (e.g., Edwards, 2000; Tidd, 2001); this again emphasizes the necessity of incorporating the respective industry focus within a comprehensive framework in order to analyze the top managerial influence in the context of a particular industry.

6 Conclusion, Implications and Limitations

The prior state of knowledge has significantly lacked insights on a combined view of the most central perspectives regarding TMs' influence on innovations. This academic void, which is of essential significance against the background of their key impact on organizational operations, has directly been addressed by setting up a holistic framework. Yet this approach, as research in general, not only advances the state of knowledge by gaining new insights, but also discloses research gaps requiring further investigation. Hence, the outlook on implications and the identification of future research paths as well as the paper's limitations are outlined in the following.

6.1 Implications and Further Research

The implications addressed in the following lay the foundation and provide an orientation for future research paths, which based on the setup of the comprehensive framework on TM's impact on innovations require more investigation. As mentioned, the past empirical research conducted on this topic has predominantly put focus on one of the perspectives (e.g., the individual influence on culture, network influence, etc.), not considering any effects which derive from a conjoint investigation of the different influence areas. The holistic framework developed within this paper yet provides the theoretical basis for implementing more profound (empirical) analyses of the top managerial influence regarding an integrated view of perspectives.

With focus on the individual top managerial level, an investigation of the significance of the available and above all also accessible internal and external resources for the individual impact on firm innovativeness is required. Further, this paper's implications allude to the fact that a more detailed examination of the individual impact on the firm's overall innovation performance is overdue. Regarding the future research paths, the holistic investigation of perspectives detects a further necessity to also analyze TMs' influence on innovations according to the respective position within the TMT, as the comparison of the executed influence between distinct positions is expected to be perceptive (some previous studies accredit the role of the CEO with better access to a broader-oriented information basis, e.g., Six et al., 2013). Moreover, a detailed examination of TMs' practically executed level of influence moves to the center of attention, as there possibly is a deficit between potential and realized top managerial influence (Linder & Sperber, 2017), which raises the following questions: are TMs not willing to invest more effort into the advancement of organizational innovations, do they consider it as unnecessary due to already prevailing innovation orientation, or do they rather lack appropriate tools to realize a higher level of influence? One aspect which further requires investigation based on the developed comprehensive framework is the top managerial innovation-related network: as it was outlined, the industry focus can have a significant effect on the overall TM's innovation influence, which amongst others is due to the different network structures built up by the TM within the industry. Hence, the allocation of ties between internal and external organizational sphere might differ for specific industries: for instance, the trend-based and fast moving lifestyle industry contains a high level of confidentiality, which can lead to resistance against the open exchange of ideas with the external sphere in comparison to other, less trend- or innovation-focused industries. Regarding future research approaches, it moreover will be beneficial to investigate the company size as decisive factor for the single TM's innovation impact, as the size (e.g., also affecting size of the TMT, the size of the workforce the TM is responsible for, etc.) can significantly influence the TM's possibilities and constraints regarding the individual innovation influence.

Focusing on the collective top managerial level, the insights through the integrated view over all four perspectives shed light on the fact that not only aspects embedded in the single TM, but rather in the collective of TMs as a group play a role. As for instance, the decision of how the single TM influences innovations is often not only dependent on the individual willingness and/or ability to influence, but rather on the scope of influence bestowed on the single TM. Hence, the process of decision making within TMT and the allocation of decision power needs to be addressed further. In this context, the demographic factors also come into play: especially when focusing on the collective top managerial level of all TMs within the firm, the composition of specific factor combinations (e.g., age groups, functional backgrounds, etc.) can influence the single TM's innovation impact.

In general, these and other aspects will require further attention by (empirical) research studies for increasing the awareness of present and future TMs for their extensive influence on innovations as well as the mutual dependencies between the different perspectives. Only if they are aware of the importance of their broad influence on the organizational management, they will be able to productively execute this important task in practice. Or as Blanchard (2007: 145) has summarized it: "*The key to successful leadership today is influence, not authority.*"

6.2 Limitations

Several limitations regarding this paper and the developed framework must be mentioned: first, the framework is built up on the four central perspectives, which have been identified based on previous studies to have the most severe impact on the TM's influence. The framework hence pictures the fact that a holistic approach compulsory needs to consider the perspectives of management, culture, leadership and network; however, it is unquestioned that further aspects influence the comprehensive relation and in addition could further complement an even more comprehensive approach of displaying the single factors of influence. Second, the framework is directed towards the relation of TMs and organizational innovativeness, while the further relation between innovativeness and firm performance, and thus the important impact of firm innovations on output, remains disregarded and requires detailed investigation in the future.

References

Adair, J. E. (2009). *Leadership for innovation. How to organize team creativity and harvest ideas.* Kogan Page Limited.

Amabile, T. M. (1996). Creativity and innovation in organizations. *Harvard Business School*, 9-296-239. Background Note 396–239.

Amabile, T. M. (1998). How to kill creativity. *Harvard Business Review, 76*(5), 77–87.

Amabile, T. M., & Khaire, M. (2008). Creativity and the role of the leader. *Harvard Business Review, 86*(10), 101–109.

Anderson, N., Potočnik, K., & Zhou, J. (2014). Innovation and creativity in organizations: A state-of-the-science review, prospective commentary, and guiding framework. *Journal of Management, 40*(5), 1297–1333.

Balkundi, P., & Kilduff, M. (2005). The ties that lead: A social network approach to leadership. *The Leadership Quarterly, 16*(6), 941–961.

Bass, B. M. (1990). From transactional to transformational leadership: Learning to share the vision. *Organizational Dynamics, 18*(3), 19–31.

Blanchard, K. H. (2007). *Heart of a leader: Insights on the art of influence* (2nd ed.). David C. Cook Publication.

Bledow, R., Frese, M., Anderson, N., Erez, M., & Farr, J. (2009). A dialectic perspective on innovation: Conflicting demands, multiple pathways, and ambidexterity. *Industrial and Organizational Psychology, 2*(3), 305–337.

Boeker, W. (1997). Strategic change: The influence of managerial characteristics and organizational growth. *Academy of Management Journal, 40*(1), 152–170.

Boso, N., Story, V. M., Cadogan, J. W., Micevksi, M., & Kadić-Maglajlić, S. (2013). Firm innovativeness and export performance: Environmental, networking, and structural contingencies. *Journal of International Marketing, 21*(4), 62–87.

Bowen, F. E., Rostami, M., & Steel, P. (2010). Timing is everything: A meta-analysis of the relationships between organizational performance and innovation. *Journal of Business Research, 63*(11), 1179–1185.

Burt, R. S. (1997). A note on social capital and network content. *Social Networks, 19*(4), 355–373.

Carpenter, M. A., Geletkanycz, M. A., & Sanders, Wm. G. (2004). Upper echelons research revisited: Antecedents, elements, and consequences of top management team composition. *Journal of Management, 30*(6), 749–778.
Carroll, G. R., & Teo, A. C. (1996). On the social networks of managers. *Academy of Management Journal, 39*(2), 421–440.
Cheung, M. F. Y., & Wong, C.-S. (2011). Transformational leadership, leader support, and employee creativity. *Leadership & Organization Development Journal, 32*(7), 656–672.
Chua, R. Y. J., Roth, Y., & Lemoine, J.-F. (2015). The impact of culture on creativity: How cultural tightness and cultural distance affect global innovation crowdsourcing work. *Administrative Science Quarterly, 60*(2), 189–227.
Collins, C. J., & Clark, K. D. (2003). Strategic human resource practices, top management team social networks, and firm performance. *Academy of Management Journal, 46*(6), 740–751.
Cooper, R. G. (2005). *Product leadership: Pathways to profitable innovation* (2nd ed.). Perseus Books.
Cooper, R. G., & Kleinschmidt, E. J. (1995). Benchmarking firms' new product performance and practices. *Engineering Management Review, 23*(3), 112–120.
Cooper, R. G., & Kleinschmidt, E. J. (1995). Benchmarking the firm's critical success factors in new product development. *Journal of Product Innovation Management, 12*(5), 374–391.
Cooper, R. G., & Mills, M. S. (2005). Succeeding at new product development the P&G way: A key element is using the "Innovation Diamond." *PDMA Visions, 29*(4), 8–13.
Daellenbach, U. S., McCarthy, A. M., & Schoenecker, T. S. (1999). Commitment to innovation: The impact of top management team characteristics. *R&D Management, 29*(3), 199–208.
Damanpour, F., & Evan, W. M. (1984). Organizational innovation and performance: The problem of "organizational lag." *Administrative Science Quarterly, 29*(3), 392–409.
Davies, A. E. (1900). The concept of change. *The Philosophical Review, 9*(5), 502–517.
Dawson, P., & Andriopoulos, C. (2014). *Managing change, creativity and innovation* (2nd ed.). SAGE Publications Limited.
De Massis, A., De Minin, A., & Frattini, F. (2015). Family-driven innovation: Resolving the paradox in family firms. *California Management Review, 58*(1), 5–19.
De Sousa, F. C., Pellissier, R., & Monteiro, I. P. (2012). Creativity, innovations and collaborative organizations. *The International Journal of Organizational Innovation, 5*(1), 26–34.
Edwards, T. (2000). Innovation and organizational change: Developments towards an interactive process perspective. *Technology Analysis & Strategic Management, 12*(4), 445–464.
Elenkov, D. S., Judge, W., & Wright, P. (2005). Strategic leadership and executive innovation influence: An international multi-cluster comparative study. *Strategic Management Journal, 26*(7), 665–682.
Elenkov, D. S., & Manev, I. M. (2005). Top management leadership and influence on innovation: The role of sociocultural context. *Journal of Management, 31*(3), 381–402.
Ettlie, J. E., Bridges, W. P., & O'Keefe, R. D. (1984). Organization strategy and structural differences for radical versus incremental innovation. *Management Science, 30*(6), 682–695.
Feld, S. L. (1981). The focused organization of social ties. *The American Journal of Sociology, 86*(5), 1015–1035.
Fennell, M. L. (1984). Synergy, influence, and information in the adoption of administrative innovations. *Academy of Management Journal, 27*(1), 113–129.
Finkelstein, S., & Hambrick, D. C. (1996). *Strategic leadership. Top executives and their effects on organizations.* West Publishing Company.
Fliaster, A., & Schloderer, F. (2010). Dyadic ties among employees: Empirical analysis of creative performance and efficiency. *Human Relations, 63*(10), 1513–1540.
Flynn, F. J., & Chatman, J. A. (2001). Strong cultures and innovation: Oxymoron or opportunity? In C. L. Cooper, S. Cartwright, & P. C. Earley (Eds.), *The international handbook of organizational culture and climate* (pp. 263–288). John Wiley & Sons.
Frankort, H. T. W. (2008). Structural holes, technological resources, and innovation: A study of an interfirm R&D network. *Best Paper Proceedings of the Academy of Management, 1*, 1–6.

Geletkanycz, M. A., & Hambrick, D. C. (1997). The external ties of top executives: Implications for strategic choice and performance. *Administrative Science Quarterly, 42*(4), 654–681.
Hagen, E. E. (1962). *On the theory of social change*. The Dorsey Press.
Hambrick, D. C., & Mason, P. A. (1984). Upper echelons: The organization as a reflection of its top managers. *Academy of Management Review, 9*(2), 193–206.
Hayes, R., & Abernathy, W. (1980). Managing our way to economic decline. *Harvard Business Review, 57*(4), 11–25.
Hodgkinson, G. P., & Healey, M. P. (2008). Cognition in organizations. *Annual Review of Psychology, 59*(1), 387–417.
Hoffman, R. C., & Hegarty, W. H. (1993). Top management influence on innovations: Effects of executive characteristics and social culture. *Journal of Management, 19*(3), 549–574.
Howell, J. M. (2005). The right stuff: Identifying and developing effective champions of innovation. *Academy of Management Executive, 19*(2), 108–119.
Howell, J. M., & Avolio, B. J. (1993). Transformational leadership, transactional leadership, locus of control, and support for innovation. *Journal of Applied Psychology, 78*(6), 891–902.
Hueske, A.-K., & Guenther, E. (2015). What hampers innovation? External stakeholders, the organization, groups and individuals: A systematic review of empirical barrier research. *Management Review Quarterly, 65*(2), 113–148.
Hult, G. T. M., Hurley, R. F., & Knight, G. A. (2004). Innovativeness: Its antecedents and impact on business performance. *Industrial Marketing Management, 33*(5), 429–438.
Hunter, S. T., & Cushenbery, L. (2011). Leading for innovation: Direct and indirect influences. *Advances in Developing Human Resources, 13*(3), 248–265.
Ibarra, H., & Hunter, M. (2007). How leaders create and use networks. *Harvard Business Review, 85*(1), 40–47.
Jaussi, K. S., & Dionne, S. D. (2003). Leading for creativity: The role of unconventional leader behavior. *The Leadership Quarterly, 14*(4–5), 475–498.
Jung, D. I., Chow, C. W., & Wu, A. (2003). The role of transformational leadership in enhancing organizational innovation: Hypotheses and some preliminary findings. *The Leadership Quarterly, 14*(4–5), 525–544.
Jung, D. I., Wu, A., & Chow, C. W. (2008). Towards understanding the direct and indirect effects of CEO's transformational leadership on firm innovation. *The Leadership Quarterly, 19*(5), 582–594.
Kahn, K. B., Barczak, G., Nicholas, J., Ledwith, A., & Perks, H. (2012). An examination of new product development best practice. *Journal of Product Innovation Management, 29*(2), 180–192.
Khazanchi, S., & Masterson, S. S. (2011). Who and what is fair matters: A multi-foci social exchange model of creativity. *Journal of Organizational Behavior, 32*(1), 86–106.
Kitchell, S. (1995). Corporate culture, environmental adaptation, and innovation adoption: A qualitative/quantitative approach. *Journal of the Academy of Marketing Science, 23*(3), 195–205.
Kraiczy, N. D., Hack, A., & Kellermanns, F. W. (2015). The relationship between top management team innovation orientation and firm growth: The mediating role of firm innovativeness. *International Journal of Innovation Management, 19*(1), 1550005-1 – 1550005-24.
Landsperger, J., Spieth, P., & Heidenreich, S. (2012). How network managers contribute to innovation network performance. *International Journal of Innovation Management, 16*(6), 1240009-1 – 1240009-21.
Li, Q., Maggitti, P. G., Smith, K. G., Tesluk, P. E., & Katila, R. (2013). Top management attention to innovation: The role of search selection and intensity in new product introductions. *Academy of Management Journal, 56*(3), 893–916.
Li, V., Mitchell, R., & Boyle, B. (2016). The divergent effects of transformational leadership on individual and team innovation. *Group & Organization Management, 41*, 66–97.
Linder, C., & Sperber, S. (2017). If what you want is not what you get: A communication-based approach to top managers' intended firm creativity and employees' failure to deliver. *European Management Review, 14*(3), 227–246.

Makri, M., & Scandura, T. A. (2010). Exploring the effects of creative CEO leadership on innovation in high-technology firms. *The Leadership Quarterly, 21*(1), 75–88.
Martins, E. C., & Terblanche, F. (2003). Building organisational culture that stimulates creativity and innovation. *European Journal of Innovation Management, 6*(1), 64–74.
Michael, J., & Yukl, G. (1993). Managerial level and subunit function as determinants of network building in organizations. *Group & Organization Management, 18*(3), 328–351.
Miller, P., & Brankovic, A. (2011). Building a creative culture for innovation. *Expert Insight/IESE Expert, 11*, 51–58.
Mumford, M. D., & Gustafson, S. B. (1988). Creativity syndrome: Integration, application, and innovation. *Psychological Bulletin, 103*(1), 27–43.
Nonaka, I., Umemoto, K., & Senoo, D. (1996). From information processing to knowledge creation: A paradigm shift in business management. *Technology in Society, 18*, (2), 203–218.
Nonaka, I., von Krogh, G., & Voelpel, S. (2006). Organizational knowledge creation theory: Evolutionary paths and future advances. *Organization Studies, 27*(8), 1179–1208.
Peteraf, M. A. (1993). The cornerstones of competitive advantage: A resource-based view. *Strategic Management Journal, 14*(3), 179–191.
Pfeffer, J., & Salancik, G. R. (2003). *The external control of organizations: A resource dependence perspective.* Stanford University Press.
Porter, M. E. (1985). *Competitive advantage: Creating and sustaining superior performance.* The Free Press.
Read, A. (2000). Determinants of successful organizational innovation: A review of current research. *Journal of Management Practice, 3*(1), 95–119.
Rüegg-Stürm, J. (2003). *Das neue St. Galler Management-Modell: Grundkategorien einer integrierten Managementlehre, Der HSG-Ansatz* (2nd ed.). Haupt.
Ruttan, V. W. (1959). Usher and Schumpeter on invention, innovation, and technological change. *The Quarterly Journal of Economics, 73*(4), 596–606.
Schumpeter, J. A. (1934). *The theory of economic development: An inquiry into profits, capital, credit, interest, and the business cycle.* Harvard University Press.
Shalley, C. E., & Gilson, L. L. (2004). What leaders need to know: A review of social and contextual factors that can foster or hinder creativity. *The Leadership Quarterly, 15*(1), 33–53.
Shin, S. J., & Zhou, J. (2003). Transformational leadership, conservation and creativity: Evidence from Korea. *Academy of Management Journal, 46*(6), 703–714.
Six, B., Normann, M., Stock, R. M., & Schiereck, D. (2013). Strategic leaders' impact on corporate policies and firm performance: Insights from CEOs and CFOs of large listed firms in Germany. *Schmalenbach Business Review, 65*, 82–111.
Smith, M., Busi, M., Ball, P., & van der Meer, R. (2008). Factors influencing an organization's ability to manage innovation: A structured literature review and conceptual model. *International Journal of Innovation Management, 12*(4), 655–676.
Smith, W. K., & Tushman, M. L. (2005). Managing strategic contradictions: A top management model for managing innovation streams. *Organization Science, 16*(5), 522–536.
Sperber, S. C. (2017). The top managers' impact on opening the organizational culture to innovation. *International Journal of Innovation Management, 21*(2), 1750014–1 – 1750014–42.
Tang, F. (2011). Knowledge transfer in intra-organization networks. *Systems Research and Behavioral Science, 28*(3), 270–282.
Tesluk, P. E., Farr, J. L., & Klein, S. R. (1997). Influences of organizational culture and climate on individual creativity. *The Journal of Creative Behavior, 31*(1), 27–41.
Tidd, J. (2001). Innovation management in context: Environment, organization and performance. *International Journal of Management Review, 3*(3), 169–183.
Tierney, P., Farmer, S. M., & Graen, G. B. (1999). An examination of leadership and employee creativity: The relevance of traits and relationships. *Personnel Psychology, 52*(3), 591–620.
Ulrich, H., & Krieg, W. (1974). *St. Galler Management-Modell* (3rd ed.). Haupt.
Utterback, J. M. (1994). *Mastering the dynamics of innovation: How companies can seize opportunities in the face of technological change.* Harvard Business Review Press.

Wissema, J. G., & Euser, L. (1991). Successful innovation through inter-company networks. *Long Range Planning, 24*(6), 33–39.

Wong, S. K. S. (2013). The role of management involvement in innovation. *Management Decision, 51*(4), 709–729.

Woodman, R. W., Sawyer, J. E., & Griffin, R. W. (1993). Toward a theory of organizational creativity. *Academy of Management Review, 18*(2), 293–321.

Yuan, X., Guo, Z., Fang, E. (2014). An examination of how and when the top management team matters for firm innovativeness: The effects of TMT functional backgrounds. *Innovation: Management, Policy & Practice, 16*(3), 323−342.

Yukl, G. A. (2012). *Leadership in organizations* (8th ed.). Pearson Education Limited.

Change or Be Changed—Online Education and Organizational Culture at Universities

Jürgen-Matthias Seeler, Desiree Wieser, Anita Zehrer, and Karin Sixl-Daniell

1 Introduction

Online education has become an increasingly important sector within universities. It can provide potential for growth of the institutions and enables learners who are otherwise not able to commit to studies in traditional university programs. Online education is more than just recording traditional classroom lectures and making them available via internet. Instead, it integrates digitization and the internet in the learning process (Volery & Lord, 2000).

This paper elaborates on the various challenges within universities when adopting online education. It aims to identify areas in which universities will have to consider changes of organizational culture to meet upcoming demands resulting from the shift to online education. The report is partly based on previous research findings as well as experiences from two universities, namely Management Center Innsbruck, Austria (MCI), and IUBH International University of Applied Sciences, Germany (IUBH). It uses the results in order to discuss potential changes in the way universities operate and prompts at respective changes in organizational culture.

Using secondary data from previously conducted research and experiences in university management, this report is case study oriented and shall be understood as a position paper. It indicates potential challenges which university leadership must address in order to adopt digitization trends. The call for cultural change at universities results from the understanding of organizational culture underlying this paper: Organizational culture is a set of traditional values and norms of a group, which are guiding individuals' behavior within that group (Engelen & Tholen, 2014;

J.-M. Seeler (✉)
IU International University of Applied Sciences (formerly IUBH), Erfurt, Germany
e-mail: juergen-matthias.seeler@iu.org

D. Wieser · A. Zehrer · K. Sixl-Daniell
Management Center Innsbruck, Innsbruck, Austria

T. Herberger and J. Dötsch (eds.), *Digitalization, Digital Transformation and Sustainability in the Global Economy*, Springer Proceedings in Business and Economics, https://doi.org/10.1007/978-3-030-77340-3_9

Hofstede et al., 2010). Therefore, changes in university management will inevitably modify culture of the organization. At the same time, it can be assumed that the success of organizational changes depends on respective changes in culture, given that committed employees are precondition to sustainable change (Patel, 2014).

The Covid pandemic in 2020 forced many industries to consider digitizing business models more seriously. In fact, it acted like a catalyst for forced change and/or forced innovation in many instances. Likewise, most universities had to adopt some elements of online education. Given this paper is developed at end of 2020, there is still a lack of research into the impact of the immediate shift to online education during the Covid pandemic. As a position paper, this report does not claim to provide all necessary answers to cultural change at universities, but may raise important questions and address crucial issues, which will be relevant for many institutions of higher education. Therefore, the guiding question for this paper is:

What are likely implications of online education on organizational culture at universities?

The paper holds that online education provides important growth potential for universities. At the same time institutionalizing online education at universities requires changes in organizational culture and ultimately also changes in leadership behaviour.

The report will subsequently explain the context of online education in higher learning institutions and elaborate on previous research findings. It will then explain the background of the two universities that serve as cases for this paper. In this part, a brief explanation of the methodological approach in this paper will be included. Then, the report will elaborate on the implications of the shift towards online education on organizational culture at universities. For this, developments from other industries will also be taken into account in order to understand better the dynamics of the shift from traditional university activities towards online education. Lastly, the summary will draw together most important insights and provide for an outlook on potential future research.

2 Previous Research Findings and Experiences

Given its relative novelty, the effects of online education on organizational culture have not been researched in depth yet. However, there are some key characteristics of online education, which underpin the claim for change of organizational culture at universities. Important features of higher learning institutions offering online courses are (Wieser & Seeler, 2018, p. 135, 139–141):

- Student centered approach of facilitation
- High level of responsiveness of lecturers to student queries needed
- Learning Management Systems (LMS) as the center of all study-related activities with clear structures and rules for learners, lecturers and administrative staff
- Strong commitment to student–student and lecturer-student collaboration

- An understanding of lecturers as facilitators in the co-construction of knowledge
- Commitment to development of synchronous and asynchronous lectures and teaching material which empower active student engagement and participation
- Dedication to quality assurance systems with strong monitoring and evaluation measures
- Lack of direct social interaction may increase stress levels of learners, lecturers and administrative staff
- Self-guided learning by students requires high levels of motivation
- Self-guided learning by students requires close monitoring of student progress in order to limit student drop-out.

In addition, one key aspect of online education programs is that they are based on study material such as course books etc. This is important in order to provide a reliable knowledge base for students during their self-directed learning phases—a cornerstone of scalability in online studies. At the same time, it requires lecturers to facilitate content, which may have been developed by other academics.

Despite the perspective of universities on online education, the perspective of students should be taken into account as well. This will help shaping a better idea of the cultural changes in higher learning institutions. Seemingly, students' expectations in online programs differ from those enrolling in traditional classroom courses (Wieser et al., 2017, 2018). It is known that motivated and satisfied students are more likely to succeed in online courses (Bekele, 2010; Cho & Heron, 2015; Yukselturk & Bulut, 2007), however the expectations of online learners have not received the same amount of attention. Expectations are in fact a key factor for learners' level of satisfaction (Appleton-Knapp & Krentler, 2006; Yukselturk & Bulut, 2007) and therefore it is assumed that they can also influence students' success (Bekele, 2010; Cho & Heron, 2015; Yukselturk & Bulut, 2007).

Various studies showed cognitive skills, time management, self-regulation, study skills, personal factors (Bitzer & Janson, 2015; Dabbagh, 2007; Muilenburg & Berge, 2005; Yukselturk & Bulut, 2007), as well as communication and cooperation with peers and instructor(s) (Eom & Ashill, 2016), realistic expectations (Mandernach et al., 2006; Moessenlechner et al., 2015) and motivation as major, and in fact decisive, components of student success in online courses (Bitzer & Janson, 2015; Castillo-Merino & Serradell-López, 2014; Chua & Don, 2013; Dabbagh, 2007; Eom & Ashill, 2016; Huet et al., 2011; Mandernach et al., 2006; Moessenlechner et al., 2015; Muilenburg & Berge, 2005; Yukselturk & Bulut, 2007).

On average, student cohorts in online education tend to be older and more diverse concerning background, nationality and prior education compared to those in classroom courses as such courses permit working adults to study while working. These students expect challenges in time-management, given that many of them study and work simultaneously. With more work experience, online students also have higher expectations in the professional relevance and applicability of course content. At the beginning of their studies, online students often wonder about the level of collaboration in respective programs and there seems to be a concern of being left alone when assuming online studies. Students who are just starting their academic career are afraid of not having personal contact with fellow students. They also wonder whether lecturers will be available at all. Finally, there is a general sentiment that online education may be regarded as less credible by recruiters (Wieser et al., 2017, 2018). However, the 2020 Covid pandemic made online education a necessity for all students, full-time and part-time students alike.

3 Methodological Aspects and Background of the Cases

This report represents a position paper and aims at providing an answer to the guiding question: "What are likely implications of online education on organizational culture at universities?" However, it is not based on empirical evidence obtained for the specific purpose of this paper. Rather, it uses research findings, which the authors and colleagues generated previously and regarding different research questions. Furthermore, it employs experiences from two universities with substantial, yet different, online education offerings. The report uses these insights to draw conclusions in that it suggests likely changes in organizational culture of universities driven by the shift towards online education. Therefore, this paper does not provide for the academic rigor usually expected in qualitative and/or quantitative research. The findings may rather be used to develop future research approaches.

The two universities and their experiences employ quite different approaches to online education. Considering the aforementioned characteristics of universities and expectations of students it becomes obvious that the wider scope of digitization trends in higher learning matter when it comes to online education. This is why two institutions with very different traditions and approaches to online teaching are selected for this paper.

Most universities have certainly operated for years, if not decades or centuries, in a traditional lecturing mode. Some of them have adopted digitization trends and started online activities in recent years. On the other hand, there are a few universities, which were established as online institutions. An example for the former is Management Center Innsbruck, Austria, which is strongly affiliated to Innsbruck University and started as traditional higher learning institution. It then introduced its first online degree program in 2014. Indicative for the latter is IUBH International University of Applied Sciences, Germany, which started its online education entity in 2011 with the clear commitment to center all activities in the digital sphere.

MCI is a privately established, yet state funded university in Austria, which offers traditional classroom studies and—since 2014—online degree programs. The following information can be found on MCI's website (MCI, 2020). MCI employs a workforce of approximately 320 employees and additionally a large number of lecturers from professional practice on a freelance basis. More than 15% of the 3200 students are now enrolled in online programs and almost all on-campus courses employ at least some elements of online education. All online degree programs still contain a number of residential school activities. For this, students must attend classroom lectures in Innsbruck and typically spend up to 20 days per academic year on site. In addition, the overall course facilitation is bound to the traditional semester structure. These cornerstones are obligatory, to some extent due to the regulatory framework in Austria (Fachhochschulstudiengesetz FHStG). Written exams are typically held on site. Course presentation on MCI's learning management system is increasingly standardized. Quality assurance systems are in place. Given the history of MCI, and the restrictions set by legal regulations, one can hold that MCI attempts to translate traditional classroom lectures into an online learning concept, which is marked by blended learning techniques, and based on a quality assurance framework adopted from its attendance courses. Interactive course facilitation can probably be seen as most important feature of MCI's online courses.

IUBH International University of Applied Sciences is a private university in Germany with more than 600 staff members, more than 40,000 students enrolled, and a vast number of study programs offered solely online. All information presented here can be obtained from the university's website (IUBH, 2020). Its online education branch only started operating in 2011 and is rapidly growing ever since. For the purpose of this paper, only this part of IUBH will be taken into account. Its online degree programs are fully facilitated online with no residential school or any other attendance requirements. All exams—written tests, assignments, oral exams etc.—are performed online. For written tests, students can also opt for a paper-based version of the exam which is offered once per month in designated study centers throughout Germany and Austria. However, the majority of students is sitting written tests online and these are then live camera monitored and, in addition, recorded for later inspection. Written assignments are standardized regarding its structures across all study courses. So is the content offered in most of the courses. Written course books, live lectures, shortcasts etc. are all structured in the same way. The same applies to the Learning Management System, in which the structure of all courses is presented in the same way. This helps students to get used to the way courses are offered, and thus makes it easier for them to find their way through their studies. An important element of IUBH's course facilitation is the commitment to responsiveness to student queries. On weekdays, lecturers must respond to every student question within 24 h. There are, however, usually no on-campus classes.

IUBH also offers rolling admission and students are able to commence studies at any time. All study courses are based on what can be called a performance semester, meaning that students study at their own pace and a semester is successfully completed, once a student has obtained the 30 ECTS allocated to the semester. This provides students with a maximum of flexibility but also requires a high level of discipline. To conclude IUBH's approach, one could describe it as an attempt to rethink university education from a digital perspective and essentially create study courses and academic and administrative support functions based on online technology only. Student centered standardization of course facilitation is probably the key element of this approach.

There is no superiority of either approach, given they both turned out to be success stories for their organizations. Rather, the two concepts describe the scope within which online courses and degree programs are often designed.

4 Insights from Other Industries

This part is supposed to explain disruptive changes, which happened and are still ongoing in some industries. They indicate how fast even the university sector may be subject to new developments caused by the wider area of digitization.

Most notably, there are a number of highly successful companies, which managed to change business models of entire industries. Amazon is one prominent example. It has not only changed the way people order books, but actually fostered the shift towards online shopping overall. Amazon managed to become one of the most valuable companies in the world, in that it offered customers immediacy, reliability, and convenience of its services. The same is true for Facebook, Instagram and other social networks. Google never operated a physical information office. Tinder never advertised customers' relationship wishes in newspapers. MPesa and Airtel Money never operated bank branches, yet became important players in mobile phone money transfers. There is also not a single travel agency office to be found run by Booking.com, yet, the company has become one of the most successful intermediaries for the sale of travel services.

It is difficult to tell which the driving factors were for these companies to arrive at the current status. But certainly, they allowed themselves to completely rethink their industries' traditional approaches. It is also obvious that these companies are all allocated in the services sector. What was described earlier for Amazon, is probably true for all these companies: Their success is based on services which are available immediately, based on reliable processes, and conveniently available at a fingertip on a smartphone.

Can such features be blueprints for universities? Many may argue that this is not the case. However, the dynamics of such changes should at least be considered when thinking about online education at universities.

5 Implications for Organizational Culture of Universities

How are the formal and informal organizational culture of a university affected by online education? When looking at the trends mentioned above, probably the most important change is to develop a mentality of immediacy within the workforce of the university. This claim is not limited to lecturers but needs to be adopted by all staff. Operating in an online environment means responding to all student needs as fast as possible, usually faster than in traditional settings. Openness to new technological and pedagogical trends is necessary as well. Online education is not just migrating classroom lectures into the virtual space but developing a way of facilitation, which fosters participation and collaboration in an online environment. Immediacy and openness also require more flexibility by lecturers and administrative staff as the occurrence of tasks becomes less predictable. This is also relevant regarding working hours of staff members. Cooperation among staff members and across departments is necessary and thinking in silos, e.g. departments etc. is likely to compromise efficiency.

An absolute commitment to service provision to students, clear rules and regulations, and the use of technology to assess the performance of staff members, particularly lecturers, is needed. Technology, and more specifically the fact that simply everything in online education is recorded, cares for stringent quality management systems. This will eventually result in a high reputation of the university and its programs. Lecturers must be ready to facilitate content developed by other academics and accept to be fully monitored in their teaching performance. The claim for freedom of research and teaching is certainly limited in highly standardized processes and it may well be that new academic staff struggles with rather narrow boundaries of course facilitation.

The same is relevant for administrative staff. Online students are typically learning remotely. They will usually not be in the position to enter an administration office at the university for questions. Therefore, for many typical information requests—e.g. release of exam results, recognition of prior learning, questions regarding internships, student fees etc.—standardized online processes must be established. For further queries, unambiguous communication channels are necessary. Most importantly, service commitments regarding administrative issues require clear timeframes within which students will receive answers to their questions especially given the lack of typical face to face interactions.

It may appear to be easy to put such structures and rules into practice, however, some academics are used to working at their own pace, using modes and structures of teaching and supervising, which they developed for themselves over some or many years. For some, it may be a limitation of their academic freedom, when they are supposed to put the content of a course in a strict course book structure or follow such a pre-defined structure. The same may be true for examination modes. If a university requires a certain structure for written exams—e.g. 20 Multiple Choice questions and 4 open questions with a clearly prescribed allocation of points per question—it is not uncommon that some lecturers will argue the prescribed exam structure would not match the requirements of their course. In addition, acting as a facilitator as opposed to an instructor and observing strict deadlines in response to student queries may be rather difficult for some.

Similarly, such debates will most likely come up as far as the standardization of administrative processes are concerned. In general, standardization and process-orientation increase the possibility for quantitative performance assessment. It is obvious that this may be helpful for a university's leadership to identify potential weaknesses in an organization. At the same time, it is also understandable that at least some academic and administrative staff members may not be fond of the idea of being monitored more closely in their performance.

Online education can be viewed as a kind of open system with three interacting entities (students, instructor/lecturer, and LMS), influenced by the environment (Bitzer & Janson, 2015; Eom & Ashill, 2016). What can be done in order align a university to the demands accompanying the trend towards online education?

Firstly, hiring the right people is a key factor (Sixl-Daniell et al., 2006; Mandernach, 2005). Online education and the trend towards digitization in university operations underpins the need for facilitators who are ready to accept continuous changes in their workplaces. The openness to new developments must be assessed already during recruitment. It is also important, to clearly communicate respective expectations (standardization of processes, working at evening hours, responsiveness etc.) to applicants.

The demand for more flexibility, responsiveness and service orientation also requires to offer something to academic and administrative employees in return. Online degree programs and digitization of processes provide for the opportunity to grant a maximum of flexibility concerning working from home. With solid structures and robust IT systems in place, staff members will often be able to work from home. In addition, a considerable share of the work—e.g. grading exams, thesis supervision, developing of teaching material etc.—can be performed at times most convenient for those performing those tasks. For many lecturers, this offers great potential to meet professional and private commitments and it also limits commuting times to a minimum. However, especially the Covid pandemic has shown that working from home is not ideal for everyone and has its drawbacks due to e.g. limited face to face interactions, blurred lines between working and after work hours, a tendency towards increased availability, potential issues concerning insurance, taxes and costs to name only a few. Numerous studies are currently (2020, early 2021) undertaken to highlight potential issues when working from home. Again, hiring the right people is important when employing staff members who may (often) work from home and rather independently. It also changes the role of leadership. While control is important where certain standards—e.g. response times—must be met, trust is crucial for most of the remaining academic and administrative work. The role of trust is crucial in organizational culture and even more so in institutions offering online learning programs as lecturers' physical presence is no longer a must.

Leadership must ensure that all processes allow for an IT-based system of monitoring and evaluation, by which a follow up on lecturers' performance (e.g. recordings of lectures, response time to student queries etc.) is provided. This provides the timely availability of data and allows speedy identification of service weaknesses. In order to create a conducive work atmosphere, clear communication of service expectations is necessary. In particular, standardization of academic teaching materials may not be popular with all lecturers. While it can always be argued that some courses require different structures, the general advantages of standardization may outweigh the potential disadvantages in some instances. Therefore, creating an atmosphere of pragmatism and avoiding a mindset of resistance to change (e.g. "That can't work; we have never done tit this way!") is crucial. Once leadership and academic and administrative staff have agreed on processes and standards, it should be common that everyone in the organization unreservedly puts the decisions into action.

Furthermore, it is important to develop a tolerance to error. In fast paced environments driven by digitization trends, it is highly likely that some decisions made turn out to be wrong or—by the time the come into effect—outdated given new technological trends led to unexpected changes. An example for this could be the use of a certain tool for facilitating online classes. Many of them are offered, some are free of charge, and others attract a license fee. A university has to assess the various systems, and then decide for the one that is best suited for the specific requirements of its online lectures. While using the system it may well happen that the webinar system turns out to be instable or other, better tools emerge. In such cases, it is important that open-mindedness and pragmatism in evaluating the tools used prevails leading to the use of the best suited systems and tools. This may appear to be common sense. However, often debates commence in which reasoning is shaped more by personal vanity than by rationally comprehensible reasons.

To conclude the implications of online education on culture at universities, it is seemingly necessary to act and think as a digital organization. As far as the formal culture of a university is concerned, it would be worthwhile to digitize all processes. This requires digitizing a student's journey from requesting information on study courses and enrolment to graduation and alumni events. With such changes, new challenges arise and new questions must be answered. If universities commit to online education and the respective flexibility for lecturers concerning location and time of work, then labour and working hours laws need to be considered. As far as existing workforces are concerned, it cannot be assumed that all will be supportive in the necessary change processes. Some services may become redundant or will be subject to considerable changes. Library services are an example for this. Many universities have put efforts in developing physical libraries but online library provisions can probably serve the needs of students and academics better, and more flexibly. Even the role of lecturers will most certainly change in the near future. With the potential of and adaptive learning techniques, teaching will be—at least in parts—more student oriented and more efficient. Therefore, lecturers could become more needed as coaches of students during their journey through the course content.

6 Concluding Remarks

This position paper intended to provide answers to the question: "What are likely implications of online education on organizational culture at universities?" As a position paper, it is based on some research carried out previously in the field of online education and uses experiences and insights from two universities, which employed different approaches towards online education. Given the potential of digitization, the report discusses the changes that universities will most certainly undergo in regard to teaching, but also more holistically concerning structures and processes in the organization of higher learning.

Summarizing the paper, some of the most important features of a university's culture may be a mindset of immediacy, openness, and flexibility. This is necessary for academic and administrative processes. Online teaching and operating a higher learning institution digitally requires standardized processes at all levels. Therefore, a commitment to service provision, strict obedience to rules and regulations and a stringent, quantifiable quality assurance system is necessary. The latter should be linked to a performance assessment system for all staff members. Clear communication channels for students must accompany standardization of processes in academia and administration. In order to operate in a highly digitized, fast-paced environment, hiring the right people is crucial. Academic freedom will likely be limited through standardization. At the same time, academic and administrative staff may enjoy more flexibility regarding location and time of work. This will change the role of leadership towards a trust-based approach of staff guidance. Acting and thinking like a digital organization requires an atmosphere of pragmatism and tolerance to error. Otherwise, digital collaboration among university staff and between students and university employees may remain below its potential. Lastly, leaders and employees of universities should be open to further changes. Some services will become redundant in traditional ways given the potential of digitization. In addition, the looming introduction of systems using artificial intelligence will most certainly change the role of those who have always been in the center of university education: lecturers.

This position paper does not claim to have all the answers concerning the various challenges resulting from rapid technological changes, but aims to act as a starter for further discussions. Experiences from other sectors strongly suggest that game changers often approach markets with a completely new business model. Looking at the rapid developments in other industries, it is certainly a valid idea for universities to embrace the potentialities of digitization proactively. The trend towards more online education and digitization of university processes is inevitable, and the Covid pandemic served probably as a wake-up call for many higher learning institutions. Therefore, the call for change of organizational culture at universities must not be underestimated.

References

Appleton-Knapp, S. L., & Krentler, K. A. (2006). Measuring student expectations and their effects on satisfaction: The importance of managing student expectations. *Journal of Marketing Education, 28*(3), 254–264. https://doi.org/10.1177/0273475306293359

Bekele, T. A. (2010). Motivation and satisfaction in internet-supported learning environments: A review. *Educational Technology & Society, 13*(2), 116–127.

Bitzer, P., & Janson, A. (2015). Towards a holistic understanding of technology-mediated learning services—a state-of-the-art analysis. *International Conference on Information Systems,* (2014), 0–19.

Castillo-Merino, D., & Serradell-López, E. (2014). An analysis of the determinants of students' performance in e-learning. *Computers in Human Behavior, 30*, 476–484. https://doi.org/10.1016/j.chb.2013.06.020

Cho, M.-H., & Heron, M. L. (2015). Self-regulated learning: The role of motivation, emotion, and use of learning strategies in students' learning experiences in a self-paced online mathematics course. *Distance Education, 36*(1), 80–99. https://doi.org/10.1080/01587919.2015.1019963

Chua, Y. P., & Don, Z. M. (2013). Effects of computer-based educational achievement test on test performance and test takers' motivation. *Computers in Human Behavior, 29*(5), 1889–1895. https://doi.org/10.1016/j.chb.2013.03.008

Dabbagh, N. (2007). The online learner: Characteristics and pedagogical implications. *Contemporary Issues in Technology and Teacher Education, 7*(3), 217–226. Retrieved from http://go.editlib.org/p/22904

Engelen, A., & Tholen, E. (2014). *Interkulturelles Management*. Schäffer-Poeschel.

Eom, S. B., & Ashill, N. (2016). The determinants of students' perceived learning outcomes and satisfaction in university online education: An update. *Decision Sciences Journal of Innovative Education, 14*(2), 185–215. https://doi.org/10.1111/dsji.12097

Hofstede, G., Hofstede, G. J., & Minkov, M. (2010). *Cultures and organizations* (3rd ed.). McGraw-Hill.

Huet, N., Escribe, C., Dupeyrat, C., & Sakdavong, J.-C. (2011). The influence of achievement goals and perceptions of online help on its actual use in an interactive learning environment. *Computers in Human Behavior, 27*(1), 413–420. https://doi.org/10.1016/j.chb.2010.09.003

IUBH. (2020). IUBH Internationale Hochschule. (URL: https://www.iubh-fernstudium.de/. Last access December 29, 2020.

Mandernach, B. J., Donnelli, E., Dailey-Hebert, A. (2006). Learner attribute research in dialogue with classroom practice: Predictors of success in the accelerated, online classroom. *The Journal of Educators Online, 3*(2), 1–17. http://www.thejeo.com/Volume3Number2/MandernachFinal.pdf

Mandernach, B. J. (2005). A faculty evaluation model for online instructors: mentoring and evaluation in the online classroom. *Online Journal of Distance Learning Administration,* VIII(III). http://www.westga.edu/%7Edistance/ojdla/fall83/mandernach83.htm

MCI. (2020). Management center innsbruck–the entrepreneurial school. (URL: https://www.mci.edu/en/. Last access December 28, 2020.

Moessenlechner, C., Obexer, R., Sixl-Daniell, K., & Seeler, J.-M. (2015). E-learning degree programs: A better way to balance work and education? *ICELW International Conference Focused on E-Learning in the Workplace, 23*(24), 25.

Muilenburg, L. Y., & Berge, Z. L. (2005). Student barriers to online learning: A factor analytic study. *Distance Education, 26*(1), 29–48. https://doi.org/10.1080/01587910500081269

Patel, T. (2014). Cross-cultural Management. A transactional approach. Routledge

Sixl-Daniell, K., Williams, J.B., Wong, A. (2006). A quality assurance framework for recruiting, training and retaining virtual adjunct faculty. *Online Journal of Distance Learning Administration, Volume IX, Number I, Spring 2006.* https://www.westga.edu/~distance/ojdla/spring91/daniell91.htm

Volery, T., & Lord, D. (2000). Critical success factors in online education. *International Journal of Educational Management, 14*(5), 216–223.

Wieser, D., Seeler, J.-M., Sixl-Daniell, K., & Zehrer, A. (2017). "Online students' expectations differ: The advantages of assessing students' expectations in online education". In Conference Paper/Proceedings, 3rd International Conference on Higher Education Advances (HEA'd). Valencia.

Wieser, D., Seeler, J.-M., Sixl, K., & Zehrer, A. (2018). Assessing the study experience in online education and the relevance of expectations: Seeing the successful implementation of online education in a new light. In EURAM 2018 Research in Action. University of Iceland, Reykjavík: European Academy of Management. ISBN 9782960219500.

Wieser, D., & Seeler, J.-M. (2018). Online, not distance education: The merits of collaborative learning in online education. In A. Altmann, B. Ebersberger, C. Moessenlechner, & D. Wieser, D. (2019). *The disruptive power of online education: challenges, opportunities, responses*, Emerald Publishing Ltd., (pp. 125–146).

Yukselturk, E., & Bulut, S. (2007). Predictors for student success in an online course. *Educational Technology & Society, 10*(2), 71–83.

Digital Sustainable Leadership

Angelika Kölle

1 Introduction—The Human Being as an Individual

Nature gives us many examples and pictures of networks, symbioses, mutations and adaptations to permanently changing environmental conditions. In plants and animals we speak of evolution, in economics we use change and challenging processes. Changing environmental conditions are comparable to the economic terms. We do not only see these processes at play in economy and ecology but also societal and political contexts. These processes are fueled further by technological and economic progress, globalization and crises. The speed, intensity and efficiency of change is a very complex system, which can only be properly dealt with by using artificial intelligence (AI), swarm intelligence and adaptive tools, processes and management methods.

This results in co-existences, co-evolutions, co-operations, collaborations, as well as the working together of up to now separate specialist subjects: digitization, sustainability and leadership. The New Normal or the solution of new problems of today cannot be solved in the long term by relying on old methods, which worked in the past. The required courage, the speed of adaptation and the ability to adapt to new and different phenomena is the basis needed for successful change.

The human being as an individual is at the heart of this change, as the individual can change him- or herself or the situation, as well as adapt the processes. Digital sustainable leadership is one option in a globalized changing world to act as a responsible and future oriented manager, to be courageous when innovating processes and to continuously develop one's own potential and grow.

A. Kölle (✉)
6th Generation Pflanzen Kölle, Heilbronn, Germany
e-mail: mail@angelika-koelle.de

Entrepreneur / Consulting and Training, Heilbronn, Germany

T. Herberger and J. Dötsch (eds.), *Digitalization, Digital Transformation and Sustainability in the Global Economy*, Springer Proceedings in Business and Economics, https://doi.org/10.1007/978-3-030-77340-3_10

2 Purpose Giving Leadership for Future Leaders

In our fast-paced modern world, a dynamic process has established itself—"higher, farther, faster"—resulting in an overstraining of people, organizations and whole societies. In particular the speed of communication and information leaves marks and impacts the quality of communication and information processing in people. This becomes evident when specialist terminology is used imprecisely or even in distorting ways. Comparing leadership versus management clearly shows, how the impact of acting is different, merely by looking at the definition.

It is surprising how terminology is used in economic contexts. We primarily speak of and write about management and managers and much less of leadership and leaders. But it's people who create, decide and work. Processes and organizations are but framework and structure. When we build organizations and processes around people and we know their needs and fulfill them, the result is a connecting unit. But if we try to adapt people to organizations and processes, this is not helped by natural or organic growth and thus has no sustainable foundation. Maslow contributed with his research and observation results to and more comprehensive understanding of human motivation, needs and behavioral norms. The well-known pyramid as depiction shows in a simplified way the complexity of Maslows research and was never published by Maslow in this form by himself.

Figures 1 and 2 show that the factors which are difficult to quantify, such as feelings, emotions, needs and motives form the basis of all human action. In planning and decision making it is thus essential to know these drivers of human action, to take them into account and to steer them, when necessary.

Simon Sinek researched why some companies are much more successful than their competitors (Reference Website). His result shows that it depends on the attitude and the type of leadership personality. This he showed in his model "the golden circle". He makes visible the hidden core, the soul of the enterprise and focuses it in his visualization like a dartboard. It is not a question of what someone does but why and for what they are doing it. Also focusing on the quality of action before examining the result proper is a completely new way of looking at leadership in management literature (Fig. 3).

To know the purpose of our actions and our work and define it is not a new approach. The realization regarding the import and power of this approach has been

Fig. 1 Leadership versus management. *Source* Own figure

Leadership	*versus*	**Management**
People		Organisation/Processes
Feelings		Facts and Figures
Emotional Level		Factual Level
Direct Interaction		Indirect Interaction

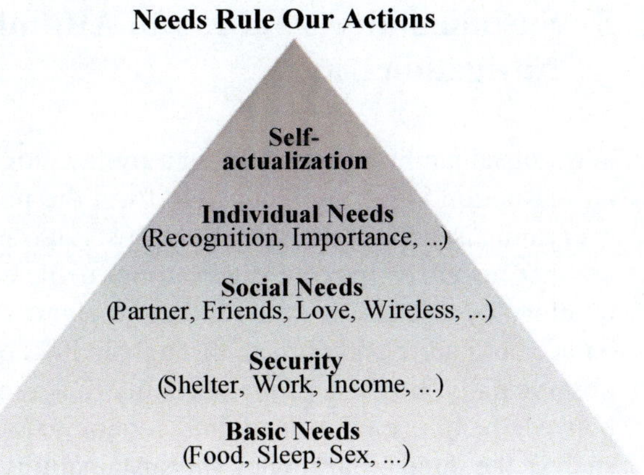

Fig. 2 Maslows Pyramid. Based on: Maslow (1943)

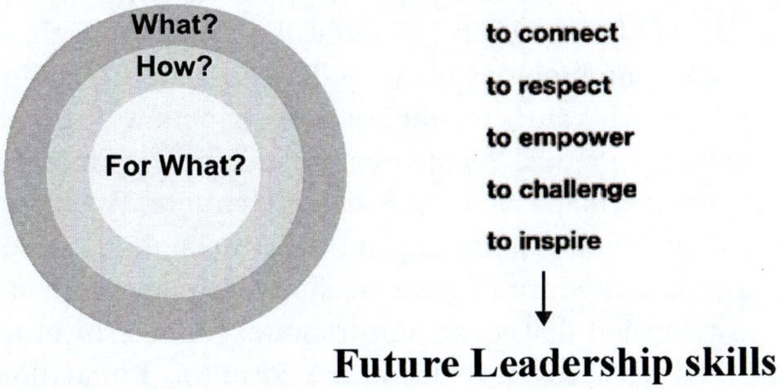

Fig. 3 Golden circle. *Source* Sinek (2009)

brough back into focus by Simon Sinek. Purpose-giving leadership means not only understanding the "why" of an enterprise but also being able to practice the "how". In applied leadership and from my 30-year experience, the big five of how to lead are a challenge.

Future Leadership Skills:

To connect
To respect
To empower
To challenge
To inspire.

The challenge lies in keeping the order of 1–5. Skipping a step or switching the order causes problems depending on the type of interference—which leads to energy loss on all sides. leadership competences are changing. The competence of communication, social and empathetic competences gain importance. The role of leadership personality changes and adapts more and more towards the ideal of a team captain, coach and mentor.

3 Sustainability—Value and Attitude for Behavioral Navigation

Why sustainability started out as a trendy slogan and was subsequently treated as an old notion is incomprehensible from the point of view of a gardener. On earth everything is in limited supply and is lost if it is not carefully used and treated. Nature and her resources may be used but not depleted and we may only use as much as to allow for regenerative processes to replenish them. Humankind has disturbed the balance of nature and climate through endless exploitation, a process which we can observe daily. Because of the necessity to act responsibly to allow a proper balance between people, environment and economy, models of sustainability were created, such as the three pillar model, the sustainability triangle or the tilt model (Fig. 4).

The dimensions of sustainability impact one another and thus improve or limit the balance. Sustainability is a fundamental attitude and should be one of the fundamental values of our society. Without this foundation the co-existence and the individual appreciation on our planet will become more and more fragile and more and more destroyed. Values are the basis of our actions, our behavior and our leadership. In the following model "value tree" foundational values, functional values, and behavioral norms form the basis of leadership culture. When looking at change and challenging factors, such as climate change and technological progress, putting leadership culture at the center is not only sensible and valuable but decisive for success. It is well established that leadership requires values. In order to grow tall like a tree, deep roots are necessary. Our values form this foundation, these roots, without which no tree can stand up (Fig. 5).

How do leaders know which values make their company grow? Why do we spend much more time looking at future plans than looking at our foundation? These questions show that the focus is shifting and from quantitative growth towards qualitative growth. Quality includes the inner quality and the inner values of both the leadership personality and the company and the society itself. Changes in the environment cause automatically changes in the inner values. Values are subject to temporal, political and social change. Ethical values and fundamental rights of people are defended by the United Nations. The times required states to establish common mandatory targets for sustainable development in all three levels of sociology, economy and ecology

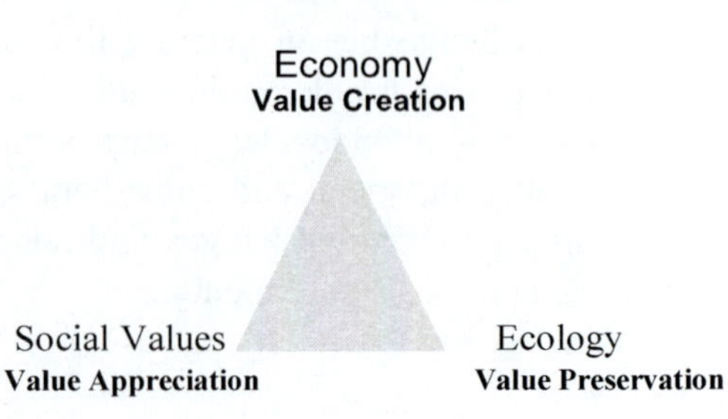

Fig. 4 Sustainability triangle. Based on: Walker et al. (2019)

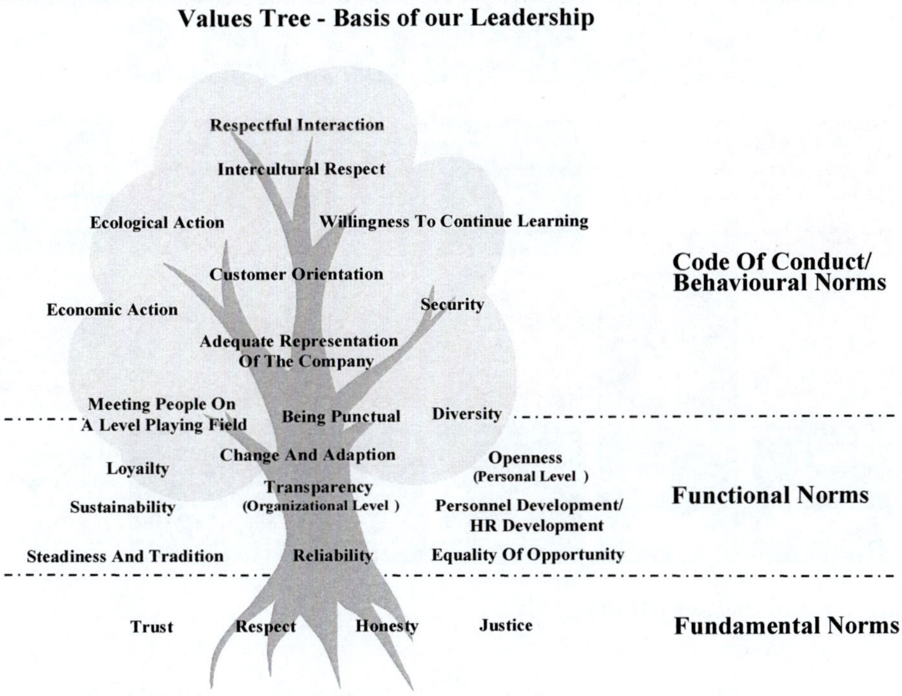

Fig. 5 Value tree. Based on: VDV-Akademie e.V (2016)

and the values that are fundamental to these disciplines. Since January 1, 2016, the 17 sustainable development goals are mandatory for the entire world, all states and all peoples (Fig. 6).

4 Analog and Digital Ways for Decision Making

Changes are sped up in times of crisis. In 2011 an earthquake with following tsunami has caused the nuclear catastrophe in Fukushima, Japan, which caused political change and change of attitude towards climate change in Germany and in many other countries overnight. This event caused Baden-Wuerttemberg to become the first German federal state to be led by a minister president of the green party and the German government under Angela Merkel decided to exit nuclear energy. A crisis is often speeds up change or is a catalyst for change—this is also true in the Corona crisis. Analog methods, such as school teaching in person had to be switched within a few days to digital and surprisingly this was possible within a very short period using online technology. Digital technology has become an irreplaceable component. The ability to adapt and the speed of adaptation of digital communication, digital interaction made the crisis strategy of the politics of lockdown, Corona-App, home office and home schooling and Corona tracing possible. Hybrid models, i.e. a

Fig. 6 SDGS. *Source* UNESCO (2021)

combination of analog and digital processes are becoming more and more important and have become part of our daily norm. What this means and what is important to us, has been made clear by the Corona crisis. The necessity and the desire of local freedom and social closeness have become evident. This can be seen in Fig. 7 of digital and leadership.

What has to happen to make a functional unit out of digital technology and leadership? All new technology, every new form of organization and every new law forms our thinking and acting. If you look at it from the point of view of ethics, morality, and sustainability, there will be some kind of unifying symbiosis. The decision for an inner attitude towards sustainability will bring human and technological systems into co-evolution.

Digital		Leadership
Virtual Rooms	**Where?**	Analog und virtual Rooms
Machines/ Devices	**Who?**	People
Language (1-0 unambiguous)	**What?**	Spoken And Written Word
KW	**How?**	Kcal/ Felings/ Social Energy
Efficiency/ Information Medium	**Why?**	Leadership/ Communication Medium
→ **Technology**		→ **Society**

Fig. 7 Digital technology and leadership. *Source* Own figure

5 Future Prospects-Analog and Digital Ways

We have the privilege and the opportunity to co-shape our world. Growth is different every time and that is key. Individual worlds are created by new and different ways of creating. Joy and courage are important energies. With great confidence in the next leadership generation one thing is clear: they will think and hopefully also act differently in order to build a peaceful society on a healthy planet earth. Albert Einstein once coined the phrase: "We cannot solve our problems with the same thinking we used when we created them."

Live and love what you do!

Be smart—follow your heart—invest in SDGs.

6 Question Thinking for Digital Sustainable Leadership

- What has influenced you most?
- What change history can you tell about yourself and your company?
- What are your roots?
- What kind of responsibility do you like to take on?
- What is your motivation?
- Are you rather cost or quality oriented?
- Which three values unite you and your company?
- Do you feel like an ambassador of your company?
- Are you thinking in terms of problems or solutions?
- Do you prefer thinking of people or processes?
- For what do you get up in the morning?
- What strengthens and what inspires you?
- What kinds of value appreciation do you know?
- Which code of conduct you think most necessary/appropriate/suitable for you?
- Which SDGs are you already following in your life?
- Which virtual rooms do you use most frequently?
- Are you equally competent in the digital and the analog world?
- Are you in charge of your smart phone or is your smart phone in charge of you?
- Do you know your values? Do you know your non-values?

References

Maslow, A. H. (1943). A theory of human motivation. *Psychological Review, 50*(4), 370–396. https://doi.org/10.1037/h0054346

Ogunyemi, O., & Ogunyemi, K. (2020). Authentic leadership: leading with purpose, meaning and core values. In S. Dhiman & J. Marques (Eds.), *New horizons in positive leadership and change.* Springer International Publishing (Management for Professionals) (pp. 369–380).

Sinek, S. (2009). *Start with why. How great leaders inspire everyone to take action.*

UNESCO. (2021). UNESCO and sustainable development goals. Online verfügbar unter https://en.unesco.org/sustainabledevelopmentgoals, zuletzt geprüft am 26.01.2021.

VDV-Akademie e.V. (2016). Leitfaden aus dem Projekt MIGEMA. Moderne Personalführung in Verkehrsunternehmen - wertschöpfend und gesund für Mitarbeiter/-innen und Betriebe. Online verfügbar unter https://docplayer.org/storage/67/57540756/1611660593/ayn9CS5YkAHKIqNM8CnEvQ/57540756.pdf, zuletzt geprüft am 26.01.2021.

Walker, J. I., Pekmezovic, A., & Walker, G. R. (Eds.). (2019). *Sustainable development goals. Harnessing business to achieve the SDGs through finance, technology and law reform.* Wiley.

Russia's Place Vis-à-Vis the EU28 Countries in Digital Development: A Ranking Using DEA-Type Composite Indicators and the TOPSIS Method

Zoltán Bánhidi, Imre Dobos, and Madina Tokmergenova

1 Introduction

The International Digital Economy and Society Index (I-DESI) is a composite index comprising a set of indicators that was designed to measure progress towards a digital economy and society of all EU and selected non-EU countries, including the Russian Federation. Aiming to mirror and extend the results of the European Commission's EU-only Digital Economy and Society Index (Bánhidi et al., 2020), I-DESI measures performance in five dimensions or policy areas: Connectivity, Human Capital (digital skills), Use of Internet by citizens, Integration of Digital Technology and Digital Public Services. The latest edition of I-DESI (European Commission, 2018) combines 24 individual indicators from various databases (including those of the World Economic Forum, OECD, World Bank and ITU etc.) measured over a four-year time period from 2013 to 2016. The I-DESI composite index uses a scoring model to rank each country according to its digital performance and to track the evolution of the EU as a whole and its member states in digital competitiveness. This has the drawback that the dimension weights used in the DESI "were selected to represent the EU's digital policy priorities" (European Commission, 2016), which might not be identical to the policy priorities of the selected non-EU countries, rather than being based on objective criteria or the statistical properties of the dataset (Tokmergenova et al., 2021). Although we do not consider these to be unreasonable, and acknowledge that the rationale behind the weights are partly rooted in theoretical considerations about enablers and synergies, we are still on the opinion that the exact values selected by the Commission experts are somewhat arbitrary. In this paper, we

Z. Bánhidi · I. Dobos (✉) · M. Tokmergenova
Deptartment of Economics, Faculty of Economic and Social Sciences,
Budapest University of Technology and Economics Budapest, Budapest, Hungary
e-mail: dobos.imre@gtk.bme.hu

T. Herberger and J. Dötsch (eds.), *Digitalization, Digital Transformation and Sustainability in the Global Economy*, Springer Proceedings in Business and Economics, https://doi.org/10.1007/978-3-030-77340-3_11

sought to demonstrate how other models of decision theory can provide a viable alternative to this pre-defined weighting system.

In an earlier paper, the authors have already endeavored to assess the digital competitiveness and level of digital development of the Russian Federation vis-à-vis the countries of the European Union. Bánhidi et al. (2019) ranked the countries of the Russian Federation and the EU using six methods. Three of the methods ranked the 29 countries with equal weights. One of these methods was a scoring model with the weights proposed by the European Commission (2018). With these weights, Russia ranked 26th out of 29 countries. Another method using Data Envelopment Analysis (DEA) using the same weights was the DEA Common Weights Analysis (DEA/CWA) method. Using this method, the authors performed two analyses that are distinguished by the procedure according to which the available data were transformed. Since the DEA basically organizes the criteria for evaluating Decision Making Units (DMUs) into two groups according to whether the criteria can be considered input or output criteria, the criteria need to be transformed by some method. There are two possible options for this: one is to transform the inputs to be minimized, which are arranged according to the maximum by reciprocals, and the outputs, which are arranged to the minimum by reciprocal, are also transformed; the other option is to scale the data to a specified scale according to preference. The five dimensions of I-DESI are each arranged to a maximum, so there is the preferred one that takes on the highest value. In this sense, it is difficult to define an input here, but if we look for one, Connectivity and Human Capital are the best candidates, because the other three dimensions can be understood as a consequence of these two variables, i.e. they are the output dimensions. Performing the ranking with these two methods using the reciprocal procedure, Russia took the 29th, last place, while scaling the data to a scale of 1–20, the 25th place.

Using the multidimensional scaling (MDS) method of multivariate statistics, the Russian Federation finished in 27th place.

Using the classical method of the DEA and using two methods of data transformation, Russia can already show better results. With reciprocal data, the Russian Federation ranked 20th, while with scaled data, it ranked 19th.

As the results of the six methods used showed a fairly large standard deviation, further studies with the use of basic data seemed necessary. These methods are the DEA-type Composite Indicators (DEA/CI) method (Cherchye et al., 2007) and the TOPSIS method (Technique for Order of Preference by Similarity to Ideal Solution) proposed by Yoon and Hwang (1981).

The DEA-type Composite Indicators method is practically the same as a special case of DEA, with the difference that then each of the criteria is either an input, i.e. to be minimized; or an output, i.e. to be maximized. Since each of the DESI dimensions is to be maximized, the latter case occurs, we only have output criteria. This also means that data transformation can be omitted in this case, which can avoid the distortions caused by transformations.

The TOPSIS method is essentially a very simple, geometric approach based on a decision theory method that attempts to eliminate procedures based on data transformation. The method consists of three consecutive steps. (It is often summarized in six steps, but this is based on the three basic methods we describe.) In the first step, the scale problem between the data is brought to the same scale as a normalization transformation. That normalization can be a Euclidean distance on the unit sphere or transforming the data to a [0, 1] interval with an affine transformation. The resulting nominated data is then weighted by a weight vector. The weights can be subjective, given a priori, or objectively determined from the statistical properties of the available data by theoretical or mathematical statistical considerations. Finally, in the third step, the calculated efficiency is determined using the ratio of the distance between the normalized, weighted data to ideal and nadir (negative ideal) points, the order of which gives the ranking.

The paper will consist of the following sections. In the second part, we provide a brief literature review of the Digital Economy and Social Index and the analyses performed with it. In the next chapter, we determine the position of the Russian Federation among the 29 countries using the DEA/CI method. In chapter four, we do the same examination using the TOPSIS method. Finally, in the fifth part, we interpret our results and compare our ranking obtained with the two methods of decision theory, above all the place of the Russian Federation among the countries of the European Union.

2 Literature Review

Literature review highlights studies of DESI index analysis and its methodology problems in general and specifically for EU countries. Bilozubenko et al. (2020) applied a cluster method to evaluate the digital development of the EU-27. They divided EU countries into three clusters (using the Euclidean distance metric and the k-means algorithm) and sought to identify the key parameters of the "digital divide" that separates these groups. Jovanović et al. (2018) examined the DESI methodology and used correlation analysis to assess how the digital performance of EU countries affects the economic, social and environmental dimensions of sustainable development, highlighting the importance of digitalization as an additional, crucial component of sustainable development. Karnitis et al. (2019) developed a country-level model explaining the dependence of economic growth on the level of digitalization, focusing primarily on the Baltic countries. The results of the research indicate that two dimensions of the DESI index, Use of Internet and Digital Public Services, have a significant impact on the growth of the economy. Stavytskyy et al. (2019) analyzed three hypotheses and found that a high level of consumption and low unemployment are associated with a high DESI index score. The authors also suggest that in emerging and developing countries that are not presented in the official DESI reports, such as Ukraine, significant efforts are required to increase their digital development to levels that are comparable to those in Western European countries. Orbán (2020) combines the Digital Public Services dimension of DESI and her own survey results to assess the performance of e-administration services in Hungary. While she mainly focuses on "the causes of underperformance" in her paper, she also criticizes the European Commission's measurement framework for its lack of robustness and stability. Bánhidi (2021) analyzes the significance of broadband penetration for economic development with an econometric model for nine South American countries. According to this model, increased broadband penetration is associated with significant spillover effects, excess societal returns over and above the expected returns of other investments in financial capital. Soltész and Zilahy (2020) studied the features of a popular ride-sharing platform and a related network with a network theory approach, showing that the internal structure of this network shows scale-free characteristics. However, the authors also suggest that while these networks have significant growth potential, they should eventually run out of "free nodes" and reach a saturation point.

Literature review also highlights the main problems of digital development of Russia and studies present which specific areas of digital development in Russia require more sources. Ermolaev et al. (2019) assessed the development of the digital economy in Russia based on international indices. Their results show that further efforts are required to increase the percentage of Internet users, enhance the quality of digital infrastructure and the availability of ICT technologies. Revinova and Lazanyuk (2018) assessed the level of digitalization in the regions of Russia. The level of digital development varies highly between regions: among the Federal Districts the leading position belongs to the Northwestern district, and among subjects to Moscow and Saint-Petersburg. In lagging regions, the main problems identified by the authors are the lack of digital infrastructure and funding. Korovin (2018) indicates risks of digitalization of industry in Russia in terms of low level of technological development, equipment and software products. Labor productivity is also crucial in achieving leading positions in industrial digitalization by Russia. Statistical research demonstrates a positive trend in increasing the number of university graduates in such specialties as automation, IT and communications, but the demand for these specialists in Russia remains low. Baskakova and Soboleva (2019) analyzed functional illiteracy in Russia based on access to internet and level of computer literacy. The research shows that older generation, low educated, population with low income, rural population are associated with increased risk of functional illiteracy. The regional factor of Russia also contributes to unequal development of digital economy. Mironova et al. (2019) studied the importance of digital education and digital literacy in Russia as the main factor of development of economy and society. The factor of difference in generations development should be considered in transition to digitization. Akberdina (2018) indicates that industrial digitalization is impossible without a developed industrial sector, and demonstrates that the level of digitalization, automation determines the degree of using high technologies in industry. Certain regions of Russia are developed less that refers to historical factor and the author proves the fact that concentration of high technologies impacts differentiation in digital development. Kuvayeva (2019) assesses the readiness of Russia to digital integration. The author highlights the lack of unified statistical measures for assessing digital readiness of all countries, including Russia. Analyzed dimensions in the article such as investments in technologies, high-tech industry development, readiness to digital transitions are low in comparison to developed countries. Miethlich et al. (2020) analyzed the digital economy and its influence on national competitiveness on the examples of Switzerland, Russia and Azerbaijan. Their study suggests that Switzerland and Russia both excel in IT education services, but Russia lags behind Switzerland in the protection of intellectual property rights. The authors also performed cluster analysis based on data regarding the share of TCI (telecommunications, computer and information) in total service exports. According to their results, Russia is placed in the third cluster, which means that the country is not geared towards exporting TCI.

3 Ranking with DEA-Type Composite Indicators

The Data Envelopment Analysis (DEA) method was first described and applied by Charnes et al. (1978). In the last more than forty years, the procedure has since had numerous theoretical extensions and practical applications (Cook & Seiford, 2009).

The method used in this paper is a special property model of DEA. In the basic DEA, the criteria that evaluate DMUs can be divided into two different groups according to whether the criteria can be considered input or output. The basic DEA CCR-I (1)–(3) model can be written in the following form, where vectors ($\mathbf{u}, \mathbf{v}$) are the weights vectors of DEA, and vectors $(\mathbf{y}_j, \mathbf{x}_j)(j = 1, 2, \ldots, p)$ are the output and input evaluations of the jth DMU, and the number of DMUs is value p:

$$\mathbf{u} \cdot \mathbf{y}_1 / \mathbf{v} \cdot \mathbf{x}_1 \rightarrow \max \tag{1}$$

s.t.

$$\mathbf{u} \cdot \mathbf{y}_j / \mathbf{v} \cdot \mathbf{x}_j \leq 1; \; j = 1, 2, \ldots, p \tag{2}$$

$$\mathbf{u} \geq 0, \mathbf{v} \geq 0 \tag{3}$$

However, the model in its original form could not be used to rank DMUs in the absence of input criteria among our quantitative sub-indicators. In this case, we can rewrite model (1)–(3) as follows if we assume that the input does not exist or assume it to be a single one, i.e. $\mathbf{v} \cdot \mathbf{x}_1 = 1$.

$$\mathbf{u} \cdot \mathbf{y}_1 \rightarrow \max \tag{4}$$

s.t.

$$\mathbf{u} \cdot \mathbf{y}_j \leq 1; \; j = 1, 2, \ldots, p \tag{5}$$

$$\mathbf{u} \geq 0 \tag{6}$$

Table 1 Weights of dimensions in TOPSIS calculations

	CN	HC	UI	DT	PS
Weights	0.082	0.297	0.233	0.194	0.194

Source Own calculation

The latter model is called in the literature the DEA-type Composite Indicators (DEA/CI) method (Cherchye et al., 2007; Dobos & Vörösmarty, 2014). The new model (4)–(6) must be solved for each DMU, in our case for all countries, in order to determine the efficiency of that country. Dataset is Table 2 in the Appendix. We are looking for the $\mathbf{u}$ weight vector, and the $\mathbf{y}_j$ vector represents the digital dimensions of the jth country.

The solutions of the linear programming models (4)–(6) are given in Table 3 of the Appendix. This shows that the Russian Federation ranks 19th, i.e. in the second third of the countries of the European Union. This suggests that Russia's digital development is considered moderate. After the DEA/CI method, the results obtained with the TOPSIS method are presented.

4 Ranking with TOPSIS Method

In the introduction, we gave a short overview of the TOPSIS method, which is not repeated here. The three steps described are illustrated by the methods we use.

In the *first step*, we perform the normalization of the basic data. Suppose that the data for criterion i according to each country are contained in the vector $\mathbf{x}_i$. (Dataset used is Table 2 in the Appendix.) Then the data transformation is as follows

$$y_{ji} = \frac{x_{ji} - x_j^{min}}{x_j^{max} - x_j^{min}}, \ (j = 1, 2, \ldots, n; i = 1, 2, \ldots, m),$$

where the minimal and maximal values of criterion i is x_j^{min} and x_j^{max}, number n is the number of countries, and number m is the number of criteria/dimensions. With this transformation, the values of each criterion for each country were transformed to the interval [0, 1]. Let the value of the new vectors be $\mathbf{y}_i$.

In the *second step*, knowing the values of the individual variables, in our case dimensions, we use the entropy-based method to determine the weights of the variables (Zhou et al., 2006). We chose entropy-based weighting because then the weights are objective, that is, they are determined from the data. The formula for the transformation is as follows:

$$H_i = -\frac{1}{\ln(n)} \cdot \sum_{j=1}^{n} \frac{y_{ji}}{\sum_{j=1}^{n} y_{ji}} \cdot \ln\left(\frac{y_{ji}}{\sum_{j=1}^{n} y_{ji}}\right), \ (i = 1, 2, \ldots, m),$$

The weights will thus be as follows:

$$w_i = \frac{1 - H_i}{n - \sum_{i=1}^{m} H_i}, \ (i = 1, 2, \ldots, m)$$

The weighted normalized values are denoted by z_{ji}, which is equal to $z_{ji} = w_i \cdot y_{ji}$. The ideal and nadir points are then determined using the z_{ji} values.

Finally, in the *third step*, we use the weighted data to determine the efficiency index using the ideal (I_i) and nadir (N_i) points, which are calculated in the following way:

$$I_i = \max_{j=1,2,\ldots,n} z_{ji}, N_i = \min_{j=1,2,\ldots,n} z_{ji}, \ (i = 1, 2, \ldots, m).$$

In this last, third step, the distances from the preferred and non-preferred dimensions are determined, after which the efficiencies can be calculated. The distance of the jth country from the ideal and nadir is determined as follows:

$$d_j^I = \sqrt{\sum_{i=1}^{n} \left(z_{ji} - I_i\right)^2}, d_j^N = \sqrt{\sum_{i=1}^{n} \left(z_{ji} - N_i\right)^2}, \ (j = 1, 2, \ldots, n),$$

A final calculation is the determination of the TOPSIS efficiency E_j, which shows the ratio of the distance from the two awarded points:

$$E_j = \frac{d_j^N}{d_j^I + d_j^N}, \ (j = 1, 2, \ldots, n),$$

After a brief description of the TOPSIS method, we describe the results of our calculations performed on the dataset. We omit the detailed calculations, only the objective weights, and the TOPSIS efficiencies and the order are presented in Table 1 (CN—Connectivity, HC—Human Capital, UI—Use of Internet, DT—Integration of Digital Technology and PS—Digital Public Services) and Table 3 in the Appendix.

It is immediately apparent that the weight of the dimensions is highest among Human Capital and Use of Internet. This means that countries with a high level of development in education are at the top of the list. This is also true for the Russian Federation. This puts Russia in 18th place among the countries of the European Union, which corresponds to a medium level of development.

5 Conclusions

In this paper, we demonstrate how the DEA/CI and TOPSIS methods can be used to provide a viable framework for ranking the 28 countries of the European Union and the Russian Federation in the absence of explicit input criteria or predetermined weights that are required by the classical DEA method and the European

Commission's scoring model. These methods can eliminate the need for a pre-defined weighting system used by the original composite index, rather than an intrinsic one based on the statistical properties of the dataset. The entropy-based method identifies Human Capital as the dimension with the highest "objective weight" (0.297), highlighting the importance of digital literacy in driving the digital transformation of the economy and society. The original weighting system proposed by the European Commission (2020) also attributes the joint-highest weight (0.25) to this dimension and Connectivity, which they group together as "digital infrastructure" and suggest that two of the other dimensions, Use of Internet and Digital Public Services "are enabled by the infrastructure and their contribution is strengthened by the quality of such infrastructure". While we can accept this thesis as a sensible policy recommendation, we would also note that the entropy-based method attributes a much lower weight to the Connectivity dimension (0.082).

According to our rankings, the Russian Federation demonstrates respectable results in digital economic and social development relative to Eastern and Southern member states of the European Union, on account of its solid results in the field of Human Capital. In order to further improve its digital competitiveness, Russia would have to improve its scores in the Integration of Digital Technology and Connectivity dimensions. As for the latter, the Russian Ministry of Communications and Mass Media has set quite ambitious national broadband coverage targets to overcome its connectivity gap, which are not yet reflected in our I-DESI database. However, achieving these might prove extremely challenging, owing to the fairly low population density and vast territory of the country. On the other hand, the other dimension, the use of ICT by the business sector should not be neglected either, since it should be regarded as one of the most important drivers of productivity and economic growth.

Appendix

See Tables 2 and 3.

Table 2 The basic data (x_i)

Country	CN	HC	UI	DT	PS
Austria	0.63	0.59	0.60	0.59	0.72
Belgium	0.68	0.60	0.62	0.61	0.61
Bulgaria	0.61	0.47	0.42	0.36	0.45
Croatia	0.54	0.45	0.49	0.46	0.56
Cyprus	0.54	0.45	0.54	0.39	0.49
Czechia	0.67	0.58	0.58	0.39	0.43
Denmark	0.77	0.80	0.79	0.71	0.71
Estonia	0.62	0.66	0.70	0.53	0.85

(continued)

Table 2 (continued)

Country	CN	HC	UI	DT	PS
Finland	0.72	0.73	0.78	0.67	0.83
France	0.59	0.62	0.59	0.53	0.82
Germany	0.64	0,62	0.66	0.59	0.69
Greece	0.50	0.48	0.46	0.45	0.48
Hungary	0.60	0.62	0.55	0.51	0.46
Ireland	0.63	0.77	0.56	0.51	0.66
Italy	0.51	0.50	0.42	0.47	0.68
Latvia	0.65	0.47	0.58	0.32	0.56
Lithuania	0.61	0.53	0.58	0.46	0.63
Luxembourg	0.65	0.67	0.79	0.77	0.64
Malta	0.64	0.48	0.57	0.57	0.66
Netherlands	0.75	0.69	0.76	0.75	0.76
Poland	0.53	0.53	0.51	0.33	0.57
Portugal	0.60	0.43	0.47	0.39	0.55
Romania	0.61	0.43	0.48	0.27	0.39
Russia	0.39	0.64	0.49	0.30	0.57
Slovakia	0.57	0.65	0.59	0.40	0.38
Slovenia	0.60	0.44	0.53	0.43	0.67
Spain	0.64	0.62	0.58	0.55	0.82
Sweden	0.75	0.69	0.78	0.65	0.73
United Kingdom	0.74	0.65	0.72	0.68	0.90

Source https://ec.europa.eu/digital-single-market/en/news/international-digital-economy-and-society-index-2018

Table 3 DEA/CI and TOPSIS Efficiencies and ranking of countries

	DEA/CI Efficiencies	DEA/CI Ranking	TOPSIS Efficiency	TOPSIS Ranking
Austria	0.854	14	0.522	12
Belgium	0.883	11	0.521	13
Bulgaria	0.792	21	0.145	28
Croatia	0.712	27	0.230	24
Cyprus	0.700	28	0.211	25
Czechia	0.870	12	0.355	19
Denmark	1.000	1	0.855	1
Estonia	0.972	7	0.672	7
Finland	1.000	1	0.846	2
France	0.928	9	0.554	11

(continued)

Table 3 (continued)

	DEA/CI Efficiencies	DEA/CI Ranking	TOPSIS Efficiency	TOPSIS Ranking
Germany	0.860	13	0.584	9
Greece	0.653	29	0.196	26
Hungary	0.779	23	0.416	15
Ireland	0.963	8	0.616	8
Italy	0.761	25	0.289	20
Latvia	0.844	15	0.274	22
Lithuania	0.804	18	0.377	17
Luxembourg	1.000	1	0.722	6
Malta	0.844	16	0.381	16
Netherlands	1.000	1	0.787	3
Poland	0.714	26	0.264	23
Portugal	0.779	24	0.189	27
Romania	0.792	22	0.119	29
Russia	*0.801*	*19*	*0.365*	*18*
Slovakia	0.813	17	0.418	14
Slovenia	0.800	20	0.289	21
Spain	0.928	10	0.557	10
Sweden	0.990	6	0.759	4
UK	1.000	1	0.734	5

Source Own calculation

References

Akberdina, V. V. (2018). Digitalization of industrial markets: Regional characteristics. *Upravlenets/the Manager, 9*(6), 78–87. https://doi.org/10.29141/2218-5003-2018-9-6-8

Bánhidi, Z. (2021). The impact of broadband networks on growth and development in South America. *Periodica Polytechnica Social and Management Sciences, 29*(1), 33–39. https://doi.org/10.3311/PPso.14905

Bánhidi, Z., Dobos, I., & Nemeslaki, A. (2019). Comparative analysis of the development of the digital economy in Russia and EU Measured with DEA and using dimensions of DESI. *Вестник Санкт-Петербургского университета. Экономика/St. Petersburg University Journal of Economic Studies, 35*(4), 588–604. https://doi.org/10.21638/spbu05.2019.405

Bánhidi, Z., Dobos, I., & Nemeslaki, A. (2020). What the overall digital economy and society index reveals: A statistical analysis of the DESI EU28 dimensions. *Regional Statistics, 10*(2), 42–62. https://doi.org/10.15196/RS100209

Baskakova, M., & Soboleva, I. (2019). Novye grani funktsional'noy negramotnosti v usloviyakh tsifrovoy ekonomiki [New Dimensions of Functional Illiteracy in the Digital Economy]. *Voprosy obrazovaniya/Educational Studies Moscow*, no1 (pp. 244–263). https://doi.org/10.17323/1814-9545-2019-1-244-263

Bilozubenko, V., Yatchuk, O., Wolanin, E., Serediuk, T., & Korneyev, M. (2020). Comparison of the digital economy development parameters in the EU countries in the context of bridging the digital divide. *Problems and Perspectives in Management, 18*(2), 206–218. https://doi.org/10.21511/ppm.18(2).2020.18

Charnes, A., Cooper, W. W., & Rhodes, E. (1978). Measuring the efficiency of decision making units. *European Journal of Operational Research, 2*(6), 429–444. https://doi.org/10.1016/0377-2217(78)90138-8

Cherchye, L., Moesen, W., Rogge, N., & Van Puyenbroeck, T. (2007). An introduction to 'benefit of the doubt' composite indicators. *Social Indicators Research, 82*(1), 111–145. https://doi.org/10.1007/s11205-006-9029-7

Cook, W. D., & Seiford L. M. (2009). Data envelopment analysis (DEA)–thirty years on. *European Journal of Operational Research, 192*(1), 1–17. https://doi.org/10.1016/j.ejor.2008.01.032

Dobos, I., & Vörösmarty, G. (2014). Green supplier selection and evaluation using DEA-type composite indicators. *International Journal of Production Economics, 157*, 273–278. https://doi.org/10.1016/j.ijpe.2014.09.026

Ermolaev, K. N., Trubetskaya, O. V., Shnyakin, K. V., & Pavlova, J. A. (2019). Platforms and tendencies for the development of the digital economy in Russia. *SHS Web of Conferences, 62*, 01001. https://doi.org/10.1051/shsconf/20196201001

European Commission. (2016). DESI 2016 digital economy and society index—methodological note, [online] Available at: http://ec.europa.eu/information_society/newsroom/cf/dae/document.cfm?action=display&doc_id=8846. Accessed December 05, 2020.

European Commission. (2018). International digital economy and society index 2018", Publications Office of the European Union, Luxembourg, Rep. SMART 2017/0052, [online] Available at: https://ec.europa.eu/digital-single-market/en/news/international-digital-economy-and-society-index-2018. Accessed July 05, 2019.

European Commission. (2020). Digital economy and society index (DESI) 2020—methodological note, [online] Available at: http://ec.europa.eu/newsroom/dae/document.cfm?doc_id=67082. Accessed December 05, 2020.

Jovanović, M., Dlačić, J., & Okanović, M. (2018). Digitalization and society's sustainable development—measures and implications. *Zb. Rad. Ekon. Fak. Rij., 36*(2), 905–928. https://doi.org/10.18045/zbefri.2018.2.905

Karnitis, G., Virtmanis, A., & Karnitis, E. (2019). Key drivers of digitalization; EU context and Baltic case. *Baltic Journal Modern Computing, 7*(1), 70–85. https://doi.org/10.22364/bjmc.2019.7.1.06

Korovin Grigory, B. (2018). Problems of industrial digitalisation in Russia. *Journal of New Economy, Ural State University of Economics, 19*(3), 100–110. https://doi.org/10.29141/2073-1019-2018-19-3-9

Kuvayeva, Y. V. (2019). Digital economy: Concepts and Russia's readiness to transition. *Izvestiya Uralskogo gosudarstvennogo ekonomicheskogo universiteta/Journal of the Ural State University of Economics, 20*(1), 25–40. https://doi.org/10.29141/2073-1019-2019-20-1-3

Miethlich, B., Belotserkovich, D., Abasova, S., Zatsarinnaya, E., & Veselitsky, O. (2020). Digital economy and its influence on competitiveness of countries and regions. *Revista ESPACIOS, 41*(12). http://revistaespacios.com/a20v41n12/20411220.html

Mironova, O. A., Bogdanova, R. M., & Kolesnikov, Y. A. (2019). Aspects of the generational theory application in terms of digital education development in Russia. *Медиаобразование. 2019*(1), 93–104. In: Шамис Е., Антипов А. (2016) Теория поколений. М.: *Институт Синергия.* 398, https://doi.org/10.13187/me.2019.1.937

Orbán, A. (2020). Measuring the development of the hungarian electronic administration. *Central and Eastern European EDem and EGov Days, 338*(6), 93–102. https://doi.org/10.24989/ocg.v.338.7

Revinova, S., & Lazanyuk, I. (2018). Prerequisites for development of the digital economy in russia: Differentiation of regions. *International Journal of Business and Management Studies (IJBMS), 7*(2). http://universitypublications.net/ijbms/0702/html/U8K792.xml

Soltész, P., & Zilahy, G. (2020). A network theory approach to the sharing economy. *Periodica Polytechnica Social and Management Sciences, 28*(1), 70–80. https://doi.org/10.3311/PPso.12597

Stavytskyy, A., Kharlamova, A., & Stoica, E. A. (2019). The analysis of the digital economy and society index in the EU. *Baltic Journal of European Studies, 9*(3), 245–261. https://doi.org/10.1515/bjes-2019-0032

Tokmergenova, M., Bánhidi, Z., & Dobos, I. (2021). Analysis of I-DESI dimensions of the digital economy development of Russian Federation and EU28 using multivariate statistics. *Вестник Санкт-Петербургского университета. Экономика/ St. Petersburg University Journal of Economic Studies* (Accepted).

Yoon, K., & Hwang, C. L. (1981). *Multiple attribute decision making methods and applications: A state-of-the-art survey*. Springer Verlag.

Zou, Z., Yun, Y., & Sun, J. (2006) Entropy method for determination of weight of evaluating indicators in fuzzy synthetic evaluation for water quality assessment. *Journal of Environmental Sciences, 18*(5), 1020–1023.https://doi.org/10.1016/S1001-0742(06)60032-6

The Impact of Big Data and Sports Analytics on Professional Football: A Systematic Literature Review

Tim A. Herberger and Christoph Litke

1 Introduction

The usage potential of big data analysis is not limited to industrial companies only. In 2001, Billy Beane, the manager of Oakland Athletics, recognized big data analysis and successfully used it in the baseball professional league. Beane revolutionized the baseball game with innovative data-driven management style. He made decisions based only on statistical analysis and achieved a unique winning streak of 20 games won. This success story is described in the book titled *Moneyball: The Art of Winning an Unfair Game* and illustrates how statistics could make sport predictable (Lewis, 2004). "Moneyball" took a decisive turn in high-performance sport and influenced it beyond baseball (Gerrard, 2016: 213). The increasing awareness of a possible success through the combination of increased computing power and better availability of data rapidly increased the proportion of quantitative analyses in sports and led to the widespread use of data analytics in professional sports (McHale & Relton, 2018: 339ff).

The use of data analytics based on innovative technologies is also widely used in professional football, as football companies expect data analytics to improve their competitiveness and thus secure their medium- and long-term sporting and economic success (Möller & Schönefeld, 2011: 1; Gassmann & Perez-Freije, 2011: 394; Werner, 2017: 17ff.). However, to design innovation processes effectively and efficiently and thus ensure the innovation success of a football company, suitable analysis methods are needed, that is, a further clarification of the rather broad term

T. A. Herberger (✉) · C. Litke
Chair of Business Administration, specifically Entrepreneurship, Finance and Digitalization, Andrássy University, Budapest, Hungary
e-mail: tim.herberger@andrassyuni.hu

C. Litke
e-mail: christoph.litke@icloud.com

T. Herberger and J. Dötsch (eds.), *Digitalization, Digital Transformation and Sustainability in the Global Economy*, Springer Proceedings in Business and Economics, https://doi.org/10.1007/978-3-030-77340-3_12

data analytics toward sports analytics (Reichmann et al., 2017). However, the implementation of new technologies and thus new process structures in a company – also in a football company – poses great challenges to the various stakeholders (e.g., owners, top management, athletes, and coaches). This is all the more true for the more disruptive and penetrating innovation. These challenges are reflected not only in the use of financial resources but also in the coverage of personnel capacities and competencies.

The analysis and target-group-specific evaluation and processing of the large data collected during a football match, which are still unspecific and unstructured to a large extent, are only possible with appropriate software tools. IT providers such as SAP and IBM provide specific cloud solutions for big data and sports analytics at football companies. For example, "SAP Sports One" offers Team Management, Training Planning, Fitness, Performance Analysis, Scouting, and Talent Finding modules via a uniform platform (Biermann, 2018a: 40).

However, can these additional instruments (better) answer the main question in football against the background of a balanced cost–benefit ratio: How do you win matches? In this study's context, the following questions will be examined based on a structured literature review (SLR) according to Massaro et al. (2016):

1. *How does the use of big data and sports analytics change professional football?*
2. *Can big data and sports analytics increase the team's competitiveness in football?*
3. *Which chances and risks are to be considered with the use of big data and sports analytics for the different stakeholders in a football company?*

The remainder of the paper is structured as follows: Sect. 2 defines the essential concepts and theoretical framework. Section 3 presents the methodology of the SLR. Section 4 discusses the results from the SLR and transfer on the three research questions. Section 5 concludes the paper.

2 Definitions and Theoretical Framework

In the age of the Internet of Things (IoT), the digitalization of the physical world and its networking with the virtual world continues to increase. The term IoT was first mentioned in 1999 and was used for the networking of clearly identifiable objects using Radio Frequency Identification technology (Ashton, 2009). Today, the definition of IoT goes further. For example, the European Commission defines the future of the IoT in its roadmap as follows:

> *Things having identities and virtual personalities operating in smart spaces using intelligent interfaces to connect and communicate within social, environmental, and user contexts* (IEEE, 2015: 31).

Other definitions go one step further and add people and processes to networking in addition to things (Bardley et al., 2013). The networking of any objects within the framework of the IoT can be used in various areas. Especially, the mobile Internet and the associated increased use of devices and applications offer the possibility of technological reorientation (e.g., wearables) to the sports industry. The most important applications of IoT in the sports world are performance measurement and continuous monitoring. Until a few years ago, quantitative data used in football were hardly considered; if they were, the processes were evaluated qualitatively, mostly subjectively and emotionally. Due to the randomness and the supposed absence of patterns, no direct benefit of quantitative data was discernible in football, as in other sports, such as baseball (Quirling et al., 2017: 324).

A negative example for the quantitative evaluation of certain measured variables would be the 2014 World Cup semi-finals. Due to the "traditional" notation analysis, the Brazilian national team was superior to the German team in almost all categories (including passes into the penalty area, crosses, corners, and tackles won), but the match ended negatively for the Brazilian national team with 1:7 (Biermann, 2018a: 40). The result was due to the exclusion of tally lists in which actions are counted individually in the data analysis. Instead of a notepad and eyewitness reports, algorithms, and video technology should be used to collect and record game data. After all, victory and defeat are not only determined by the meticulous noting of procedures on the pitch but also concretely require sports analytics to predict a reliable correlation (Biermann, 2018b).

According to Memmert and Raabe (2017), both worlds—big data and IoT—combine to form "Game Analysis 4.0," "which uses sensors, applications, and technologies to collect and analyze data from physical objects or other sources. With the correct analysis, for example, basic tactical settings can be calculated from the player position data (Memmert & Raabe, 2017: 7ff.).

The rapid growth of the IoT was favored by numerous IT-supported devices using radio technology, which communicates with each other and generates large amount of data (Fasel & Meier, 2016: 5ff.). Sports companies are investing increasingly in big data in the form of cloud data storage, artificial intelligence (AI), and on-premise-solutions. The basic idea behind big data is the use and analysis of data generated in a wide variety of forms in everyday life (Marr, 2015: 9ff.). The term big data stands for the transition to a new model of dealing with data and the use of huge amounts of data, which are usually combined, made available, and evaluated within the scope of a second use (Weichert, 2013: 133). Nonspecific data are therefore condensed into specific information that is useful for the interest group, depending on the motivation of the respective interest groups in the data.

Moreover, big data is the term used to describe extensive and disproportionately growing data volumes and data stocks that have the following three main characteristics: a comprehensive data volume (or data volume) in the Tera to Zettabyte range (volume); various structured, semi-structured, and unstructured data types (variety); and a high processing speed of data streams (velocity) (Fasel & Meier, 2016: 375; Freiknecht & Rapp, 2018: 7ff).

Many "V" terms play an important role in many definitions of big data and thus seem to confirm Francis Galton's assumption that everything can be measured (Gould, 1996: 107). However, one problem in the past was the nonexistence of the development of useful applications for the evaluation of large amounts of data or databases. Applications for the use of big data are also used in sports, especially in the football industry. For the analysis and interpretation of the video and position data of the players, for example, new ways are needed. Thus, the professional field of the so-called game analysts who used big data and have the skills to evaluate it also emerged (Memmert & Raabe, 2017: 2). Through the IoT, recording important performance data of the players for football is already possible to create performance analyses by match analysts and to support the medical department, the fitness sector, or scouting (Gramlich, 2018: 13ff.). Especially, the stakeholders of a football company such as management, coaches, and players can optimize their strategies and tactics based on big data analyses.

The "moneyball principle" has given sports analytics a new dynamic. The expansion and shift of the sports industry toward an increasingly business- and IT-oriented approach led to increased demand. Sports analytics is now a fast-growing industry and is becoming an ever-greater necessity to survive in a competitive environment. Big data and cloud technology played a major role in this growth development (Gowda et al., 2017: 499). The first known use of the prioritization of statistics and data by Billy Bean is also referred to in the literature as Sabermetrics (developed by the statistician Bill James) and is still a central area of sports analytics today, like the search for patterns in sports-related data (Fried & Mumcu, 2017: 57). Sabermetrics (Society for American Baseball Research metrics) has emerged in the literature and is a synonym for the numerical approach to sport (Memmert & Raabe, 2017: 92). Even though no final definition of sports analytics has yet been established, the ultimate goal is to search for, collect, and process sports-related data. These are analyzed with the help of IT systems to realize the user's competitive advantages that are used in two directions: to increase the performance and efficiency of the teams and to improve marketing concerning economic advantages (Link, 2018a: 3). To achieve competitive advantages in the performance area, data-supported decision-making is used to provide action aids for trainers and management. However, both player recruitment and tactical game decision can benefit from it. In addition, key performance indicators (KPIs) are analyzed based on trends and patterns to identify the most relevant KPIs (Gerrard, 2016; Hughes & Barlett, 2002: 739f; O'Donoghue, 2005: 104ff.). The KPIs aim to break down a complex system behavior into individual values for scaling, rating, and ranking systems or system components (Perl & Memmert, 2017: 65). In addition to sports performance and economics, information technology can be regarded as the third topic complex in the field of sports analytics. Sensors generate much information, data volumes are linked via the Internet, and memory chips enable larger data transactions without time restrictions. In this way, data from various sources can be merged in real time and searched for anomalies using new methodological and conceptual approaches from data sciences (Link, 2018a: 3). However, information technology is undergoing a considerable upheaval: the interaction between technical and IT experts and the associated programming of complex systems is being abandoned in favor of machine learning and the development of cognitive systems. The breakthrough of machine learning and thus the paradigm shift was achieved only with the availability of large amounts of data. Today, task solutions can be implemented with the help of computers that did not seem possible with classical programming (BaFin, 2018: 24ff). AI develops very quickly through machine learning. One successful approach is Deep Learning (Lewanczik, 2018). On the basis of existing information and with the help of a neuronal network, the system can link what has been learned with new content repeatedly and thus learns again. In addition, the machine can make its own forecasts and decisions and in turn question them. Once decisions have been made, they are confirmed or changed during the next run (Zoph et al., 2017; Davenport, 2018: 1ff.).

The areas of application of AI in sport are currently still manageable, as the development of new methods for data analysis and the interpretation associated with it is proving to be difficult. In Germany, Fraunhofer IIS makes intensive use of the technical innovations, such as AI and machine learning, for sports and markets the results under the lemma "sports analytics." In the USA, a market worth billions has established itself for the collection, analysis, and marketing of sports data (Research & Markets, 2016). Moreover, a competition for the best data analytics tools has emerged between the major providers (IBM, Intel, Microsoft, SAP, and Google) and their products and services (Link, 2018b: 13).

The beginning of sports analytics in professional football lies in manually recorded and evaluated descriptive statistics, which decomposed football into its numerical components, such as ball contacts, pass quotas, and mileages. Ultimately, however, these were only analytical tools that could support an evaluation with arguments but excluded the possibility of forecasting. In particular, technological innovations enable improved performance measurement and thus analysis and evaluation of individual players or the entire team. Meanwhile, big data and its immediate availability enable the coaching team to make decisions and assumptions about the players and teams' performance potential (Castellano et al., 2014: 701ff.). Monitoring makes it possible to resolve disputed decisions into individual sequences. In addition, thermal images can visualize the sphere of influence or the playing strategies of individual athletes or the entire team and thus allow conclusions to be drawn about effectiveness and efficiency. Furthermore, gaps in defensive formations can be detected by computer-generated grids in still images of the live broadcast.

Real-time training analyses would also be conceivable. Wearable technologies such as Global Positioning System (GPS) integrated into clothing or fitness trackers use software applications to visualize movement and performance profiles. These enable information about the physical constitution of a player and his cognitive abilities, such as anticipation and overview. To conclude the effectiveness of tactical variants, player-tracking programs can be used for tablets and data glasses (Gehrmann, 2017). Wearables are small, lightweight technological devices that can appear in various designs, such as bracelets, belts, or rings. These devices are equipped with sensors that can record a certain type of activity (van der Westhuizen & van der Haar, 2018: 226ff.). The subsequent analysis of the data collected would be conducted either with the same device or with the help of appropriate software programs on a computer belonging to the infrastructure. However, not only the one-sided delivery of collected data via a computer network but also the feeding of data from other data sources (clouds) to the wearable carrier are conceivable. Clouds are the most important development platforms for big data analytics in the environment of 24/7 always-on operations, that is, the constant availability of services or the continuous operation of devices and machines (Kobielus, 2018). This means that huge amounts of data not only can be analyzed and applied in the shortest possible time but are also available everywhere (Pickup, 2018).

Another form of wearable technology is Intelligent Clothing, which can track every movement of a football player. Complete movement sequences including all movement data can be evaluated in real time. Intelligent Clothing assumes special functions for the player at those points where wearables cannot provide adequate data and functions. For example, "smart bandages" measure strain on the joints and make preventive recommendations based on these data. Moreover, activating muscles via low-current stimuli to improve training effects is possible with Intelligent Clothing (Meyer, 2017: 28).

The market for tracking players is highly competitive and diverse (Memmert & Raabe, 2018: 36ff.). Therefore, we only briefly described basic systems for position tracking based on the following: GPS, video, and radio and microwave (Baca, 2015). GPS is the buzzword commonly used for satellite positioning and navigation. The actual GPS receivers in sports are similar in functionality to modern smartphones. Each player is equipped with a transponder (radio communication device). The hardware records position data and fitness parameters such as the athlete's heart rate and respiratory rate. In addition, acceleration sensors, gyro instruments, and compasses can be used to record the players' movements. The subsequent evaluation of the data occurs either in real time or after the game, and it is finally processed during training. However, this technology has two limitations: (1) the need for outdoor use and (2) a tradeoff between the accuracy of measurements and evaluation of data. Video-based systems do not require any additional electronics on the player's body. These are based on the setting of different camera perspectives that can be generated by a large number of different video systems. High-resolution cameras, installed under the stadium roof, the hall roof, or on the training ground, for example, can take at least 25 frames per second. Relative to 22 single players, the amount of data can consist millions of single images. To date, video-based systems have been used in competitions without any problems (Memmert & Raabe, 2018: 38). The systems function rather semi-automatically; for example, if players are concealed during goal celebrations, assigning players is often impossible because their identification no longer functions unambiguously. A manual assignment for recovery is then required (Memmert & Raabe, 2018: 39). In radar- and microwave-based systems, the players carry small transponder units on the body. The positioning is conducted with the help of several receivers at the edge of the pitch of the stadium, the hall, or the training area. The system continuously provides real-time position data. In contrast to GPS tracking, however, the installation effort in the stadium, in the hall, or on the training ground is considerably higher, making it almost impossible to use the system for away games (Laukenmann, 2017).

Two further technologies, namely, augmented reality (AR) and virtual reality (VR), have opened up new possibilities recently. AR is about augmenting the reality and the real environment with additional virtual information, thereby possibly improving the decision-making skills of users. Meanwhile, AR mixes virtual characters with the real world (Azuma, 1997: 2). Different human sensory modalities are addressed by a computer-aided extension of the perception of reality with additional information in different forms (videos, text, graphics, and 3D objects). AR offers the possibility of the user's perception of the virtual elements in his real environment. By contrast, in VR, the user identifies himself completely with a 360° world. VR creates the feeling of being at the scene of the action, whereas AR requires the user to be present to receive further information. The world of VR is supported by VR glasses or cardboard, whereas AR uses smartphones, tablets, or augmented reality glasses (Kipper & Rampolla, 2013: 1; Mangold, 2017).

AR and VR are used in professional football. For example, in the Spanish football league, viewers have access to 360° slow-motion and AR statistics. Moreover, in the National Basketball Association and National Football League, these technologies are standard and enable the user to immerse in other worlds (Zobel et al., 2018: 123ff.).

3 Methodology

Within the framework of the SLR, we applied the procedure of Massaro et al. (2016). The keywords used were "big data" along with "sports," "football," "analytics," and "match analysis." These terms were also searched for their German equivalents. Three databases were initially used to cover the relevant literature. By entering these keywords in (1) Google Scholar, (2) Scopus, and (3) Business Source Premier (EBSCO) (3), we identified the relevant literature.

Whether and to what extent the identified sources fulfilled the following criteria were also examined:

- The work is intended to shed light on the digitization based on measures relating to certain stakeholders and categories in the football field, which is why only those sources that contain explanations on these instruments are used for the SLR.
- The sources can be all types of publications (books, journal articles, research papers, etc.), provided they are officially or scientifically recognized documents.
- The sources must be published in English or German to analyze and compare the results.

Based on these exclusion/inclusion criteria, 102 literature sources in the period 2002 and 2018 were used for the SLR.

Accordingly, a suitable research framework that sets out the various interests and goals of the stakeholders in the digitization process must be developed. The purpose of this research framework is to find an adequate approach for the SLR to analyze and aggregate the relevant information from the selected articles (Vanini & Rieg, 2017: 9). The research framework contains bibliographic information, characteristics of the research design, and first results of the sources used for the SLR (Cooper, 2010: 45; Tranfield et al., 2003: 214).

Our applied research framework includes eight categories (see Table 1). The first category (1.1) organizes the sources used for the SLR according to literary attributes such as the number of sources used, the number of authors, and the period of observation. A constantly increasing development of publications in this research field can be observed. This can of course be explained by the increased processing of the key terms in media and society. The second category (1.2) lists the locations where the authors are predominantly active or conducting research. For a detailed overview, the third category (2.1) classifies the sources according to their type. The fourth category (2.2) shows how many sources are in German or English. In addition,

Table 1 Research design and descriptive (see Vanini & Rieg, 2017: 12)

Category	Variable	Results
1 Bibliographic information		
1.1 Sources, authors, research period	Sources Authors Research period	102 251 2002–2018
1.2 Authors' regions	Africa Asia Australia Europe North America (Canada/USA) South America	3 10 13 163 61 1
2 Research framework		
2.1 Type of sources	Books Book chapter Research papers Journal articles Conference papers	16 13 5 62 6
2.2 Language	German English	13 89
3 Results		
3.1 Stakeholder	Athlete Trainer Medical support Scouting Management	12 25 22 31 23
3.2 Interests of stake holder (in %)	Performance diagnostics, input for training design, and strategy development Injury Prophylaxis, rehabilitation Player rating Contract design, marketing	44% 40% 40% 33%
3.3 Sports analytics	Technique Economy Performance	54 22 46
3.4 Notes on strengths/weaknesses	Yes No	63 39

the fifth category (3.1) shows on which stakeholder groups the explanations of the respective sources are based. The sixth category (3.2) presents the metrics of the sources used that appeared most frequently. The interests and aims of the stakeholders were extracted and aggregated from all sources used for the SLR. Moreover, the seventh category (3.3) refers to the topic complexes of sports analytics. Finally, the eighth category (3.4) shows how many sources considered also discuss the strengths and weaknesses of the categories.

In addition, the citations were analyzed to identify the researchers and sources with the greatest influence. To ensure the validity of the sources, the citations were counted using Google Scholar (Dumay, 2014: 5).

The total number of citations is an indicator of the validity and quality of a source. The higher the number of citations received, the more meaningful or qualitative the source. However, the differences are large as there are seven sources with zero citations received and 26 sources with more than 100 citations received. The large differences can also be seen in the standard deviation. On average, a source receives about 117 citations (see Table 2).

Moreover, because older sources may receive more citations due to their "head start in time," citations per year were used. Table 3 shows the top three sources with the most total citations and the sources with the most citations per year.

The contributions of Davenport and Harris (2007), Di Salvo et al. (2007), and Lewis (2004) can be seen to play a significant role in the framework of our study.

The 102 sources used for the SLR were written by 251 authors. Only 26 sources were written by a single person, whereas most sources were written by two or more authors. Since only 26 authors have written more than one article, book, etc., the defined research field can be characterized as quite fragmented. Moreover, this probably does not lead to the expectation of a "dominant" opinion in the research area.

Table 2 Citation analysis(see Vanini & Rieg, 2017: 13f)

	Min	Max	Average	Median	Standard deviation
Total number of citations	0	1.627	116.73	27	252.49
Citations per year	0	197	18.77	8.07	29.21
Number of authors	1	18	3.24	2	2.67
Number of pages of the sources	1	320	44.67	13	79.34
Number of sources	0	156	40.32	33.5	33.15

Table 3 Citation analysis(see Vanini & Rieg, 2017: 15)

Rank	Source	TNC	Rank	Source	CPY
1	Davenport and Harris (2007)	1.627	1	Gabbett (2016)	197.00
2	Lewis (2004)	1.275	2	Davenport and Harris (2007)	147.91
3	Di Salvo et al. (2007)	1.004	3	Di Salvo et al. (2007)	91.07

The number of pages can also be an indicator of the quality of the sources, as longer articles, books, etc. usually suggest more comprehensive and detailed analyses. The results show that the average of about 45 pages does indicate longer articles, but this depends on the type of source, as not only journal articles but also more extensive books and book sections were used. Therefore, the median should also be considered at this point. Thus, of 102 sources, 37 sources have a page count of less than or equal to 10 pages.

The number of source citations is an indicator of the level of detail and thus the informative value of a source. Here, the range is wide with a minimum of 0 and a maximum of 156. However, this depends on the type of source and its number of pages. Books, for example, have more source citations due to their length.

Our SLR also has some limitations: This concerns the selection and analysis of sources, which is ultimately based on subjective elements despite the systematic and intersubjectively comprehensible procedure. In addition, only German and English language sources were used for the SLR. Studies from other language areas were not considered, which is tantamount to not having a fully comprehensive literature evaluation on this topic, albeit an extensive one.

4 Results and Discussion

Based on the SLR, an increasingly important role that big data play in professional football, one of the most common sports, can be confirmed. This role enables the consolidation of information and knowledge and thus the analysis and interpretation of correlations and patterns. In doing so, the sports uses digital technologies to improve performance in a competitive environment. The proliferation of tracking technology in sports and the associated desire to record and monitor the activities of athletes have led to a significant increase in the volume of data, the variety of data in circulation, and the rapidity of data transmission. (Millington & Millington, 2015: 140).

The use of connected electronic performance and tracking systems components and data analytics is now commonplace in almost every sport. The interplay of innovations in hardware and software is shaping the history of data analytics in sports (Memmert & Raabe, 2018: 26). However, the data obtained are worthless if not accompanied by analysis. Statisticians and analysts are playing an increasingly important role in human resources in the sports industry. However, interest in sports analytics is not yet compelling among many stakeholders in professional sports, even though various data, technologies, new metrics, and analytics exist on the market (Davenport, 2014: 2). One major reason cited for this is that many professional sports teams cannot afford to employ multiple analysts with their specialized skills due to their own economic realities (Davenport, 2014: 13).

In the field of professional football, the situation is different, probably also because of the economic size of this industry. FC Barcelona, Manchester City, FC Liverpool, and FC Bayern are now conducting intensive research into digital match analysis, mostly in a highly secretive manner. They employ renowned scientists or hold seminars on data analysis and AI with experts (Biermann, 2018: 42). Moreover, clubs, such as Chelsea FC and Manchester United, employ data scientists to meticulously track and record every move of players to maximize their chances of winning games (Marr, 2015: 213).

In the majority, however, the performance analysts do not interact directly with individual players (Carling et al., 2018). Rather, it seems to be about a knowledge edge in holistic digital match analysis. The German Football Association (DFB), for example, is planning cutting-edge research on this topic in Frankfurt (Saam, 2017). It's not surprising, then, that the analytics team of the German national team has embarked on a big data project with software company SAP, focusing on how to control space on the pitch and, by extension, the opposition (Biermann, 2018: 42).

For example, FC Barcelona uses an algorithm developed by Daniel Link in Germany. With the help of a large amount of game data, this allows production of statements about how great the goal threat is when the team is on the ball. At any time, the analyst can follow the game and determine how well a team is attacking or the opponent is defending. Link's (2018a: 29ff) concept of "Dangerousity" is used extensively by many professional stakeholders in professional football, and based on our SLR, it appears to be a leading product on the market.

Meanwhile, Benfica Lisbon, a Portuguese football club, is considered a pioneer of professional sports analytics and has become known for its intelligent, data-driven transfer policy (Craig, 2018). The club thus controls 100% of the development of its top performers and subsequently acts as a feeder club for even larger football clubs. Within 6 years, Benfica Lisbon sold 13 top performing players for 270 million UK pounds. By using machine learning and predictive analytics, players can use their personal data and the insights gained to optimize their performance and continuously improve. The basis of the success is mainly based on the fact that the young players can develop without major injuries (Wired, 2018).

The Benifca Lisbon coaching staff can do little to prevent injuries caused by direct contact during a game, that is, traumatic injuries. However, in the case of non-traumatic soft tissue injuries, especially muscle and ligament injuries, big data provide an opportunity to predict and, in the best case, even prevent them altogether. The Benfica Lisbon medical staff supports the coaching team in analyzing the physical stress of athletes with an accurate, predictive injury model. This model provides information about the peak loads an athlete can be exposed to before an injury occurs. The main questions in this model are the kind of injuries that can occur in certain risk situations and the convalescence period in case of an eventual occurrence.

FC Midtjylland has taken a similar but more rigorous approach to Benfica Lisbon (Memmert & Raabe, 2017: 120ff). This club from the 1st Danish Football League is pursuing the objective of eliminating the factor of chance as completely as possible. FC Midtjylland not only wants to be not only a professional football club but also a laboratory for innovative experiments. At the center of all decisions, whether scouting or evaluating games, is analytics. Scientific methods are used to replace irrational, subjective, and emotional decisions. This experimental approach shows that a football club can be successfully managed based on statistical analysis (De Hoog, 2015).

Creating a talent pool, for example, is driven by data and information. The use of scouts for talent management still consists only of recognizing whether the players sighted are fit into the team from a personal and psychological perspective. At this point, at least, efficiency and success are still influenced not only by data but also by the "synthesis of cold analysis and heart" (Thite, 2018: 82). Meanwhile, in the evaluation of games, mathematical models are used almost exclusively (Biermann, 2016). Large football clubs in particular have excellent analysts and scientists with outstanding ideas and innovation potential in the field of data and sports analytics. However, they have no final decision-making impact on strategic decisions; these are ultimately made by the top management. For instance, a personal union exists in Midtjylland: the revolution comes from top management because the chairperson Rasmus Ankersen is himself an analyst (De Hoog, 2015). Therefore, the clear mantra from top management is "we are a club without ears and eyes" (Memmert & Raabe, 2017: 122).

In 1st German Bundesliga, TSG 1899 Hoffenheim, in particular, is often cited as an example of the consistent use of big data to optimize performance. The data from the game and player analysis are used for systematic performance diagnostics. In addition to the athletic performance factors, the psychological performance factors are identified, stored, and used to make statements for training control, individualization, and so on (Görlich & Mayer, 2018: 22).

Moreover, other new technologies are being integrated into the training process to support players' conscious thinking with the help of video games (e.g., software called "Helix") (Söhnlein & Borgmann, 2018: 23ff). The athletes are confronted with VR situations in which their own team and the opposing team meet. It is hoped that this technology will improve the athletes' positional awareness. Another advantage of this software is that the exercises can be adapted and tailored to the positional requirements of different players. For the intuitive aspects of the players, the "Footbonaut" (Fiedler, 2018: 59ff) is additionally used to test the players' reactions to unpredictable technical contexts. Reaction times or technical accuracy are registered to generate a profile of the player and monitor his development. The combination of the conscious thinking approach with tactical and intuitive aspects potentially brings an improvement in a player's decision-making as he perceives game situations more consciously.

Finally, the use of the "SAP Sports One" product as a common platform for the mobile provision of medical, psychological, and performance diagnostic parameters and other live information is an essential component of the football club's big data strategy. The derivation of data from the system for new or optimized applications is available to various team-related groups at any time (Görlich & Mayer, 2018: 22).

The case studies of Benfica Lisbon, FC Midtjylland, and TSG 1899 Hoffenheim, which are presented in the structured literature analysis, show how big data can help football clubs to achieve a competitive advantage in the context of a more efficient usage of their human capital (player squad). The evaluation shows that professional sports analytics especially fixates on human resources, because only selecting and owning the best players at the lowest price makes the difference and represents the most important competitive advantage (Davenport & Harris, 2007: 37). However, a spiral of innovative competition has been initiated among the football clubs, which seems to be spinning much faster and is forcing the clubs to permanently expand their analytical capabilities and to tie up considerable financial resources in the process. (Davenport & Harris, 2007: 67ff).

Results from the SLR reveal the seemingly important role played by big data for the trainer in the field of performance analysis/diagnostics in the future, as many performance indicators are made measurable through data collection and analysis methods. In this context, an important future topic for coaching staff will be prevention, the objective of which is sustainable health promotion with measures to prevent injuries and illnesses. Current trends in the medical field include regeneration, prevention, and individual training (SportHeads, 2018: 33).

The number of games and training sessions and the enormous pressure to perform placed on athletes during a season can have far-reaching effects on the athletic success or failure of the individual athlete and, consequently, on the entire team. If the training load is an important determinant of injury, it must be measured accurately daily over weeks and months (Gabbett, 2016: 273). The goal is clearly the critical analysis and evaluation of a player's physical activities and the associated creation of an optimal training plan (Davenport, 2014: 22). In addition, the medical staff can use the training data to minimize the risk of injury from overuse through preventive treatment (Link, 2018a: 17). The key here is targeted load control of individual players and a possible early warning system for signs of fatigue (Memmert & Raabe, 2018: 72f). McCall et al. (2015) suggested that fatigue is one of the most important factors in football injuries.

The number of kilometers ran, the sprints performed, and the average daily speed achieved by a player are information that is not decisive for the pure medical care of professional football players. Rather, it is a matter of collecting data that can be used to identify specific stress control measures for individual athletes and act as an early warning system for signs of fatigue (Memmert & Raabe, 2017: 134). However, the biggest problems are the indicators themselves: How is fatigue measured in concrete terms? How quickly and when can a player be reintegrated into the daily routine after an injury? The answers cannot yet be answered unambiguously by the scientific community (Memmert & Raabe, 2018: 73). Currently, scientifically based models in practice that enable sensible load control with suitable specifications is still lacking (Memmert & Raabe, 2017: 135). That said, many football organizations today are using existing technology in their training sessions to minimize the risk of injury and prevent long-term negative health effects (van der Westhuizen & van der Haar, 2018: 226ff; Ikram et al., 2015: 1). This was also the main reason why the International Football Association Board allowed wearables in the game, to be able to detect possible health problems at an early stage with targeted stress monitoring (Memmert & Raabe, 2017: 134f).

Another major approach being pursued with big data is the improvement of players' cognitive abilities. In football, considerable importance is attached to understanding the game and decision-making ability, not only for the outcome of individual matches but also, as a consequence, for the position in the table at the end of a season (Frick, 2004: 71). The goal is to develop the players' procedural knowledge and to increase their decision-making speed in game situations. In a football game, the context is constantly changing as players must make decisions based on the position of the ball, the current position of teammates, opponents, their own position on the field, and the estimated distance to the different participants. Because of this variability, each player interprets game situations according to his own experience and preparation for these moments. This effective decision-making is called tactical skill and is a basic requirement for a good football player. In particular, this skill of the experienced player refers to deciding which action to perform at a particular moment of the game. Thus, it is an important feature for performance differentiation and simultaneously serves to distinguish it from purely physical characteristics (Kannekens et al., 2011: 846f).

Today's modern game of football also demands an increase in the speed of the decision-making process among players (Bush et al., 2015: 1ff). An analysis of the differences between the 1966 and 2014 World Cup showed that players were 35% better at targeted passes and speed in 2014 than in 1966. The contact time for a player on the German national team changed from 2.9 s at the 2006 World Cup to 0.9 s at the 2014 World Cup (Mckenna, 2017). However, the fast execution of actions does not mean that the player must run faster than his opponent. Instead, it means that he can be better positioned on the field or play better passes. Thus, the player's tactical skills increase the likelihood of reading the opponent's play and effectively making game decisions based on it (Gerrard, 2016: 214).

Football is highly complex, not least because of the number of players and the size of the field; therefore, the coaching staff must be able to reduce the unpredictability of a game by simulating game situations. This should optimize players' decision-making processes under simulated competition conditions (Di Salvo et al., 2007: 222ff). Today, software solutions can assess the temporal-spatial behavior of players and the movement patterns of teams in terms of their effectiveness and efficiency.

To better prepare for the next game, coaching staff must know exactly which tactical variants should be used depending on the respective opponent. The basis for this sports game analysis is the movements of the athletes, which are recorded by several cameras or body sensors. This enables a reconstruction of the movement sequences. Thus, coaching staff can make an evaluation by visual information. For example, the trainer could suggest a different field position for each player or analyze whether the distances between the players correspond to the strategies defined in training. Even the concrete determination of distances between players can improve the team's positioning in the long term and thus increase performance. It also allows for constructive engagement with players to establish structural patterns of play. Overall, data analysis via games provides the coaching team with the legitimacy of objectified feedback to the players to standardize team strategy (Gudmundsson & Wolle, 2013).

Many coaches see great potential in the cognitive optimization of players. The focus is on players' faster thinking, recognition, anticipation, and decision-making. However, scientific research in the cognitive field is still in its infancy. In the future, imaging techniques such as functional magnetic resonance imaging or electroencephalography will be increasingly used in mobile applications. In addition, an increased individualization in recovery and stress control is expected (SportHeads, 2018: 21).

Based on our SLR, professional sports clubs show a strong tendency to use big data and its analysis to try minimizing the chance of losing in their respective sports. In football, for example, coaching is likely to become even more technology- and computer-assisted in the future. Football analysts will in all likelihood use big data to elicit patterns and to develop new individual algorithms for training control and match analysis. However, the networking of science and sport is only just the beginning (SportHeads, 2018: 21). With the help of big data and its evaluation, the coaching staff can analyze the opponent, even determine the individual game behavior, possibly also the respective game intelligence. Important impulses can be given to determine the optimal team formation in the context of the respective opponent and its strengths and weaknesses. Performance and fitness data provide coaches, physiotherapists, physicians, and psychologists with information for the individual design of training sessions or rehabilitation measures for each player and thus connect to the aforementioned anticipatory measures against signs of fatigue and corresponding injuries (Gehrmann, 2017).

The tactical analysis will play an even greater role in football in the future because continuous-time position data are particularly available in large quantities. Three fundamentally different approaches can be distinguished: trivial methods, system models, and metamodels (Link, 2018a: 19): Trivial methods are cumulative statistics based on player results or measures of running intensity. However, since football is a complex system due to its dynamic, non-linear nature, these data are, in principle, not meaningful enough for strategy development or performance evaluation (Carling et al., 2014: 2ff; Mackenzie & Cushion, 2013: 639ff). System modeling tries interpreting the interaction and coupling behavior of teams, groups of players, and individual players with the help of relative phase or entropy. This should help make statements about the system dynamics a football game is subject to (Rein & Memmert, 2016; Frencken et al., 2012: 1207ff). The network analysis for passing behavior in games and thus for the identification of recurring patterns also provide promising results and belongs to the type of system modeling (Ribeiro et al., 2017: 1689ff). Another possible approach is based on a metamodel that recognizes tactical constructs according to position data (Beetz et al., 2009: 1ff). Moreover, data on ball possession (team ball possession, individual ball possession, or ball control), actions (pass, cross, or one-on-one) and tactics (pressing, synchronization, or playability) are recorded electronically based on raw data such as player position, the ball position, and game status. This allows strategies or playing styles to be defined for various situations (Link, 2018a: 19).

The extraction of tactical structures from raw data is done either by conventional rule-based approaches or by machine learning. When using explicit rules, the knowledge is usually modeled by human experts. However, in machine learning, there are no predefined rules, but they are derived from existing datasets. With the help of artificial neural networks and supervised learning, data analysts determine a so-called ground truth to subsequently use this as a training basis for the network. In unsupervised learning, the ground truth is omitted by the data analysts; that is, the network does not know what it is supposed to recognize. In both cases, algorithms do not need to be defined fixedly because they emerge during the learning process. Therefore, machine learning is mainly about pattern recognition and relationship detection (Kempe et al., 2015: 249ff; Rein & Memmert, 2016).

With conventional models, the results are better if a detailed design is available. However, if the design is too complex, a multiplication of rules and a high error rate can occur. Machine methods are excluded from this problem (Link, 2018a: 20). Supervised learning requires the correct answers to the model constellations. These must be supplied as a unique ground truth. The specification of the ground truth is often associated with a high manual effort in the preparation of the data. Objects cannot always be unambiguously classified, and values cannot always be estimated or predicted. In football, for example, the attacking play of one's own team should be structured in such a way that the constant playability of the athletes is possible. However, playability cannot be fully objectified. Ground truth is lacking, and thus, the net lacks the ability to learn. In unsupervised learning, the advantage is the partially fully automated creation of models. By training the models, the input data are increasingly adapted to the models. The basic challenge in unsupervised learning is to recognize when a model is sufficiently trained based on patterns and relationships. This is the involved verification process (Fraunhofer, 2018: 23ff).

For the 2018 FIFA World Cup, methods based on machine learning were used for the first time. Hence, the so-called random forest method was used for forecasting purposes (Groll et al., 2018: 7ff). A random algorithm gains access to parts of a data set and creates thousands of possible decision trees. This can then be used, for example, to determine expected values for goals. It could be proven that the amount of data plays a decisive role. The larger the number of games to be evaluated, the smaller the percentage deviation between the prediction and the actual result (Schauberger & Groll, 2018).

Predictive analytics is another method from the field of data mining that is used in sports and especially in football after the evaluation of our SLR for data analysis. Here, a statistical or machine learning technique is used to create a quantitative prediction of the future. Often, predictive analytics occurs along with supervised machine learning to predict a probability (e.g., how likely is this player to delay a shot on goal?) or a future value (e.g., how long can a player be used before needing a recovery period?) (Burns, 2020). Although machine learning techniques are improving forecasts, even in the unlikely event that a model could take all relevant variables into account, the emergence of "predictable" football is unlikely and thus no certainty about the actual match outcome. With big data as a basis, almost everything in professional football can be measured: ball possession, passing rates, or running distances of individual players. For a long time, data such as ball possession and running performance were considered factors in winning a game. However, successful teams like FC Barcelona or Bayern Munich often have lower running performance and are still successful (Memmert & Raabe, 2018,: 256).

The collection of biometric player data is highly visible as a useful information tool for training. According to the literature, intelligent technologies offer players great opportunities, but also considerable risks. The potential benefits lie in the optimization of players' physical performance. As a result, many professional sports clubs have become "laboratories" dedicated to injury prevention and performance enhancement (King & Robeson, 2007, 2013: 13f). Football companies in particular monitor their players in private by observing their diet and sleep patterns. In addition, emotional well-being is recorded via social networks (Marr, 2015). The interest in comprehensive information about the health and performance of players on the part of club managers is understandable, especially since a player's absence represents a considerable cost factor. However, the boundary of the relationship between employee and employer in terms of privacy and monitoring can quickly be crossed. Therefore, biometric data also raise questions about players' rights and data protection, as it carries the risk of compromising players' privacy and autonomy by no longer guaranteeing the confidentiality of the data. Moreover, this may negatively influence contract negotiations with the consequence of career damage or curtailment (Karkazis & Fishman, 2017: 45–50).

A digital divide can be seen between athletes who have access to their own biometric data and the knowledge of how to use them and those who have neither access nor the necessary knowledge of what to do with the provided data. For athletes, the logical question is whether this digital divide can be bridged and a degree of data sovereignty can be ensured (Baerg, 2017: 9). With the help of the so-called "quantified self-movement," self-tracking can be performed, and the players can generate their own analysis (Nafus & Sherman, 2014: 1785). At first glance, digital self-measurement and data analysis in training work can be viewed positively in terms of data sovereignty for the players, but in practice, this approach raises the question of the effectiveness of data collection and data evaluation.

Another risk from player's perspective is that other parties (e.g., advertising partners and third-party ownership investors[1]) are interested in the data of individual players and may acquiring them for sale. Third-party use of biometric data raises ethical concerns: a) validity and interpretation of data; b) increased surveillance and privacy threats; c) confidentiality risks and data security concerns; d) conflicts of interest; and e) resulting dependence and coercion (Karkazis & Fishman, 2017: 48). On a positive note, all players' data that are measured and recognized can be presented with complete transparency (Memmert & Raabe, 2018: 147). However, from a negative viewpoint, there is a risk of the "glass player." A buyer of these detailed statistics could not only develop strategies to exploit the weaknesses but also impart insider market knowledge when buying and selling (Marr, 2015). In addition, data analytics procedures can be used to de-anonymize data once it has been anonymized; that is, "harmless" data are eliminated. Personal data can be used for correlations that may reveal, for example, political orientation or sexual orientation of a player (Thür, 2015: 5). This would then have a concrete impact on the player's relevant advertising marketing. Apart from the sporting attributes of the athlete, this factor also has a major influence on the evaluation of a player.

[1] For further information about third-party ownership arrangements see Herberger et al. (2018) and Herberger et al. (2019).

One potential drawback of data analytics in sports is the ever-increasing number of data sources, and consequently, coaches and management must handle and process this large amount of information. Almost all factors can be collected to measure performance; thus, the challenge is to distill the most relevant information from the data. Doing so creates the risk of digging too deep into the data, thereby increasing the problem of incorrect conclusions based on statistically significant results that lack causality. AI and machine learning can assist in this problem by developing algorithms that independently support and significantly improve the decision-making process; however, the fundamental problem cannot be eliminated (SportTechie, 2018). In individual cases, this can also lead to incorrect conclusions by decision-makers.

The evaluation of the SLR shows that the influence of chance will be further minimized in the coming years. The supervision, training, and coaching of players will be supported even more by technology and computers. Analysts will increasingly try exploiting opportunities in the field of big data by searching for patterns and creating individual algorithms for training control and game analysis. However, the potential from the networking of science and sport has not yet been fully developed (SportHeads, 2018: 21).

Sports data analysts must also be able to effectively communicate discoveries to decision-makers, typically various stakeholders within the professional football club. Currently, this communication can be a bottleneck, as executives often lack the ability and familiarity to translate quantitative data into qualitative thinking. Consequently, the demand from decision-makers within the professional football club for sports analytics is significantly less than the potential supply of data, technology, new metrics, and analytics (Davenport, 2014: 2; Biermann, 2016).

Professional football is undergoing sustainable and strong changes, mainly due to the influence of big data. Moreover, professional football clubs are increasingly investing in deep learning, predictive analytics, and the entire sports analytics sector. Given the large investments in transfer rights trading, foregoing sports analytics in player signings to reduce uncertainty would also be negligent.

However, investments in big data may not have the positive effects hoped for if professional football clubs are unable to make adequate decisions with the information they obtain from data analytics. The purchase of analysis tools does not automatically develop the competence to produce meaningful arithmetically developed results and especially to draw the appropriate conclusions from them. As long as a professional football club has not learned to use data and analytics to support its decisions, it will not be able to benefit from big data and sports analytics (Ross et al., 2013).

5 Conclusion

This study aims to show the changes caused by the use of technologies in the context of big data and sports analytics based on an SLR concretely in football. We also aim to analyze in this context to what extent the use of big data and sports analytics changes the strategies of professional football clubs and their stakeholders.

Based on our SLR, for the first research question, the emergence of digital methods and technologies in football is apparent. Modern computer-aided systems can be used to record individual players or the entire team to analyze tactical behavior. Moreover, kinematic characteristics, such as running paths, can be determined. The use of automatic tracking methods leads to a considerable reduction of the acquisition effort. Since modeling the course of a game proves to be complex, promising methods of data mining, such as the random forest method or predictive analytics, are conducted with the help of machine learning to support strategic planning. In practice, data mining has only been used in a few areas so far, as the trainers ultimately want to make the decisions themselves (Schoop & Brauchle, 2016: 20).

In the future, data analysts will become indispensable consultants. Big data and digital analysis tools will support the stakeholders of a professional football club. Moreover, software will help merge an increasing amount of measured and predicted data. The analysis of every game movement will serve as a primary factor for evaluating the game and recognizing the opponent's strategy. At the same time, it will serve as a basis for making informed decisions and calculating chances of winning.

For the player as human capital, digitalization means that the head coach can use objective data to justify his decisions in the debriefing of a match, resulting in better traceability and clear error analysis of the player. This transparency provides the club with the so-called "transparent player." However, the ethical component must not be forgotten. Many active football players are now asking about the whereabouts of the data collected. In particular, attention should be paid to the global scouting companies, which monitor and measure players at a young age to provide current market values to potential buyers.

Concerning the second research question on the benefits of big data and sports analytics for increasing competitiveness, the main purpose is to transform raw data into meaningful, value-adding, and actionable information. Data analysts make their strategic decisions based on these data, which leads to improved performance and generates a measurable and sustainable competitive sports advantage, ultimately resulting in a concurrent economic competitive advantage (Bukstein, 2016: 25ff).

The quantifiable performance indicators controlled by advanced tracking tools allow coaches to try achieving optimal load and maximum performance of their players. Big data and sports analytics are a great help to develop adequate strategies based on interdisciplinary synergies and maximize value creation from the potential of coaches and players. However, results on the field are not only determined by predictable facts.

Due to technological growth, real-time data can now be extracted and made immediately available to trainers on smart devices. This enables decisions to be made in a fraction of a second (van der Westhuizen & van der Haar, 2018: 226ff). To ensure this, coaches are increasingly reliant on data scientists and their analytics. Therefore, big data and sports analytics can be used to effectively improve performance in training and competition.

Our third research question addressed the chances and risks to be considered in using big data and sports analytics for the different stakeholders in a professional football club. Big data applications allow supporting, accelerating, and critically evaluating the decision-making ability of players based on predefined game situations or performance indicators. In addition, sports-specific software will be used to improve players' perceptual abilities and thus train conscious and unconscious thinking, which can lead to competitive advantages and should therefore be viewed positively from the perspective of stakeholders within a professional football club. However, the collection and analysis of a large amount of highly sensitive personal data can lead to transparency but has negative effects, especially for the player himself.

The football of the future is also facing a digital transformation, but this does not mean that big data and sports analytics will decode it tomorrow. In the next decade, football will be more modern and advanced from an analytical perspective. However, how will players, coaching and medical staff, management, and fans react to the different methods, approaches, analytics, and other innovations? Is it even possible to finally analyze the interpersonal factors in such a complex game like football?

Sports analytics will most likely change football on the field, but chance will continue to be a determining factor (Lucey et al., 2013: 2706ff). With sports analytics, a wide variety of data types are generated during data storage and use. An integrated database or data warehouse should be available for this purpose. However, not only the physical integration of data but also stronger cross-functional coordination of analysts must be present, for example, between performance analysts (qualitative video analysts and quantitative data analysts) and sports scientists (Gerrard, 2016: 216).

Acknowledgments We do not receive any grants or funds for our paper. All remaining errors are our own.

References

Ashton, K. (2009). That 'Internet of Things' Thing: In the real world, things matter more than ideas. Retrieved February 28, 2021, http://www.rfidjournal.com/articles/view?4986

Azuma, R. T. (1997). A survey of augmented reality. *Presence: Teleoperators and Virtual Environments*, *6*(4), 355–385.

Baca, A. (2015). *Computer science in sport. Research and practice*. Routledge.

Baerg, A. (2017). Big data, sport, and the digital divide: Theorizing how athletes might respond to big data monitoring. *Journal of Sport and Social Issues*, *41*(1), 3–20.

BaFin. (2018). Big Data trifft auf Künstliche Intelligenz. Bonn, Frankfurt am Main: Bundesanstalt für Finanzdienstleistungsaufsicht.

Bardley, J., Reberger, C., Dixit, A., & Gubta, V. (2013). Internet of everything: A $4.6 trillion public-sector opportunity: More relevant, valuable connections will boost productivity, revenue, and citizen experience, while cutting costs. Retrieved February 28, 2021, https://www.cisco.com/c/dam/en_us/about/business-insights/docs/ioe-public-sector-vas-white-paper.pdf

Beetz, M., Hoyningen-Huene, N., Kirchlechner, B., Gedikli, S., Siles, F., Durus, M., & Lames, M. (2009). ASPOGAMO: Automated sports game analysis models. *International Journal of Computer Science in Sport, 8*(1), 1–21.

Biermann, C. (2016). Moneyball im Niemandsland. *11 Freunde*. Retrieved February 28, 2021, https://www.11freunde.de/artikel/midtjyllands-revolution

Biermann, C. (2018a). Ohne Mathe geht es nicht. Wie die digitale Datenanalyse den Fußball verändert. *Rotary Magazin, 2018*(6).

Biermann, C. (2018b). Matchplan: Die Neue Fußballmatrix. Köln: Kiepenheuer & Witch.

Bukstein, S. (2016). Evolution and impact of business analytics in sport. *Sport Business Analytics*, 25–46.

Burns, E. (2020). Predictive analytics. Retrieved February 02, 2021, https://www.searchenterprisesoftware.de/definition/Predictive-Analytics

Bush, M., Barnes, C., Archer, D. T., Hogg, B., & Bradley, P. S. (2015). Evolution of match performance parameters for various playing positions in the English Premier League. *Human Movement Science, 39*, 1–11.

Carling, C., Wells, S., & Lawlor, J. (2018). Performance analysis in the professional football club environment. In W. Gregson & Littlewood (Eds.), *Science in soccer: Translating theory into practice*. Bloomsbury Publishing PLC.

Carling, C., Wright, C., Nelson, L. J., & Bradley, P. S. (2014). Comment on performance analysis in football: A critical review and implications for future research. *Journal of Sports Sciences, 32*(1), 2–7.

Castellano, J., Alvarez-Pastor, D., & Bradley, P. S. (2014). Evaluation of research using computerised tracking systems (Amisco® and Prozone®) to analyse physical performance in elite soccer: A systematic review. *Sports Medicine, 44*(5), 701–712.

Cooper, H. M. (2010). *Research synthesis and meta-analysis: A step-by-step approach*. SAGE.

Craig, L. (2018). Sports analytics: How data gives teams the edge. Retrieved February 02, 2021, https://www.techerati.com/features-hub/opinions/sports-analytics-how-data-gives-teams-the-edge/

Davenport, T. H. (2018). *The AI advantage. How to put artificial intelligence revolution to work*. MIT Press.

Davenport, T. H. (2014). Analytics in sports: The new science of winning 2. International Institute for Analytics, 1–28.

Davenport, T. H., & Harris, J. G. (2007). Competing on Analytics: The New Science of Winning. Harvard Business Press.

De Hoog, M. (2015). How data, not people, call the shots in Denmark. Retrieved February 02, 2021, https://thecorrespondent.com/2607/how-data-not-people-call-the-shots-in-denmark/230219386155-d2948861

Di Salvo, V., Baron, R., Tschan, H., Calderon Montero, F. J., Bachl, N., & Pigozzi, F. (2007). Performance characteristics according to playing position in elite soccer. *International Journal of Sports Medicine, 28*(3), 222–227.

Dumay, J. (2014). 15 years of the Journal of Intellectual Capital and counting–A manifesto for transformational IC research. *Journal of Intellectual Capital, 15*(1), 2–37.

Fasel, D., & Meier, A. (2016). Was versteht man unter Big Data und NoSQL? In D. Fasel & A. Meier (Eds.), Big Data. Grundlagen, Systeme und Nutzungspotenziale. Springer Fachmedien.

Fiedler, H. (2018). Der Einsatz von KI in der Personalauswahl - Erkenntnisse aus dem "Footbonaut". In R. Lanwehr & J. Mayer (Eds.), People Analytics im Profifußball. Springer Fachmedien GmbH.

Fraunhofer. (2018). Maschinelles Lernen - Kompetenzen Anwendungen und Forschungsbedarf. Retrieved February 02, 2021, https://www.bigdata.fraunhofer.de/content/dam/bigdata/de/documents/Publikationen/BMBF_Fraunhofer_ML-Ergebnisbericht_Gesamt.pdf

Freiknecht, J., & Rapp, S. (2018). *Big Data in der Praxis. Lösungen mit Hadoop, Spark, HBase und Hive. Daten Speichern, Aufbereiten, Visualisieren* (2nd ed.). Carl Hanser Verlag.

Frencken, W., Poel, H., Visscher, C., & Lemmink, K. (2012). Variability of inter-team distances associated with match events in elite-standard soccer. *Journal of Sports Sciences, 30*(12), 1207–1213.

Fried, G., & Mumcu, C. (2017). *Sport Analytics. A Data-Driven Approach to Sport Business and Management*. Routledge.

Frick, B. (2004). Die Voraussetzungen sportlichen und wirtschaftlichen Erfolges in der Fußball-Bundesliga. In M. Bieling, M. Eschweiler, & J. Hardenacke (Eds.), *Business-To-Business-Marketing im Profifußball* (pp. 71–93). Deutscher Universitätsverlag.

Gabbett, T. J. (2016). The training—injury prevention paradox: Should athletes be training smarter and harder? *British Journal of Sports Medicine, 50*(5), 273–280.

Gassmann, O., & Perez-Freije, J. (2011). Eingangs-, Prozess- und Ausgangskennzahlen im Innovationscontrolling. *Controlling & Management Review., 55*(6), 394–396.

Gehrmann, S. (2017). Die Vermessung Des Sports. Retrieved March 03, 2021, https://www.bi-scout.com/die-vermessung-des-sports

Gerrard, B. (2016). Understanding sports analytics. Retrieved February 28, 2021, https://winningwithanalytics.com/2016/06/22/first-blog-post/.

Görlich, P., & Mayer, J. (2018). Falldarstellung: TSG 1899 Hoffenheim-Herkunft und Strategie. In R. Lanwehr & J Mayer (Eds.), People Analytics im Profifußball. Springer Fachmedien GmbH.

Gould, S. J. (1996). *Das Missverständnis Des Menschen*. WW Norton & Company.

Gowda, M., Dhekne, A., Shen, S., Choudhury, R. R., Yang, X., Yang, L., Golwalker, S., & Essanian, A. (2017). Bringing IoT to sports analytics. In *14th USENIX Symposium on Networked Systems Design and Implementation*. Boston, MA, USA.

Gramlich, D. (2018). Technische Grundlagen der Datensammlung und -analyse und ihre Auswirkungen auf den Fußball. Big Data im Fußball. Studylab 2018. Norderstedt: Books on Demand GmbH.

Groll, A., Ley, C., Schauberger, G., & van Eetvelde, H. (2018). Prediction of the FIFA World Cup. A random forest approach with an emphasis on estimated team ability parameters. Retrieved February 28, 2021, https://arxiv.org/pdf/1806.03208.pdf2018

Gudmundsson, J., & Wolle, T. (2013). Computers, Environment and Urban Systems Football analysis using spatio-temporal tools. *Computers, Environment and Urban Systems*. Retrieved February 28, 2021, https://thomaswolle.net/article-resources/GudmundssonWolle_FootballAnalysisUsingSpatioTemporalToolsEA.pdf

Herberger, T. A., Oehler, A., & Wedlich, F. (2018). Third-Party-Ownership-Konstruktionen im Profifußball: Finanzwirtschaftliche Einordnung, kritische Bestandsaufnahme und Implikationen. In T. Herberger (Ed.), *Sportökonomie im Kontext Von Governance & Gesellschaft* (pp. 129–158). Verlag Dr. Kovač.

Herberger, T. A., Oehler, A., & Wedlich, F. (2019). Third party ownership arrangements: Is a ban in football really appropriate? *Journal of Governance & Regulation, 8*(3), 47–57.

Hughes, M. D., & Bartlett, R. M. (2002). The use of performance indicators in performance analysis. *Journal of Sports Sciences, 20*(10), 739–754.

IEEE. (2015). Towards a definition of the Internet of Things (IoT). Retrieved February 28, 2021, https://iot.ieee.org/images/files/pdf/IEEE_IoT_Towards_Definition_Internet_of_Things_Issue1_14MAY15.pdf(1)

Ikram, M. A., Alshehri, M. D., & Hussain, F. K. (2015). Architecture of an IoT-based system for football supervision (IoT Football) 2nd World Forum on Internet of Things (WF-IoT) 2015 (pp. 69–74). IEEE.

Karkazis, K., & Fishman, J. R. (2017). Tracking US professional athletes: The ethics of biometric technologies. *American Journal of Bioethics, 17*(1), 45–60.

Kannekens, R., Elferink, T., & Visscher, C. (2011). Positioning and deciding: Key factors for talent development in soccer. *Scandinavian Journal of Medicine and Science in Sports, 21*(6), 846–852.

Kempe, M., Grunz, A., & Memmert, D. (2015). Detecting tactical patterns in basketball. Comparison of merge self-organising maps and dynamic controlled neural networks. *European Journal of Sport Science, 15*(4), 249–255.

King, N. M. P., & Robeson, R. (2007). Athlete or guinea pig? Sports and enhancement research. *Studies in Ethics, Law, and Technology, 1*(1).

King, N. M., & Robeson, R. (2013). Athletes are guinea pigs. *American Journal of Bioethics, 13*(10), 13–14.

Kipper, G., & Rampolla, J. (2013). *Augmented reality*. Elsevier Inc.

Kobielus, J. (2018). Wikibon's 2018 big data analytics trends and forecast. Retrieved February 28, 2021, https://wikibon.com/wikibons-2018-big-data-analytics-trends-forecast/

Laukenmann, J. (2017). Forscher *entschlüsseln* den Erfolg im Fußball. Retrieved February 28, 2021, https://www.tagesanzeiger.ch/wissen/technik/entschluesselung-des-fussballs-dank-big-data/story/30186152?track

Lewanczik, N. (2018): Was wird wirklich relevant, was bleibt Zukunftsmusik?. Retrieved February 28, 2021, https://onlinemarketing.de/news/technologie-trends-2018-relevant-zukunft. Technologie. Trends.

Lewis, M. (2004). *Moneyball: The art of winning an unfair game*. W. W. Norton, & Company Inc.

Link, D. (2018a). Data analytics in professional soccer. Performance analysis based on spatio-temporal tracking data. Springer Fachmedien GmbH.

Link, D. (2018b). Sports analytics: Wie aus (kommerziellen) Sportdaten neue Möglichkeiten für die Sportwissenschaft entstehen. *German Journal of Exercise and Sport Research*. Deutschland: Springer-Verlag GmbH, *48*(1), 13–25.

Lucey, P., Bialkowski, A., Carr, P., Morgan, S., Matthews, I., & Sheikh, Y. (2013). Representing and discovering adversarial team behaviors using player roles. In *Proceedings of the IEEE Conference on Computer Vision and Pattern Recognition* (pp. 2706–2713).

Mackenzie, R., & Cushion, C. (2013). Performance analysis in football. A critical review and implications for future research. *Journal of Sports Sciences, 31*(6), 639–676.

Marr, B. (2015). *Big data: Using SMART big data, analytics and metrics to make better decisions and improve performance*. Wiley.

McCall, A., Davison, M., Andersen, T. E., Beasley, I., Bizzini, M., Dupont, G., Duffield, R., Carling, C., & Dvorak, J. (2015). Injury prevention strategies at the FIFA 2014 World Cup: Perceptions and practices of the physicians from the 32 participating national teams. *British Journal of Sports Medicine, 49*(9), 603–608.

McHale, I. G., & Relton, S. D. (2018). Identifying key players in soccer teams using network analysis and pass difficulty. *European Journal of Operational Research, 268*(1), 339–347.

McKenna, B. (2017). T*SG* 1899 Hoffenheim gets "faster in the Head" with SAP analytics. Retrieved February 28, 2021, https://www.computerweekly.com/news/450423973/TSG-1899-Hoffenheim-gets-faster-in-the-head-with-SAP-analytics

Mangold, M. (2017). Unterschied virtual reality (VR) und augmented reality (AR). Retrieved February 28, 2021, https://magic-holo.com/unterschied-virtual-reality-vr-und-augmented-reality-ar/

Massaro, M., Dumay, J. C., & Guthrie, J. (2016). On the shoulders of giants: Undertaking a structured literature review in accounting. *Accounting, Auditing and Accountability Journal, 29*(5), 767–801.

Memmert, D., & Raabe, D. (2017). Revolution im Profifußball. Mit Big Data zur Spielanalyse 4.0. Deutschland: Springer-Verlag GmbH.

Memmert, D., & Raabe, D. (2018). *Data analytics in football: Positional data collection, modelling and analysis*. Routledge.

Meyer, J.-U. (2017). 2.0. Die Digitalisierung der Sportbranche. E. *Sport*-1st Aufl. Göttingen: BusinessVillage GmbH.

Millington, B., & Millington, R. (2015). The datafication of everything: Toward a sociology of sport and big data. *Sociology of Sport Journal, 32*(2), 140–160, Sects. 140–160.

Möller, K., & Schönefeld, C. (2011). Innovation Performance Measurement Framework - Ein Referenzmodell zur Analyse der Innovationssteuerung. *Controlling & Management, 55*(6), 367–371.

Nafus, D., & Sherman, J. (2014). Big data, big questions|This one does not go up to 11: The quantified self-movement as an alternative big data practice. *International Journal of Communications, 8*, 1784–1794.

O'Donoghue, P. (2005). Normative profiles of sports performance. *International Journal of Performance Analysis in Sport, 5*(1), 104–119.

Perl, J., & Memmert, D. (2017). A Pilot study on offensive success in soccer based on space and ball control-key performance indicators and key to understand game dynamics. *International Journal of Computer Science in Sport, 16*(1), 65–75.

Pickup, O. (2018). Three major ways cloud is transforming sport. Retrieved February 28, 2021, https://www.raconteur.net/technology/three-major-ways-cloud-transforming-sport

Quirling, C., Kainz, F., & Haupt, T. (2017). *Sportmanagement*. Verlag Franz Vahlen GmbH.

Reichmann, T., Kißler, M., & Baumöl, U. (2017). *Controlling mit Kennzahlen. Die systemgestützte Controlling-Konzeption* (9th ed.). Verlag Franz-Vahlen GmbH.

Rein, R., & Memmert, D. (2016). Big data and tactical analysis in elite soccer: Future challenges and opportunities for sports science. *Springerplus, 5*(1), 1410.

Research and Markets. (2016). Worldwide sports analytics market (2016–2022). Retrieved February 28, 2021, https://www.researchandmarkets.com/research/gpr3fw/worldwide_sports

Ribeiro, J., Silva, P., Duarte, R., Davids, K., & Garganta, J. (2017). Team sports performance analysed through the lens of social network theory. Implications for research and practice. *Sports Medicine, 47*(9), 1689–1696.

Ross, W. J., Beath, C. M., & Quaadgras, A. (2013). You may not need Big Data after all. Retrieved February 28, 2021, https://hbr.org/2013/12/you-may-not-need-big-data-after-all

Saam, S. (2017). DFB-Akademie: 'Silicon Valley' des Fußballs. Retrieved February 28, 2021, https://www.dw.com/de/dfb-akademie-silicon-valley-des-fu%C3%9Fballs/a-41669374

Schauberger, G., & Groll, A. (2018). Predicting matches in international football tournaments with random forests. *Statistical Modelling, 18*(5–6), 460–482. Retrieved February 28, 2021, https://journals.sagepub.com/doi/full/10.1177/1471082X18799934

Schoop, M., & Brauchle, A. (2016). Anwendung von Data-Mining-Technologien zu Statistischen Auswertungen und Vorhersagen Im Fußball. Universität Hohenheim.

Söhnlein, K., & Borgmann, S. (2018). Diagnostik von Exekutivfunktionen im Fußball. In R. Lanwehr & J. Mayer (Hrsg.). People Analytics im Profifußball. Springer Fachmedien GmbH.

SportHeads. (2018). Sport professionals 2018. Eine Studie zum Arbeitsumfeld des Teams Hinter dem Team. München.

SportTechie. (2018). Techie and N3XT sports state of soccer technology & innovation. *Sport*. Retrieved February 28, 2021, https://www.sporttechie.com/sporttechie-and-n3xt-sports-state-of-soccer-technology-innovation/

Thite, M. (2018). *e-HRM: Digital approaches, directions & applications*. Taylor & Francis Group.

Thür, H. (2015). Die Privatsphäre im Zeitalter von big Data. Jusletter IT, 21.

Tranfield, D., Denyer, D., & Smart, P. (2003). Towards a methodology for developing evidence—Informed management knowledge by means of systematic review. *British Journal of Management, 14*(3), 207–222.

van der Westhuizen, E. J., & van der Haar, D. T. (2018). A wearable device-based framework for determining player effectiveness on the football pitch. *ACM International Conference Proceeding Series*, 226–231.

Vanini, U., & Rieg, R. (2017). *Effects of voluntary intellectual capital disclosure—a structured literature review*. University of Applied Sciences.

Weichert, T. (2013). Big data. Eine Herausforderung für den Datenschutz. In: Geiselberger, H., & Moorstedt, T. (Eds.). Big Data. Das Neue Versprechen der Allwissenheit. Suhrkamp Verlag.

Werner, H. (2017). Performance-Messung in Forschung und Entwicklung. Controlling & management review. 3/2017, 16–26.

Wired (2018). The unlikely secret behind Benfica's fourth consecutive Primeira Liga title. Retrieved February 28, 2021, https://www.wired.co.uk/article/bc/microsoft-sl-benfica

Zobel, B., Werning, S., Metzger, D., & Thomas, O. (2018). Augmented und Virtual Reality: Stand der Technik, Nutzenpotenziale und Einsatzgebiete. In: de Witt, C., & Gloerfeld, C. (Hrsg.). Handbuch Mobile Learning. Wiesbaden: Springer Fachmedien GmbH.

Zoph, B., Vasudevan, J., Shlens, J., & Le, Q. (2017). AutoML for large scale image classification and object detection. Retrieved February 28, 2021, https://ai.googleblog.com/2017/11/automl-for-large-scale-image.html

Transnational Corporations and Fordism in the Digital Era: A Theoretical Explanation and Prediction

Daniel Lorberg and Holger Janusch

In the 1920s, innovation, especially assembly line production, gave rise to a new type of corporations and industries and a new form of capitalism that ushered in the age of mass production and mass consumption: Fordism. The production of the automobile for the masses is emblematic of this development. Digitalisation is once again bringing about a radical change in capitalism and the Fordist production structure. As a result of digitalisation, not only has an entire new industry already emerged with innovative companies such as Apple and Google, but the production of classic Fordist industries such as the automotive sector is also undergoing fundamental change. The Internet of Things, Big Data and artificial intelligence are revolutionising production processes and business models. The more efficient work and production processes generate productivity and welfare gains and promising growth opportunities for the future. However, the flip side of this development is accompanied by an increasingly unequal distribution of these gains. Despite the productivity gains, social inequality is rising in many industrialised countries and increasing the pressur on the welfare and social state due to increasing debt. At the same time, humankind is facing tough challenges like climate change, overpopulation and many more. Some might even see uprising military conflict on a large scale. Some of these challenges might be seen as results of the unequal distribution. But all of them can be easier if even overcome if humankind is able to use the gains digitalisation is bringing. Therefore we´ll try to give a few insides in this paper about why the economic cake is getting bigger, and why the pieces at the same time are more unequal divided.

D. Lorberg (✉)
Solar Decathlon Solar 21/22 and Living Lab. NRW, University of Wuppertal, Pauluskirchstrasse 7, 42285 Wuppertal, Germany
e-mail: lorberg@uni-wuppertal.de

H. Janusch
North American Studies Program, University Bonn, Regina-Pacis-Weg 5, 53113 Bonn, Germany

T. Herberger and J. Dötsch (eds.), *Digitalization, Digital Transformation and Sustainability in the Global Economy*, Springer Proceedings in Business and Economics, https://doi.org/10.1007/978-3-030-77340-3_13

Our journey begins with the changing nature of the firm. Asking the question of how does digitalisation affect the internal structure of corporations first? To answer the question, how do such changes transform the global capitalist economy in general in the end? This paper provides a theoretical explanation and prediction into how this unfinished digitalisation affects capitalism and what can be expected from this development for the future. The starting point of our consideration is the technological change in the digital revolution's course on dominant companies' structure at a micro level, which we discuss in the first part of this essay. In the second part, we will build on this and examine the consequences of this fourth industrial revolution for the economic and social macro level. In particular, we will look at what this revolution means for the structure of income distribution and ultimately for the traditional Fordist production system.

1 The Genesis of Transnational Companies: The Micro Level

In introductory economics textbooks, we learn quite early on what enterprises are. They are the places where production factors, such as capital and labour, are combined to produce goods and services. This process is also expressed in cost functions and essentially determines the market forms these enterprises meet: monopolies, oligopolies or polypolies. Even if we rarely find the perfect market with homogeneous products, no preferences of consumers besides the price and the presence of a large number of relatively small buyers and sellers, who can't influence the price; we still refer in particular to the natural monopoly as a form of market failure. This form of monopoly is natural because it arises directly from the cost function. It is characterised by permanently falling average production costs due to high initial investments and no or only low marginal costs. This structure ensures that one firm is more efficient in producing the entire market quantity than two or more firms. It excludes competition and gives the power to set prices freely to only one company. Therefore, it is a market failure. Typical examples are companies that own networks, for example, in telecommunication or rail industry, which is why they are often regulated.

We support the thesis that in course of the digital revolution, in addition to this classic natural monopoly, a new form of natural monopoly is increasingly emerging, which we call abstract natural monopoly. They are abstract because they are not based on a single asset, such as a railway network, but on many complementary assets that enable permanently falling marginal costs across many different business processes and markets. The consequence of this is that this structure is not as discriminatory against other market participants as the classic natural monopoly. What emerges is an efficiency advantage based on economies of scale at the company level that encompasses large parts of the company. These assets can be typical headquarter services but also particular but scalable technical advantages. For instance, if you have a perfect transnational tax avoidance strategy or large amounts of investment capital or many loyal clients and their data, you can gain efficiency for many different company activities and on a lot of different markets. Or you could have specific algorithms or a robotic manufacturing advantage, allowing you to make all your manufacturing or sales strategies more efficient, independent of if it's clothing or machinery. Therefore these tendencies affect all industries, from manufacturing to banking. How big this effect is, depends on how relevant scale effects are in an economy. One could think of many examples like small corner bars or different personal services that might seem to be not very much affected by scale effects. But if you look at Starbucks or McDonalds as examples, it seems those industries could be at least potentially much more efficient by using scale effects. Spending a lot for the perfect all-over business model and then scaling it up, is for many of those industries a way that has recently opened now due to the low transaction costs caused by the digital revolution.

Accordingly, comparably efficient companies can also coexist since we are talking about markets with differentiated products anyway. Therefore, this structure is not as exclusively discriminating to other companies as a classical natural monopoly is. However, it also follows that companies with a too-small size or without scalable assets often no longer participate in the market. Simultaneously, the specific markets are not mandatory boundaries for those companies forming an abstract natural monopoly. Because many scalable assets, especially those on the headquarter level, could gain efficiency benefits on many different markets. The consequence would therefore be fewer, more extensive and in many cases, more differentiated companies. Almost without exception, these would also be transnational companies, since the necessary economies of scale can typically only be realised across several countries. China's big market might be a relevant exception here.

As these companies always combine every new asset with existing assets, innovations for them often have a higher value than for the innovator. Alphabet (the company behind Google), for example, buys start-ups for immense prices, and it is not alone in this. Some of these are companies with little more than a developed idea and far from operating profits. If you look at the individual deals, you often ask yourself: for whom can this be worth so much? But the answer is simple: for Alphabet. When Alphabet buys an idea or a company, it combines it with all its other assets—vast amounts of data, customers, market access, tax structuring models and much more. These multipliers make acquisitions extremely profitable, even at high prices. The entrepreneurs who gratefully accept the money fetch a price above what their idea would ever have been worth to them since they do not have Alphabet's other assets. Therefore, Schumpeterian creative destruction is collected in a digital world before it becomes hazardous for the top dogs (Lorberg & Janusch, 2020). The system is thus not fundamentally hostile to innovation. However, innovations are primarily incorporated and do not lead to new unconnected companies.

While this is especially true of digital companies, it is not intended to give a false impression that a company must distribute digital services to generate an abstract natural monopoly. The increasing emergence of abstract natural monopolies is a consequence of the digital revolution in a general sense. We will now explain in more detail with the help of International Business Theory. This theory is a strand of business theory that deals primarily with the formation of multi- or transnational companies. The main protagonists are the Marxist Steven Hymer (1960), John H. Dunning (1988) with his eclectic paradigm and Buckley and Casson () with their Internalisation Theory.

In 1972, Steven Hymer made his mark with two striking theses on the economy of the year 2000. The first is the "law of increasing firm size" which describes genesis of the transnational company. He assumes growth of company sizes as a historical law and foresees this process's acceleration until it stabilises in global oligopolies. This system would cause wealth as well as poverty and thus leads to unequal development, also geographically. This development forms the second law, "the law of uneven development" (Hymer, 1972). Hymer therefore already offered a comparable thesis to the one presented here in the early 1970s. For him, the development of company size represents a regularity that can be observed historically: "Since the beginning of the Industrial Revolution there has been a tendency for the representative firm to increase in size from the workshop to the factory to the national corporation to the multidivisional corporation and now to the multinational corporation. This growth has been qualitative as well as quantitative. With each step, the business enterprise acquired a more complex administrative structure to coordinate its activities and a larger brain to plan for its survival and growth" (Hymer, 1982: 128). Thus, he argues that the enterprises are developing in their internal organisation and, under conditions of competition, are forming a structure that differs from that of the entrepreneurial firm, as Alfred Marshall described it as the formerly typical model.

"The new corporate form has great flexibility. Because of its decentralised structure, a multidivisional corporation can enter a new market by adding a new division, while leaving the old divisions undisturbed. (And to a lesser extent it can leave the market by dropping a division without disturbing the rest of its structure). It can also create competing product-lines in the same industry, thus increasing its market share while maintaining the illusion of competition. Most important of all, because it has a cortex specialising in strategy, it can plan on a much wider scale than before and allocate capital with more precision" (Hymer, 1982: 135). He also recognised that the order of economic activity was and is determined by two competing mechanisms: "The hallmarks of the new system were the market and the factory, representing the two different methods of coordinating the division of labour. In the factory, entrepreneurs consciously plan and organise cooperation, and the relationships are hierarchical and authoritarian; in the market, coordination is achieved through a decentralised, unconscious, competitive process" (Hymer, 1982: 131).

Hymer explained his "law of increasing firm size" primarily through organisational development and capital accumulation that develops over time. Ultimately, this also means that the firm's coordination mechanism, or we could also say hierarchy, partially replaces the market over time. Even if he does not delve further into this relationship, we find the annexes of the idea that Coase (1937) put forward in "The Nature of the Firm": the use of markets (competition) as a coordination mechanism causes costs. It should be added to this: The use of the firm (hierarchy) as a coordination mechanism also causes costs. In both cases, those are the costs incurred in undertaking an economic exchange. We call them transaction costs. The market causes those costs to occur as costs for the search for sellers or buyers and the right products, the right price, bargaining, deciding and enforcement. Companies produce those costs as costs of management. That means through handling all the information flows internally and externally for meaningful and effective planning, organising, commanding, coordinating and controlling.

This is the focus of Buckley and Casson's internalisation theory. They give us an additional perspective on the enterprise beyond that as a place of factor combination: "The result was a view of the firm as a complex of interdependent activities, linked by flows of knowledge and intermediate products" (Buckley & Casson, 2009: 3). Rational actors will consider the costs and benefits of using both modes of coordination. And therefore "(...) will internalise markets when the expected benefits exceed the expected costs" (Buckley & Casson, 2009: 5). As a result, the relative efficiency of coordination mechanisms defines the size of firms in each capitalist era: "It was the economics of coordinating this internal division of labour, and not technology, that set the limits to the boundaries of the firm. While technology might set a limit on the size of any one plant, it was diminishing returns to managerial coordination that set the limit to the size of the firm. These limits were reflected not only in the aggregate quantity of output produced by the firm, but also in the range of locations in which this output was produced and sold" (Buckley & Casson, 2009: 3). In conclusion, we find that markets' and companies' relative capacity defined by the available technology determines companies' size and the market form of a capitalistic era.

After these introductory thoughts on international business theory, we return to the core of this paper: the transformation of dominant companies' mode in the course of the digital revolution. If we follow Hymer's perspective, there is nothing new, as he foresees businesses' continued growth at the micro level with corresponding consequences for the macro level anyway. Without contradicting this, however, we see a qualitative leap in this development through the digital revolution. With recourse to the internalisation theory, the central question is whether the digital revolution enables companies to be more efficient coordination mechanisms. We assume that it is fundamentally advantageous for companies to be larger since the diversity of accumulated assets and their use across the largest possible number of value-creation processes provides them with superior efficiency based on falling average costs at the firm level.

Hymer was not the only one to deal with these assets as a starting point for transnationalisation. Also, Dunning used those, particularly in his Eclectic Paradigm. He describes the initial transnationalisation of companies, along with three aspects: Ownership Advantages (OAs), Locational Advantages (LAs) and Internalisation Advantages (IAs) (Dunning, 1988). A company must at first have OAs, which is synonymous with what we call assets. It means that a company has an exclusive advantage that, for instance, potentially enables it to generate additional sales, if enlarging its activities to other places. If they find a location enabling to use these OAs for the benefit of the company, that location includes advantages (LAs). In this example it could be a large market with a low level of competition. If these two aspects come together the company starts to act cross-border. Finally, the question arises as to whether this cross-border activity should take place on the market or within the company itself, i.e. through internalisation, whereby Dunning basically takes up Buckley and Casson. Such IAs in this example could be the internalisation of the sales structure, if it promises a higher revenue than getting a sales partner on board. In this way, he explains the cascade that leads to the initial transnationalisation of companies. However, he recognises that it is a cyclical process after that initial phase. The market access or the tax advantage or the patent acquired in transnationalisation becomes an asset itself and creates further advantages. It is the core for an ever further increase in a company's efficiency and expansion of the company itself, as Dunning himself describes in later writings (cf. Dunning, 2001: 175 ff.).

However, these efficiency gains are negated with increasing size by increasing coordination costs, as Buckley and Casson have already described. Here we find the limit of company's size depending on the underlying technology of information processing, storage and transmission. If a company overstretches itself, it may no longer be able to use its potentials and adapt efficiently to changes. In Schumpeterian creative destruction processes, even giants can then have to make way for small innovative companies. However, the question arises as to whether this logic still holds. The digital revolution is an unprecedented exponential development of information processing, storage and transmission, as one of the authors has already explained elsewhere (Lorberg, 2018: 169 ff.). The type and amount of data that can currently be handled ultimately make any historical comparison nonsensical. This leads to a new efficiency of management through digital systems and applications lowering internal transaction costs extremely. Barely a decade after the widespread availability of smartphones and mobile internet, even many of humanity's poorest parts can hardly imagine life without these technologies. Data is the new gold, and the unforeseeable development of artificial intelligence and the Internet of Things does not lead us to assume that we will encounter relevant limits in dealing with this data (for more details, see Lorberg, 2018, esp. Part IV).

2 Consequences for the Global Economy: The Macro Level

With the justification of the far-reaching negation of the limitation of company size and the enforcement of economies of scale in the digital revolution, the question further arises as to how this translates to the macro level. This is what we want to look at in the rest of this paper. After a historical context and a few words on capitalist societies' stability conditions, we ask how stable the new economic structure can ultimately be. We deliberately want to answer these questions in the form of theses to give the reader room for reflection.

Seeing the succession of history, especially economic history, in terms of ever-changing upheavals and renewed stabilisation is quite a common theme. Alongside minor cyclical ups and downs, which keep the basic structure untouched, it's the major disruptions changing the game rules and making utterly new thinking necessary. To renew stabilisation after those disruptions, new theories and social patterns can prove essential. In the case of the digital revolution, the authors assume it to be such a major disruption. Schumpeter (1939) in particular associated these developments primarily with technological change. It was less about the pure discovery of a so-called basic innovation, but rather about it becoming established in production and other value creation and becoming the new paradigm. We also find the themes in Marx's philosophy of history as the history of class struggles (Marx & Engels, 1848). The formation of classes takes place in the context of ever certain material conditions. In particular, the capitalist society was born with the technological development of the first industrial revolution that divided the society into those who had capital and those who could only carry their labour-power to the market.

Gramsci (2012) and, in his succession, Cox (1981, 1983) then thought more deeply about how such a system of exploitation could be stable and how it could become entrenched in and stabilised by ideology, culture and institutions. We take these thoughts as the basis for our analysis. For Gramsci, capitalism always remains a system of exploitation that serves the ruling class more than the ruled class. But the secret of its stability is precisely that it also benefits the latter. Therefore, capitalism in its stable phase lives on a promise. The promise that those at the top may profit more than those at the bottom, but the bottom benefits, too. This also implies a central ideological and often factual difference between capitalism and, for example, feudalism. In feudalism, it was accepted and probable that a peasant would be the father of a peasant. Social mobility or economic progress were no central themes of the time. However, capitalism, especially post-war capitalism, holds the promise of advancement, the much-vaunted American dream. The promise that the father will do better than his father and his son will do even better. Capitalism thus receives its legitimacy in the long term as output legitimacy; from the fulfilment of prosperity promise also for those less well-off. If the fulfilment of this promise is called into question, social stability will be disrupted. A common truth, stable institutions and ultimately, peace are at stake. At this point, we are leaving what Antonio Gramsci and Robert Cox call (world) hegemony. Hegemony is an order within the (world) economy characterised by a dominant mode of production expressed in universal norms accepted by the ruling and ruled classes and stabilised by (international) institutions.

There is a possibility that this promise can be renewed. With some adjustments, the system can return to output legitimacy. But there is also the possibility of formulating a fundamentally new promise; of creating a new hegemony. At the same time, however, there is also the possibility of remaining in unstable conditions for a longer period of time and of disintegrating globally into blocs that are more or less in conflict with each other. With these scenarios in mind, we will end by looking for answers to where the digital revolution will lead us.

Historically, we can date the beginning of the first Industrial Revolution to around 1780 and can locate its start in England. From there it needed 50–70 years to establish a new dominant mode of production and significant social upheavals all over Europe and even further. It is no wonder that the Communist Manifesto and revolutions, such as the French and less successful German, fall into this period and that the rise of the British Empire entered a new phase. With electrification from around 1870, the Second Industrial Revolution slowly brought about the new style of reasonably stable capitalism over the next 50–70 years, accompanied by wartime turmoil. This new style and mode of production is usually known as Fordism and Taylorism. Rationalisation of mass production, real wage increases and, on a broad basis, the possibility for the first time that workers themselves could afford the products they produced (mass consumption) were its characteristics. In this system, the United States replaced the British Empire as the world hegemon after the Second World War at the latest. Since the beginning of the Third Industrial Revolution in the 1970s, however, the stability of the Fordist capitalist system has begun to falter. Since then, there has been talking of the American Decline (cf. Müller-Jentsch, 2017: 80). After the short end of history in 1989/90, the question now arises about whether we may enter or have already entered an Asian or Chinese age. But even more, the stability of the world economy stands in question once more. The central question is not just if China will substitute the United States as the biggest economy and military power in the long-run, but if the mode of production and capitalist system fundamentally change in course of the digitalisation.

In order to describe the effects of the fourth industrial revolution, we take the described development towards large transnational companies with the possibility of distributing their processes all over the world in an efficiency-optimising manner as a starting point. We'll show that this results in an increased need for regulation as well as an increased regulatory problem. The increased need for regulation results from a more unbalanced distribution of primary income, which significantly affects developed countries. With an international choice for the best location in each step of a company's activity, factor-income is paid increasingly efficiently for smaller and smaller parts of those activities. Besides, income that is too high by international standards is increasingly being squeezed out or replaced by technical solutions. To understand the more efficient transnational use of production factors, it is necessary to look at the new type of company's geographical structure.

Let us take the stereotype of a classical company in the sense of Alfred Marshall as a starting example (cf. Hymer, 1982: 130). This enterprise creates value in one place. It may procure raw materials or intermediate products from abroad, but these are procured from unrelated companies and at a low-value level. Basically, all its processes take place in the place where the company is based. This means that it has both the processes that can be carried out particularly efficiently at this location and all others carried out there. For all the processes that are not efficient, the local wage is still paid. This leaves a social waste heat based on the payment of inefficient wages. Social waste heat, therefore, is an effect of inefficiency. It is based on high internal transaction costs, making it ineffective for companies to combine the globally ideal production factors to the lowest production costs. Before digitalisation, a worldwide production network in the modern sense was a true exception. Even if such companies became active across national borders, it was mostly sales or procurement, i.e. the parts with which the company core connects to other market levels. Another possibility was to rebuild an entire factory with all the value-added stages at another location. So, a company had more or less the same factory at different locations in different countries. In the end, however, this did not change the deep structure of location-based value creation.

However, the social waste heat of place-based production resulted from the time's technical conditions, the friction in the economic system itself (Williamson, 1990). We are talking here about transaction costs. Due to the comparatively underdeveloped possibilities of processing, storing, and transmitting information before the digital revolution, companies could not efficiently realise a less space-bound structure. Therefore, it was also the efficient structure of a pre-digital era. However, it is no longer since digitalisation took over. With significantly lower transaction costs in the course of the digital revolution, the processes can be carried out at the most suitable locations globally from a production point of view, as transaction costs are substantially less important. Thus, companies become complex global value-creation networks, and only that part of the overall process is carried out at a most efficient location there.

Interestingly, since many dominant companies in many sectors act in that way, location does not become less but more important due to decreasing transactions costs as a result of digitalisation. Locations specialise more and more in specific steps of production and value-creation due to agglomeration effects. At the same time, they become more and more unequal. For example, Porter's (2010) concept of clusters has become well known in this context, as have scaling considerations such as those made by Krugman (1979, 1980, 1991) in the New Economic Geography or the New Foreign Trade Theory. Where the conditions for specific processes were good, they become better and better. As more companies place their specific part of value creation to one specified place, it is easier for specified workers to find high-paid jobs at this place. That makes it attractive for other companies to settle there too if they search for those employees. As we see, specialised labour markets include scale effects. And the same uprising spiral can be found in infrastructure, knowledge externalities, specified suppliers and consultants and so on. With sinking transaction costs and a general restructuring of value creation, factor price equalisation also intensifies in the sense of the Lerner-Samuelson theorem (Samuelson, 1948). We find Hymer's "law of uneven development" approved by the intensified global competition, due to shrinking transaction costs. At the same time, scale effects on the company and location level boost this development.

The consequence of all this is fundamentally higher efficiency of production, a concentration of considerable added value in certain specialised regions central to global production. This leads to a reduction of poverty in those areas in the Third World who gained a role in this system, above all some regions in China. But at the same time, we see also a dwindling real income in the lower deciles of the income groups in the developed countries, while top incomes and company values are reaching new, sometimes seemingly surreal highs.

Now, the problem with this is primarily from two perspectives. First, the promise related to a capitalism of lasting prosperity for all is no longer being fulfilled. Second, the new structure of companies makes the increasingly necessary regulation much more difficult. As a result, the western liberal model of success increasingly lacks output legitimacy, which is reflected domestically in growing insecurity and lack of direction. In many cases, it favours a turn to nationalist and illiberal politics. In terms of foreign policy, China is now more likely to advertise the promise of prosperity for all and seems to be gradually establishing a new world order, as evidenced by the Belt and Road Initiative or the Regional Comprehensive Economic Partnership. Simultaneously, the West has failed to establish rules of the game for world trade above all the United States and the European Union. The negotiation breakdowns over the Trans-Pacific Partnership and Transatlantic Trade and Investment Partnership are symbolic for the West's failure to renew the upcoming capitalist system's rules in the digital era.

Thus, we are witnessing a period of weakness, at least among the developed countries, to cooperate, which can be seen in the past Trump administration and Brexit or the openly illiberal democracies in Poland and Hungary. However, a common capacity to act is of considerable importance for the stability of the global economy in the digital age. The Fordist conditions of our social and economic stability are still reasonably based are mass production and mass consumption. However, mass consumption must be covered by mass income to be stable in the long run. For quite some time now, we have been experiencing an ever-increasing level of public and private debt, which increasingly supplements income-based demand and shows no global tendency to be reduced again. Thus, the Fordist capitalist system based on mass consumption is kept alive by private and public debt because it misses the required income distribution. The digital revolution, therefore, destroys the conditions of its foundation, the Fordist mass consumption. It is just kept alive by debts. However, debt-based demand lead to bubbles that can challenge the very foundations of the global economy.

The digital economy thus decouples factor income and demand for goods not only spatially, but also factually. That means the income is not distributed to those who can and would do mass consumption. For instance, if the top 1% are getting more income, they will not buy 10.000.000 more small cars. But the dwindling middle class would do, but they only can do this through dept. Also, the rising demand coming from China and maybe other Asian countries will not bridge this gap. It is not the mass consumption needed, as the income distribution is worse than in the West and the income level of the middle class is still low. Besides this, the rising demand from China and other emerging markets is fuelled by more efficient use of production factors, as we argued in this essay. That means that the global middle-class income is shrinking relatively to the global GDP and the global low- and high-income deciles. Which is made visible in the famous elephant curve (World Inequality Lab, 2018). According to its Fordist logic, demand-effective factor incomes would have to be generated through redistribution across the board to stabilise the system. The transnational production structures and the corporations behind them could surely be regulated and included in such a redistribution by a world state. However, this is a utopia for the indefinite future. What is certain, however, is that competing nation-states will not be able to do this. Especially not when competition seems to outweigh cooperation.

In conclusion, digitalisation is taking us far away from stability conditions of Fordism and ultimately requires a form of regulation that goes beyond the nation-state, which was the form of state suitable for Fordism. A restoration of Fordist hegemony does not seem to be in sight, as the forces driving us away from economic stability are at the same time driving us away from national and global trust and cooperation. The friction between the nation-state and the global economy seems to be an unsolvable problem at the moment.

If a possible new Chinese hegemony is beginning to emerge, will it be able to restore a stable global economy? That's not very probable. China faces emerging economic problems due to a lower GDP growth rate and the upcoming demographic and maybe social issues. And under which circumstances would the West accept a world under Chinese hegemony, as it would have to question its own foundations like democracy and individual rights? Even more likely a world of two or three dominant blocks could emerge as the consequents of a rising China. Like in the cold war a double hegemony or in other words, a bipolar system could form. At least most scholars of neorealism hold that one for the most stable. Suppose the hegemony in those blocks would be strong enough. In that case, this system could have the spatial fit and the negotiating power towards transnational companies to make the world after digitalisation a world of welfare for many. Because we should not forget among all uprising problems, the digital economy makes humankind richer and more capable of acting than ever. Therefore, digitalisation can be the cure for such issues as the climate crisis, poverty and many more. But it also can be the cancer opening up an extended phase of conflict, crisis and unused chances. The only certain fact is that the world has not yet found a form of regulation for the digital era.

References

Buckley, P. J., & Casson, M. C. (1976). *The future of the multinational enterprise*. Macmillan.

Buckley, P. J., & Casson, M. C. (2009). The internalisation theory of the multinational enterprise: A review of the progress of a research agenda after 30 years. *Journal of International Business Studies, 40*(9), 1563–1580.

Coase, R. H. (1937). The nature of the firm. *Economica, 4*(16), 386–405.

Cox, R. W. (1981). Social forces, states and world orders: Beyond international relations theory. *Millennium—Journal of International Studies, 10*(2), 126–155.

Cox, R. W. (1983). Gramsci, hegemony and international relations: An essay in method. *Millennium—Journal of International Studies, 12*(2), 162–175.

Dunning, J. H. (1988). The eclectic paradigm of international production: A restatement and some possible extensions. *Journal of International Business Studies, 19*(1), 1–31.

Dunning, J. H. (2001). The eclectic (OLI) paradigm of international production. Past, present and future. *International Journal of the Economics of Business, 8*(2), 173–190.

Gramsci, A. (2012). Gefängnishefte. Kritische Gesamtausgabe. In W. F. Haug & K. Bochmann (Ed.), *Reprint of the first edition 1991–2002*. Argument-Verlag.

Hymer, S. H. (1960/ pub. 1976). *The international operations of national firms: A study of direct foreign investment*. MIT Press.

Hymer, S. H. (1972). The multinational corporation and the law of uneven development. In J. N. Bhagwati (Ed.), *Economics and world order* (pp. 113–140). Macmillan.

Hymer, S. H. (1982). The multinational corporation and the law of uneven development. In H. Alavi & T. Shanin (Eds.), *Introduction to the sociology of "developing societies"* (pp. 128–152). Macmillan Education UK.

Krugman, P. (1979). Increasing returns, monopolistic competition and international trade. *Journal of International Economics, 9*, 469–479.

Krugman, P. (1980). Scale economies, product differentiation, and the pattern of trade. *The American Economic Review, 70*(5), 950–959.

Krugman, P. (1991). Increasing returns and economic geography. *Journal of Political Economy, 99*(3), 483–499.

Lorberg, D. (2018). *Digitale Revolution, Fordismus und Transnationale Ökonomie*. Springer-VS.

Lorberg, D., & Janusch, H. (2020). Stumpfes Big Tech-Bashing reicht nicht. Demokraten und Republikaner attackieren die Digital-Giganten wegen ihrer Monopolmacht. Geht es Facebook und Co jetzt an den Kragen? *IPG-Journal*, 18.08.2020. https://www.ipg-journal.de/regionen/nordamerika/artikel/detail/stumpfes-big-tech-bashing-reicht-nicht-4571/ (03.01.2021).

Marx, K., & Engels, F. (1848/pub. 1978). *Manifest der Kommunistischen Partei*. München: Wilhelm Fink Verlag.

Müller-Jentsch, W. (2017). *Strukturwandel der industriellen Beziehungen., Industrial Citizenship' zwischen Markt und Regulierung*. 2nd ed. Springer Fachmedien.

Porter, M. E. (2010). Clusters and economic policy: Clusters and economic policy: Aligning public policy with the new economics of competition. *ISC White Paper*, Rev. 10/27/09. Harvard Business School; Institute for Strategy and Competitiveness.

Samuelson, P. A. (1948). International trade and equalisation of factor prices. *Economic Journal, 58*, 163–184.

Schumpeter, J. A. (1939). *Business cycles: A theoretical, historical, and statistical analysis of the capitalist process*. McGraw – Hill Book Company Inc.

Williamson, O. E. (1990). *Die ökonomischen Institutionen des Kapitalismus. Unternehmen, Märkte, Kooperationen*. Mohr Siebeck.

World Inequality Lab. (2018). World inequality report. https://wir2018.wid.world/files/download/wir2018-full-report-english.pdf (03.01.2021).